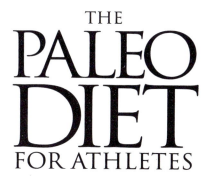

THE
PALEO
DIET
FOR ATHLETES

THE PALEO DIET

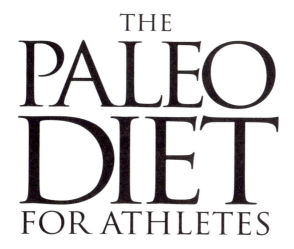

FOR ATHLETES

A Nutritional Formula for Peak Athletic Performance

Loren Cordain, PhD,
author of *The Paleo Diet*,
and **Joe Friel, MS**

RODALE

Notice

This book is intended as a reference volume only, not as a medical manual. The information given here is designed to help you make informed decisions about your health. It is not intended as a substitute for any treatment that may have been prescribed by your doctor. If you suspect that you have a medical problem, we urge you to seek competent medical help.

Mention of specific companies, organizations, or authorities in this book does not imply endorsement by the publisher, nor does mention of specific companies, organizations, or authorities imply that they endorse this book.

Internet addresses given in this book were accurate at the time it went to press.

Printed in the United States of America

Rodale Inc. makes every effort to use acid-free ♾, recycled paper ♻.

Cover design by Drew Frantzen

Interior design by DesignWorks

Library of Congress Cataloging-in-Publication Data

Cordain, Loren, date.
    The Paleo diet for athletes : a nutritional formula for peak athletic performance / Loren Cordain and Joe Friel.
        p.   cm.
    Includes bibliographical references and index.
    ISBN-13 978–1–59486–089–8 paperback
    ISBN-10 1–59486–089–0 paperback
    ISBN-13 978–1–59486–459–9 hardcover
    ISBN-10 1–59486–459–4 hardcover
    1. High-protein diet.   2. Athletes—Nutrition.   3. Prehistoric peoples—Nutrition.
I. Friel, Joe.   II. Title.
RM237.65.C669   2005
613.2'82—dc22   2005009853

Distributed to the trade by Holtzbrinck Publishers

2   4   6   8   10   9   7   5   3   1   paperback
2   4   6   8   10   9   7   5   3   1   hardcover

LIVE YOUR WHOLE LIFE™

We inspire and enable people to improve their lives and the world around them
For more of our products visit **rodalestore.com** or call 800-848-4735

Contents

Acknowledgments

From Joe Friel:

First, I want to thank my coauthor, Dr. Loren Cordain, for introducing me to the Paleo Diet in 1995. In doing so, he forever changed the way I train athletes and improved the health and well-being of my family. Second, I want to thank the scores of athletes I have coached who allowed me to change their diets in order to refine the concepts you will read about here. Chief among them is Dirk, my son, who continues to offer valuable feedback on the relationship between his training and diet. And, finally, I want to thank Joyce, my wife, for her assistance with many of the recipes included here and for allowing me the freedom to tinker in her kitchen and to get up at 4:00 a.m. to research and write about things that fascinate me.

From Loren Cordain:

On a beautiful spring morning about 15 years ago, I went out for an early-morning run on the deserted roads and trails above Fort Collins, Colorado. About 2 miles into my 7-mile run, I noticed a lean silhouette following me about a half mile behind. Being somewhat competitive in those days, I picked up the tempo and expected to shake this lone runner. Nothing doing; he picked up the pace as well. After another mile, I put it into high gear, expecting to bury this upstart. Unbelievably, this unknown figure had managed to close the distance to less than 200 yards. By the end of the run we were both in full sprint. As I was totally spent at the end of my run, Joe passed me and said, "Good morning!" I want to thank my coauthor for encouraging me to write this book in a slightly gentler manner than he pushed me on that Colorado spring morning. Finally, I want to thank my wife, Lorrie, and my three sons, Kyle, Kevin, and Kenny, for putting up with all of the lost weekends and late evenings needed to make this book happen.

Introduction

Information on the topic of nutrition for athletes has been on the market for the better part of the past century. It's interesting to note the changes that have occurred in such advice. For example, 60 years ago, Coach Willie Honeman offered the following dietary suggestions for bike racers.

> *The question of food and what to eat is one that would take much space to cover. A good rule of thumb is to eat whatever foods appeal to you, but be sure they are of good quality and fresh. Avoid too many starchy foods, such as bread, potatoes, pies, pastries, etc. Eat plenty of green and cooked vegetables.*
>
> —Willie Honeman, in *American Bicyclist*, 1945

Contrast Honeman's suggestions with what two cycling authorities recently proposed to athletes.

> *Carbohydrate supplementation is essential to meet the needs of heavy training. Greater portions of pasta, potatoes, and breads can help, but many athletes may prefer the concentrated carbohydrate found in "high-carbohydrate drinks." Such products as Ultra Fuel, Exceed High-Carbohydrate Source, and Gatorlode are used to generate additional carbohydrate intake without the bulk of solid food.*
>
> —Edmund Burke, PhD, and Jacqueline Berning, PhD, RD,
> in *Training Nutrition*, 1996

These selections illustrate what has happened to the logic of coaches, athletes, and even sports scientists since the 1970s. The current thinking is that athletes should load up on carbohydrate continuously, even to the extent of supplementing their diets with commercial products while avoiding "real" foods. The shift away from "good quality and fresh" foods, especially fruits, vegetables, and lean proteins, is widespread in the athletic world. Such a shift, while beneficial in terms of glycogen stores, which are necessary for performance—especially in endurance events—overlooks the necessity of eating foods that are also rich in other nutrients. This conventional viewpoint not only has negative consequences for health but also compromises an athlete's capacity for recovery and subsequent quality of training.

In *The Paleo Diet for Athletes,* we propose that this trend must be reversed and that the optimal model for the athlete is the same one that we as *Homo sapiens* have thrived on for nearly all of our existence on the planet—a Paleolithic, or Old Stone Age, diet, albeit one slightly modified to meet the unique demands of athletes.

The Paleo Diet is somewhat higher in protein and fat and lower in carbohydrate, relative to what sports nutritionists encourage American athletes to eat. But the greatest differences of what we propose here may be found in the timing of carbohydrate and protein ingestion, especially branched-chain amino acids; selecting foods based on glycemic load at certain times relative to training; the base-enhancing effects of our diet on blood and other body fluids; and periodization of diet in parallel with training. All of this means that you will recover faster and perform better by following our program: the Paleo Diet for Athletes. We've seen it happen in athlete after athlete for the past 10 years.

What we propose here is not intended as a quick-fix, weight-loss diet, although many of the athletes who have converted to it have reduced their excess fat stores. The dietary strategies we offer are intended for health and performance enhancement.

Performance is obvious, but why health enhancement? Unfortunately, many athletes are not truly healthy, despite being magnificently fit. Health and fitness do not always go hand in hand.

High volumes of training, often exceeding 2 hours per day, play havoc on the human immune system when it is not given adequate nutrients for renewal in the hours following training. A daily diet top-heavy in starch, especially from a single source such as grains, is bound to leave the athlete's body starved for protein and many trace nutrients. The Paleo Diet satisfies those demands daily.

Although heavily based upon science and thoroughly tested and honed in the real world of athletics, the value of eating much as our prehistoric ancestors ate is not generally accepted at face value by some scientists or athletes, as it flies in the face of much that we have been taught to believe about diet. When one suggests eating in this manner, many arguments against it are proposed. You may also be experiencing some healthy skepticism at this point—and some skepticism is a good thing. In order to continue your reading of this book in a more open manner, we need to address the most common of these concerns.

COMMON COUNTERARGUMENTS

Some of the most widespread, intuitive counterarguments against the Paleo Diet are that "they (hunter-gatherers) died at an early age" and, thus, "didn't live long enough to develop heart disease, cancer, and other chronic illnesses." Consequently, "they really were not healthier or fitter than modern people."

If you have bought into the first statement, then you are absolutely correct. There is no doubt that the average life span of hunter-gatherers and Stone Age people was quite short, compared with our own. Case in point: The average age of Neanderthals has been estimated at 12 to 15 years; pre-European-contact American Indians, 20 to 25 years. Today, US women live to age 79; men, to 72. It should be pointed out, though, that "average life span" is a misleading term. In reality, average life span is nothing more than the average age at death for an entire population; it tells us zilch about the age and health characteristics of individual, living people. For example, if two parents lived to the ages of 79 and 72, were healthy for most of their adult lives, and had two children who died at birth, the average life span of this group of four people ([79 + 72 + 0 + 0] / 4) would be 37.7 years. On the surface, based upon the low average life span, it would appear that *all* people in this group were not very healthy.

In order to more accurately portray a population's age and health characteristics, scientists have devised what are called life tables—charts that show the entire living population by age group, not just the people who have died. In a study of more than 450 !Kung hunter-gatherers in Botswana, life tables revealed that 10 percent of the population were age 60 and older. But more important, the aged populations in hunter-gatherer societies are virtually free of obesity, hypertension, high cholesterol, diabetes, and other chronic diseases that are near-universal afflictions of the elderly in Western societies. Hunter-gatherers died not from chronic, degenerative disease but from the accidents and trauma of a hazardous life spent in a perilous environment.

Think about camping out for your entire life, and you can get an appreciation for how harsh and dangerous their lifestyle was. While most of us really need not worry about death until middle or old age, hunter-gatherers commonly suffered early death from causes that claim comparatively few of us. They had no modern medicine, no advanced surgical procedures, no antibiotics, and no understanding of the germs that cause infection and disease. Civil war, strife, and regional conflict were a fact of life that continually raged throughout most of their lifetimes, and infanticide (the deliberate killing of infants) was commonly practiced. Because they lived outdoors their entire lives and were constantly challenged by the elements and the physical environment, the risk of injury from accidents was quite high over the course of their lifetimes. Hunting of big game, then as now, would have been a risky business, increasing the likelihood of accident or injury. The net result of living an entire life in a perilous environment produced a high death rate from trauma and accident in these people. It is rather remarkable that 10 to 20 percent of the population lived to 60 and beyond.

However, again, the take-home message is that the living, regardless of their age, were universally lean, fit, and free of the chronic degenerative diseases that are epidemic in our world. Figure I-1 shows that the aerobic fitness levels of young men, age 20 to 30 years, from hunter-gatherer and non-Westernized populations are far superior to the average Western couch potato, while Figure I-2 on page xiv shows that their body fat levels are much lower.

It may surprise you, but despite diets rich in animal foods, these people have healthful blood cholesterol levels that leave the average Westerner in the dust (see Table I-1 on page xiv). Further, high blood pressure—the most prevalent risk factor for coronary heart disease in the United States, affecting at least 50 million Americans—is rare or not present in non-Westernized societies.

FIGURE I-1

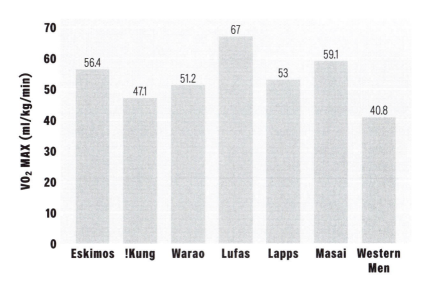

FIGURE I-2

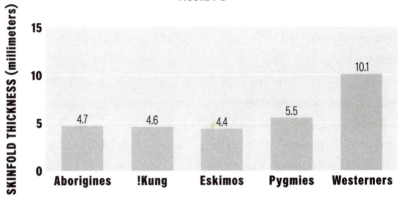

The Yanomamo Indians of South America, to whom salt was unknown in the late 1960s and early 1970s, were completely free of high blood pressure. Table I-2 shows the remarkable results of their salt-free diet in conjunction with their non-Westernized lifestyle on blood pressure. Not only is their average population blood pressure (102/64) lower than values considered to be normal (120/80) in the United States, but there is no age-associated rise in blood pressure. In the United States, by the ages of 65 to 74, 65 percent of all Americans have high blood pressure (140/90 or greater).

The superb health and fitness levels of hunter-gatherers were recorded not only in the medical literature but also in historical ac-

TABLE I-1

Blood Cholesterol Levels in Non-Westernized Populations

SOCIETY	LOCATION	MEAN SERUM CHOLESTEROL (MG/DL)
Aborigines	Australia	139
Eskimos	Canada	141
Hadza	Tanzania	110
!Kung	Botswana	120
Pygmies	Zaire	106
Yanomamo (men)	Brazil	123
Yanomamo (women)	Brazil	142
Westerners	United States	210

TABLE I-2

Blood Pressures (Systolic/Diastolic) in 506 Yanomamo Indians throughout Life

AGE	BLOOD PRESSURE	AGE	BLOOD PRESSURE
Males		Females	
0–9	93/59	0–9	96/62
10–19	108/67	10–19	105/65
20–29	108/69	20–29	100/63
30–39	106/69	30–39	100/63
40–49	107/67	40–49	98/62
50+	100/64	50+	106/64

counts by early explorers, adventurers, and frontiersmen. Cabeza de Vaca, the Spanish explorer, saw Native Americans in Florida in 1527 and described them as "wonderfully well built, spare, very strong, and very swift." Similar observations of these Indians were made in 1564 by the French explorer Rene de Laudonniere, who noted, "The agility of the women is so great that they can swim over great rivers, bearing their children upon one of their arms. They climb up, also, very nimbly upon the highest trees in the country . . . even the most ancient women of the country dance with the others."

In his 1773 account of California Native Americans, Jacob Baegert notes that "the Californians are seldom sick. They are in general strong, hardy, and much healthier than the many thousands who live daily in abundance and on the choicest fare that the skill of Parisian cooks can prepare." In his book *Across Unknown South America*, Henry Savage Landor describes the Borono Indians of the Amazon in 1913.

They displayed powerful chests, with ribs well covered with flesh and muscle. With their dark yellow skins they were not unlike beautiful bronze torsi. The abdominal region was never unduly enlarged, perhaps owing to the fact that their digestion was good, and also because they took a considerable amount of daily exercise. . . . The anatomical detail of the body was perfectly balanced. The arms were powerful, but with fine, well-formed wrists—exquisitely chiseled, as were all attachments of their limbs. Great refinement of the race was also to be noticed in the shape of their legs—marvelously modeled, without an ounce of extra flesh, and with small ankles.

Captain Cook, who visited New Zealand in 1772, was particularly impressed by the good health of the native Maori.

It cannot be thought strange that these people enjoy perfect and uninterrupted health. In all our visits to their towns, where young and old, men and women, crowd about us, prompted by the same curiosity that carried us to look at them, we never saw a single person who appeared to have any bodily complaint, nor among the numbers that we have seen naked did we perceive the slightest eruption upon the skin, or any marks that an eruption had been left behind. . . . A further proof that human nature is here untainted with disease is the great number of old men that we saw . . . appeared to be very ancient, yet none of them were decrepit; and though not equal to the young in muscular strength, were not a whit behind them in cheerfulness and vivacity.

Another common counterargument proposed by doubting Thomases is this: "We don't really know what they, our Stone Age ancestors, ate." In Chapter 8, we will delve into all the archaeological, anthropological, physiological, and fossil evidence showing us exactly what Stone Age hunter-gatherers ate. But for now, let us challenge you with a simple question that most of you could intuitively work out with little or zero knowledge of the fossil record or archaeology.

What foods could not have been consumed by Stone Age people?

This is no trick question; just do a little bit of reasoning with what you know about how some of the foods on your daily platter got there. Let's tackle some of the easy ones first. How about the cup of milk you had with your breakfast cereal—where did it come from? Well, of course, a farmer milked a cow, and the milk was processed, pasteurized, homogenized, and bottled at a dairy, then eventually made its way to your local supermarket. Bingo— as simple as that, right?

Now stop and think a moment about where that docile, milk-able cow came from. Were these peaceful, domesticated beasts always with us? Of course not! Modern-day milk cows were domesticated from wild, unruly beasts bearing enormous horns, called aurochs. Julius Caesar, who encountered these fierce brutes in Europe before they became extinct, remarked, "They are a little below the elephant in size, and of the appearance, color, and shape of a bull. Their strength and speed are extraordinary; they spare neither man nor wild beast which they have espied." Prior to do-mestication, aurochs, like all wild mammals, would not let hu-mans approach them, much less milk them. So, you can see that all of the milk and dairy products we consume today simply would not have been on the menu of our hunter-gatherer ancestors. In the average US diet, milk and dairy represent 10.6 percent of total daily energy intake.

How about refined sugars? The annual per capita consump-tion of all sugars in the United States is a staggering 152 pounds, or 18.6 percent of our total daily calories from all foods combined! Do you think it would have been possible for your Stone Age an-cestors to have consumed that much refined sugar? Absolutely not! Table sugar (sucrose) comes from either the sugarcane plant or sugar beets. Hunter-gatherers simply did not possess either the tools or knowledge to make refined sugars. In fact, sugar from sugarcane was first manufactured in northern India about 500 BC, whereas sugar extracted from sugar beets dates back to only 1747, in Germany. The ubiquitous high fructose corn syrup, the preferred sweetener in soft drinks and many processed foods, was introduced into the US food supply as recently as the late 1970s. We now consume almost as much high fructose corn syrup (63.6 pounds per capita) as we do sucrose (65.6 pounds per capita). There is no doubt that hunter-gatherers would have relished refined sugars, just as we do. However, except for honey, which was rare and only seasonally available, they simply had no readily available source of refined sugar.

Now that you are getting the drift of which foods could and could not have been on hunter-gatherers' menus, it becomes apparent that no highly processed foods were ever eaten. This isn't rocket science by any means—just simple, deductive logic that almost anyone can work out with a few basic facts.

However, here's a fact that may surprise you. Although bread, grains, and cereals symbolize "the staff of life" in virtually all Westernized societies and now represent almost 25 percent of the calories in the typical US diet, they were rarely or never consumed by our Stone Age ancestors. How do we know this? Have you ever tried to pop down a handful of uncooked whole wheat berries? How about some uncooked corn kernels or brown rice grains? If you perform these little experiments, you will see that the hard morsels come out of your body just like they went in—fully intact and undigested! Whole grains are tough as old boots unless their cell walls are first broken down by milling and their starch made digestible by cooking. Although our Stone Age ancestors had controlled fire by about 250,000 years ago, we know that grains did not become staple foods until the very recent appearance of crude stone grinding tools 13,000 years ago in the Middle East, according to fossil records. The bottom line is that grains, like dairy products and refined sugars, were not part of the native human diet.

While a cheese puff may look quite a bit different from a tortilla chip or a frozen waffle or even a bagel, all of these processed foods are almost indistinguishable from one another when you look at their individual food components. Think about it. They are really nothing more than mixtures of the same old three to six major ingredients—refined grains, refined sugars, some kind of processed vegetable oil, salt, artificial flavoring, and, perhaps, some kind of processed dairy product. Processed vegetable oils and salt, just like dairy food, refined sugars, and grains, are Johnny-come-latelies into the human diet. These ubiquitous foods and processed food mixtures made with them now compose 70 percent of all the food consumed in the US diet. By default, their inclusion into our diets displaces more healthful fruits, veggies, lean meats, and seafood—the staples of our Stone Age ancestors. As the next 12 chapters unfold, we will show you how you can improve your diet and thereby maximize your potential to improve your performance by increasing your intake of lean meats, seafood, fruits, and vegetables, along with careful and judicious consumption of certain "non-Paleo" modern foods.

Chapter 1

THE DIET REVOLUTION

Books on low-carbohydrate, high-protein diets such as *Dr. Atkins' New Diet Revolution, Protein Power, The Zone,* and *The South Beach Diet* have ruled the best-selling book lists for at least the past 5 years. Millions of Americans have successfully lost weight with diets that fly directly in the face of conventional medical and nutritional wisdom. In July 2002, these issues attained national notoriety with Gary Taubes's inflammatory *New York Times* article, "What If It's All Been a Big Fat Lie?" pitting the diet doctors' advice against big government and medical skeptics. In May 2003, the improbable became reality with the publication of the first long-term, well-controlled scientific studies of low-carbohydrate, high-protein diets. The results of these experiments, which appeared in the prestigious *New England Journal of Medicine,* decisively demonstrated that low-carbohydrate, high-protein diets were more effective in promoting weight loss than time-honored, low-fat, high-carbohydrate diets advocated by the American Heart Association.

A similar revolution in dietary thinking is just beginning to make ripples in the sports world by a small group of athletes who happen to be privy to a brand-new way of eating that has dramatically improved their athletic performances. Their dietary

1

formula for success was not accidentally stumbled upon by trial and error but resulted from a chance conversation between two old friends, Loren Cordain and Joe Friel, in the spring of 1995.

Fast-forward 8 years. Joe has become a successful coach, written five best-selling books on athletic training, and is considered by many to be an authority on endurance training. Meanwhile, Loren, a university professor, has written more than two dozen scientific papers on Stone Age (Paleolithic) diets, as well as a popular diet book based upon his research findings, and has become an internationally recognized expert in the study of Paleolithic diets. Had they not had that conversation, the small ripple that promised to become a tidal wave concerning diet and athletic performance never would have surfaced.

LOREN'S CHALLENGE: THE PALEO DIET IN A NUTSHELL

In 1995, I challenged Joe to give the Paleo Diet a try. Joe had been a longtime adherent to the standard very high-carbohydrate diet for athletes and was skeptical of my claim that eating less starch would benefit performance. Nearly every successful endurance athlete that Joe had known ate as he did, with a heavy emphasis on cereals, bagels, bread, rice, pasta, pancakes, and potatoes. In fact, Joe had done quite well on this diet as an All-American duathlete (run-bike-run) in his age group, winning national races and finishing in the top 10 at World Championships. Joe had also coached many successful athletes, both professional and amateur, who ate the same way he did.

I suggested Joe try eating a diet more in line with the Paleo Diet for 1 month. Joe took the challenge, determined to show me that eating as he had for years was the way to go. He started by simply cutting back significantly on starches and dairy and replacing those lost calories with fruits, vegetables, and very lean meats. Although a simple formula, it wasn't easy at first.

For the first 2 weeks, Joe felt miserable. His recovery following workouts was slow, and his workouts were sluggish. He figured he was well on his way to proving that I was wrong. But in week 3, a curious thing happened. He noticed that he was not only feeling better but his recovery following workouts was speeding up significantly, and he decided to experiment to see how many hours he could train. Since his early forties (he was 51 at the time), he had not been able to train more than about 12 hours per week; whenever he exceeded that weekly volume, upper respiratory infections would soon set him back. In week 4, he trained 16 hours without a sign of a cold, sore throat, or ear infection. He was amazed—he hadn't done that many hours in nearly 15 years. He decided to keep the experiment going. That year Joe finished third at the US National Championship with an excellent race and qualified for the US team for the World Championships. He had a stellar season, one of his best in years.

Joe's little experiment proved to have far-reaching effects. After making certain refinements to my basic Paleo Diet, Joe found this way of eating to be "ergogenic," a term exercise physiologists use to describe nutritional supplements that can enhance athletic performance. By the late 1990s, Joe was recommending the Paleo Diet to the athletes he coached, including Ryan Bolton, a member of the US Olympic Triathlon team in the 2000 Sydney Olympics and a winner of the Ironman USA Triathlon. Increasingly, by word of mouth and the Internet, athletes worldwide were becoming aware of the competitive edge they could gain by adopting a diet based upon my dietary principles and fine-tuned by Joe's practical experience with it.

The Paleo Diet for Athletes is not just for world-class performers like Ryan Bolton and Gordo Bryn (an ardent devotee of the Paleo Diet and winner of the Ultraman Triathlon and the World's Toughest Half-Ironman Triathlon) but also for everyday fitness enthusiasts like Don Moffat. Here's Don's story.

I wish I had known about the Paleo Diet 5 years ago, when I was a sub-3-hour marathoner before my health started breaking down due to insulin-resistance-related issues. Following a high-protein, low-carb diet for the last 2 months has created startling results in my fitness. I've lost 3 inches from my waist (down to 32), and I can't believe how, at 38, I'm putting on muscle. My run times have dropped by 25 percent. (I'm still not fast again, but I'm seeing steady, week-to-week progress.) I find the increase in muscle strength particularly gratifying, as this was always a problem for me before, even in my early twenties. It's sort of like getting some youth back.

WHY IS THE PALEO DIET FOR ATHLETES ERGOGENIC?

There is indeed a method to this madness, and I have uncovered the scientific basis for the effectiveness of the modification of the original Paleo Diet. In a nutshell, there are four basic reasons the Paleo Diet enhances athletic performance.

1. Branched-chain amino acids. First, the diet is high in animal protein, which is the richest source of the branched-chain amino acids—valine, leucine, and isoleucine. Branched-chain amino acids (BCAA) are different from other amino acids that collectively make up protein in that they are potent stimulants for building and repairing muscle. This information is quite new and has been reported in the scientific literature only in the past few years. But the dig is this: These amino acids work best when consumed in the postexercise window.

Lean meats and fish are far and away the greatest source of BCAA. A 1,000-calorie serving of lean beef provides 33.7 grams of BCAA, whereas the same serving of whole grains supplies a paltry 6 grams. Because most endurance athletes focus on starches (breads, cereals, pasta, rice, and potatoes) and sugars at the expense of lean meats, particularly following a hard workout, they get precious little muscle-building BCAA in their diets. By consuming high amounts of lean protein (and hence BCAA), athletes can rapidly reverse the natural breakdown of muscle that occurs following a workout and thereby reduce recovery time and train at a greater intensity at the next session. Joe's advice for athletes to replace starches with lean meats now makes perfect sense and explains the athletes' near-universal report of improved recovery with these dietary recommendations.

2. Blood acidity versus alkalinity. In addition to stimulating muscle growth via BCAA, the Paleo Diet for Athletes simultaneously prevents muscle protein breakdown because it produces a net metabolic alkalosis. All foods, upon digestion, report to the kidney as either acid or alkali (base). The typical American diet is net acid producing because of its high reliance upon acid-yielding grains, cheeses, and salty processed foods at the expense of base-producing fruits and veggies. The athlete's body is even more prone to blood acidosis due to the by-products of exercise. One way the body neutralizes a net-acid-producing diet is by breaking down muscle tissue. Because the Paleo Diet for Athletes is rich in fruits and veggies, it reverses the metabolic acidosis produced from the typical grain- and starch-laden diet for athletes, thereby preventing muscle loss.

3. Trace nutrients. Fruits and vegetables are also rich sources of antioxidant vitamins, minerals, and phytochemicals and, together with lean meats (excellent sources of zinc and B vitamins), promote optimal immune-system functioning. The refined grains, oils, sugars, and processed foods that represent the typical staples for most athletes are nearly devoid of these trace nutrients. From examining the training logs of numerous people he has coached, Joe found that the frequency and duration of colds, flu, and upper respiratory illnesses are reduced when athletes adopt the Paleo Diet. A healthy athlete, free of colds and illness, can train more consistently and intensely and thereby improve performance.

4. Glycogen stores. One of the most important goals of any athletic diet is to maintain high muscle stores of glycogen, a body fuel absolutely essential for high-level performance. Dietary starches and sugars are the body's number one source for making muscle glycogen. Protein won't do, and neither will fat. Athletes and sports scientists have known this truth for decades. Regrettably, they took this concept to extremes; high-starch, cereal-based, carbohydrate-rich diets were followed with near-fanatical zeal 24 hours a day, 7 days a week.

It is a little known fact, but, similar to the situation with branched-chain amino acids, glycogen synthesis by muscles occurs most effectively in the immediate postexercise window. Muscles can build all the glycogen they need when they get starch and sugar in the narrow time frame following exercise. Eating carbs all day long is overkill and actually serves to displace the muscle-building lean proteins and alkalinity-enhancing, nutrient-dense fruits and veggies that are needed to promote muscle growth and boost the immune system. Perhaps the most important refinement made to my original Paleo Diet was Joe's recognition that consumption of starches and simple sugars was necessary and useful only during exercise and in the immediate postexercise period. Joe has also found that certain carbohydrates are more effective than others in restoring muscle glycogen, particularly specific types of sugar, such as glucose and net-alkaline-producing starches found in bananas, potatoes, sweet potatoes, and yams.

NOTHING NEW IN 30 YEARS

The standard dietary advice given to athletes by sports physiologists, nutritionists, and physicians hasn't changed an iota in 30 years. It is similar to the USDA's Food Pyramid—high in grain-based carbohydrates and low in fat—the same diet that many scientists believe is responsible for the obesity epidemic in this country. The world now is aware that an alternative exists to the

Food Pyramid. Low-carbohydrate, high-protein diets have proven to be more effective in promoting weight loss than are conventional high-carbohydrate, low-fat diets. Unfortunately, the athletic world is little aware that these same types of diets (higher in protein and lower in carbohydrate) can be extremely effective in enhancing performance. Except for the few athletes privy to my research and Joe's practical implementation of it, athletes in general are unaware that an alternative diet exists—a diet that can maximize performance in a range of sports, from body building and tennis to running and triathlon.

The Paleo Diet for Athletes is revolutionary and is creating an upheaval in the sports world, similar to the commotion set in play by the diet doctors with their high-protein, low-carbohydrate diets. The information contained in this book is thoroughly supported by scientific literature, to which Loren continues to make cutting-edge contributions. More important, Joe has shown that the Stone Age diet of our ancient ancestors, with slight modifications, works extremely well for recreational athletes all the way up to Olympians. The Paleo Diet for Athletes has passed the most important test by the most critical audience of all: the athletes themselves.

THE PALEO DIET FOR ATHLETES: NUTRITIONAL CHARACTERISTICS IN A NUTSHELL

The essential dietary principles for the Paleo Diet for Athletes are straightforward: You can eat as much lean meat, poultry, seafood, fresh fruit, and veggies as you like. Foods that are not part of the modern-day Paleolithic fare include cereal grains, dairy products, high-glycemic fruits and vegetables, legumes, alcohol, salty foods, fatty meats, refined sugars, and nearly all processed foods.

There are a number of crucial exceptions to these fundamental rules that will be completely explained in coming chapters. Case in point: Immediately before, during, and after a workout or competition, certain non-Paleo foods should be eaten to promote a quick recovery. During all other times, meals that closely follow the 21st-century Paleolithic diet, described in Chapter 9, will encourage comprehensive long-term recovery and allow you to attain your maximal performance potential.

At first glance, you might think it counterproductive or even foolish to reduce or eliminate two entire food groups (cereal grains and dairy), along with most of the processed foods in your diet. One way of looking at our Paleo dietary recommendations is to compare them with the USDA Food Pyramid, the diet officially recommended by the US government and specifically designed to improve our health and reduce our risk of chronic disease. The USDA has published an extensive handbook called *Using the Food Guide Pyramid: A Resource for Nutrition Educators* (available on the Web at www.nal.usda.gov/fnic/Fpyr/guide.pdf), in which government dietitians have outlined sample 5-day menus that conform to Food Pyramid guidelines. The USDA has also been gracious enough to provide us with the vitamins, minerals, and nutrient values in their example menus. Consequently, it is a relatively simple exercise to compare modern-day Paleo diets with those officially sanctioned by the USDA.

Remember the ground rules of modern-day Stone Age diets: The diets contain no grains, dairy products, salt, processed foods, or fatty meats; they consist almost entirely of fresh fruits, veggies, lean meats, and seafood. Table 1.1 outlines a typical day for a 25-year-old woman whose daily caloric intake is 2,200 calories.

Now let's see how this representative day's worth of modern Paleo food stacks up against the USDA Food Pyramid. First, take a look at the major dietary components, which are listed in Table 1.2 on page 10. You immediately see that the Paleo Diet is much higher in protein and lower in carbohydrate than the Food Pyramid diet is. Even though more than half of the calories in our

TABLE 1.1

Sample 1-Day Menu from a Modern Diet Based on Paleolithic Food Groups for a Woman (25 years old; 2,200-calorie daily intake)

FOOD	QUANTITY (G)	ENERGY (KCAL)
Breakfast		
Cantaloupe	276	97
Atlantic salmon (broiled)	333	605
Lunch		
Vegetable salad with walnuts		
Shredded Romaine lettuce	68	10
Sliced carrot	61	26
Sliced cucumber	78	10
Quartered tomatoes	246	52
Lemon-juice dressing	31	8
Walnuts	11	70
Broiled lean pork loin	86	205
Dinner		
Vegetable avocado/almond salad		
Shredded mixed greens	112	16
Tomato	123	26
Avocado	85	150
Slivered almonds	45	260
Sliced red onion	29	11
Lemon-juice dressing	31	8
Steamed broccoli	468	131
Lean beef sirloin tip roast	235	400
Dessert		
Strawberries	130	39
Snacks		
Orange	66	30
Carrot sticks	81	35
Celery sticks	90	14

diet come from meat and seafood, the saturated fat content is quite low—even lower than recommended values (10 percent) known to reduce the risk for high blood cholesterol and heart disease. The fats you will be getting in this diet are just plain good for you! Notice that the good fats (monounsaturated and polyunsaturated fats) that lower blood cholesterol levels are considerably higher than what you would get by following the Food Pyramid diet.

Most people have heard that omega-3 fatty acids found in fish like salmon are healthful, but few are aware that a family of fats called omega-6 fatty acids, found in vegetable oils, margarine, and processed foods, can be harmful when consumed at the expense

TABLE 1.2

Dietary Characteristics in a Contemporary Diet Based on Paleolithic Food Groups and in a Recommended USDA Food Pyramid Diet for a Woman (25 years old; 2,200-calorie daily intake)

NUTRIENT	FOOD PYRAMID	MODERN PALEO DIET
Protein (g)	113	217
Protein (% energy)	20	38
Carbohydrate (g)	302	129
Carbohydrate (% energy)	53	23
Total sugars (g)	96.6	76.5
Fiber (g)	30	42.5
Fat (grams)	67	100.3
Fat (% total energy)	27	39
Saturated fat (g)	19.6	18
Saturated fat (% total energy)	7	6.4
Monounsaturated fat (g)	22.8	44.3
Polyunsaturated fat (g)	19	26.7
Omega-3 fatty acids (g)	1	9.6
Omega-6 fatty acids (g)	14.3	14.2
Cholesterol (mg)	219	461
Sodium (mg)	2,626	726
Potassium (mg)	3,450	9,062

of omega-3s. In the standard American diet, the ratio of omega-6 to omega-3 fatty acids is an unhealthy 10:1. Contrast this ratio to the wholesome 1:1 to 3:1 in the native human diet. Now take a look at the Food Pyramid: The recommendation is an appalling 14:1 and is actually worse than what the average American is currently eating! The Food Pyramid was originally conceived and thrust upon a trusting US public in 1992, prior to the widespread knowledge that an imbalance in omega-6 and omega-3 fatty acids had so much to do with health and well-being. Unfortunately, we are still saddled with this botched bit of advice.

But just wait—there are troubles with the Pyramid beyond its improper fat balance. In 1992, the concept of a glycemic load and its impact on health was unknown to the dietitians who designed the Pyramid. Should we be concerned about the glycemic load of a food? Absolutely! Does the Food Pyramid differentiate between high and low glycemic foods? Absolutely not! There is little doubt that even the recently revised Food Pyramid is badly in need of repair. It's high time that nutritionists consider the evolutionary basis for the optimal human diet rather than relying upon human foibles and biases in developing healthful, performance-enhancing diets.

As an athlete, you want to maximize your performance by maximizing your diet. This includes the amount of vitamins and minerals that you get from your food. Let's contrast the nutrient density of our sample Paleo Diet to the USDA Food Pyramid. Take a quick look at the values in Table 1-3 on page 12, and you will see that there is really no comparison. Except for calcium, the Paleo Diet simply blows away the Food Pyramid. In Chapters 5 and 9, we fully explain why a reduced calcium intake does not represent a problem, particularly if you eat ample fruits and vegetables.

An essential part of making this diet work for endurance athletes like you is to maintain an adequate carbohydrate intake so

TABLE 1.3

Trace Nutrients in a Modern Diet Based on Paleolithic Food Groups
and in a Recommended USDA Food Pyramid Diet for Women (25
years old; 2,200-calorie daily intake)

	FOOD PYRAMID		MODERN PALEOLITHIC DIET	
Nutrient	Amount	% RDA	Amount	% RDA
Vitamin A	1,659 RE	207	6,386 RE	798
Vitamin B_1	2.3 mg	209	3.4 mg	309
Vitamin B_2	2.6 mg	236	4.2 mg	355
Vitamin B_3	30 mg	214	60 mg	428
Vitamin B_6	2.6 mg	200	6.7 mg	515
Folate	453 µg	113	891 µg	223
Vitamin B_{12}	4.7 µg	196	17.6 µg	733
Vitamin C	233 mg	388	748 mg	1,247
Vitamin E	10 IU	125	19.5 IU	244
Calcium	1,215 mg	122	691 mg	69
Phosphorus	808 mg	258	2,546 mg	364
Magnesium	427 mg	138	643 mg	207
Iron	19 mg	127	24.3 mg	162
Zinc	14 mg	116	27.4 mg	228

that your muscle glycogen levels will be fully restored before your
next workout. Consequently, you will need to include additional
carbohydrates in your diet, particularly during and following long
workouts. In Chapters 2, 3, and 4, we fully explain the ins and
outs of carbohydrate ingestion relative to your workout, your
training schedule, and your personal needs.

PART I

THE ROAD MAP TO PEAK PERFORMANCE AND HEALTH

Chapter 2

STAGE I:
EATING BEFORE
EXERCISE

What should an athlete eat before, during, and after exercise? This is a question to which athletes have sought the answer for as long as there have been competitive sports. In the days of the Roman Empire, gladiators ate the heart and muscle of lions before the contest, believing this would give them the ferocious qualities of the animal. As late as the 1960s, athletes were still eating prodigious quantities of red meat before engaging in "battle." In the 1970s, there was a swing toward consuming carbohydrates on race day. That trend still continues, but recently there has been an increased interest in protein and fat in the athlete's race-day diet. And so the pendulum swings the other way once again.

While the role of carbohydrate ingestion before, during, and after exercise has been studied extensively over the past 40 years, only recently has there been much research into the role and timing of dietary protein and fat relative to exercise. Since such research is still in its infancy, there is a great deal not fully understood, and, further complicating the matter, there are contradictions in the limited research available.

THE DEMANDS OF ENDURANCE TRAINING

Training for endurance sports such as running, cycling, triathlon, rowing, swimming, and cross-country skiing places great demands on the body, putting the athlete in some stage of recovery almost continuously during periods of heavy training. The keys to optimum recovery are sleep and diet. Even though we recommend that everyone eats a diet similar to what our Stone Age ancestors ate, we realize that nutritional concessions must be made for the athlete who is training at a high volume in the range of 10 to 35 or more hours per week of rigorous exercise. Rapid recovery is the biggest issue facing such an athlete. While it's not impossible to recover from such training loads on a strict Paleo Diet, it is somewhat more difficult to recover quickly. By modifying the diet before, during, and immediately following challenging workouts, the Paleo Diet provides two benefits sought by all athletes—quick recovery for the next workout and superior health for the rest of your life.

Such high training loads require a great intake of carbohydrate for short-term replenishment of expended glycogen stores, perhaps as much as 1,200 to 1,500 calories. Eating low to moderate glycemic index foods in the Paleo-approved categories of fruits and vegetables may certainly replace such deficiencies but will be accompanied by several pounds of fiber. Such a diet will also be slow to replace expended glycogen stores in the muscles following hard workouts or races, thus delaying or substantially affecting a subsequent workout or race in the next few hours and days. This is where modification of a strict Paleo Diet is necessary for the serious athlete.

In this and the next two chapters, we will examine the times when eating in ways other than the more conventional Paleo Diet is appropriate for the serious endurance athlete. But we can't emphasize strongly enough that these are exceptions to the standards discussed in Chapter 9 and are limited to specific time windows relative to training sessions and races. In Chapters 2, 3, and 4, we discuss the five recovery stages through which the athlete passes every day that includes exercise. By dividing the day into the following stages and eating appropriate foods in adequate amounts in each, recovery will be enhanced and performance maximized.

Stage I: Immediately before the workout or race
Stage II: During the workout or race
Stage III: Thirty minutes immediately following exercise
Stage IV: A period equal to the duration of the preceding exercise session
Stage V: Long-term recovery leading to the next Stage I

Before getting into the details of these stages, let's take a look at diet during a time when most athletes seem to be unsure of what to eat—the week of the race. To differentiate the importance of all of the race events on your schedule, we classify them as priority A, B, or C. Priority A events are the most important on your schedule. Normally an athlete will have only two or three of these planned for a given season since each involves cutting back on the training load for several days to a few weeks prior. Such reductions, while allowing the athlete to fully realize race readiness, may well lead to diminished fitness if done more frequently than a few times per season. Priority C races are the least important events on your schedule. There may be many of these because they are considered little more than challenging workouts done, for example, to test fitness or to make final preparations for a higher-priority race. As you might expect, priority B events fall between A and C in terms of importance. You want to do well at these races, so you may rest for a few days before them, but you won't taper your training over the longer period that's done for the highest-priority events.

EATING DURING RACE WEEK

This is not a time to make wholesale changes in your diet. Stick with the foods you've been eating, but be aware that if this is a priority A event, you may want to reduce the amount of food that you eat this week as your training volume is reduced so you may avoid excessive weight gain. You might still put on as much as 2 or 3 pounds, but most of that is water. For every gram of glycogen your body stores away in the muscles, it also packs away 2.6 grams of water. Having extra water on board may well be an advantage, especially if you'll be racing in hot or humid conditions.

The day before the race, if you've been carefully following a Paleo Diet, shift your food choices by taking in slightly more carbohydrate than usual to ensure that your carbohydrate storage sites are full. With the reduced volume this week, your body is primed to store glycogen, so this last day of shifting your diet to increased carbohydrate should be adequate. Now is a good time to eat more fruits such as bananas, peaches, cantaloupe, watermelon, and honeydew melon, along with vegetables such as potatoes, sweet potatoes, and yams. Snack on dried fruit today. To moderate the glycemic index of these foods, include protein and fat with each meal. Good fats to select today are olive, canola, and flaxseed oils. Eating cold-water fish such as tuna, haddock, and mackerel will satisfy both the protein and fat needs. Skip the pasta party the night before the race.

In addition, reduce dietary fiber to allow for easier digestion of foods in preparation for the next day's race. Also, if your event lasts longer than about 4 hours and the weather will be hot, sprinkle a little more salt on your food. This "sodium loading" may help prevent hyponatremia (low blood sodium) the next day. Otherwise, eat at usual times and keep food types as normal as possible.

STAGE I: EATING BEFORE EXERCISE

It happens all too often: An athlete prepares meticulously for weeks and months for an important event. There is no workout that is too demanding, no sacrifice too great. Then comes race day, and an error is made in the prerace meal: choosing food that takes too long to digest or digests too quickly; eating too much too close to the race start; taking in too little fluid; or eating nothing at all. The result is a disastrous performance—all that preparation for naught. We've seen it happen too many times. In fact, we've experienced it ourselves. Live and learn.

How could this have been prevented? How, indeed, could the athletic performance have been enhanced by the foods eaten before a demanding race or training session? The purpose of this section is to help you establish a dietary routine that serves you well, whether for a workout starting at your back door or a race a thousand miles away. Of course, it's easier if you're at home than on the road. Our goal here is to establish a select menu of foods that you can find whether you're in Hometown, USA, or traveling to Hobart, Australia, for a race.

Preexercise Eating Goals

Let's start by examining the goals for preexercise foods and fluids. There are five major objectives we are trying to accomplish with nutrient intake just before the race or workout.

- **Satisfy hunger.** This is pretty basic, so it's a wonder that so many athletes ignore food first thing in the morning. If it's race day, you may be too preoccupied to be aware of telltale signs at first, but your body will soon cry out for food. The longer you put it off, the greater the risk of starting exercise underfueled. The biggest downside of such a mistake is what cyclists call "bonking" and runners call "hitting the wall." You simply run very low on muscle and liver glycogen—the body's storage form of carbohydrate. When that happens, you're forced to slow down or completely stop.

  Realizing that you're hungry in the last hour before exercise may well be too late. Eating so close to starting is likely to do

19

more harm than good. Don't start hungry and don't put off eating. If possible, eat at least 2 hours in advance of exercise. At first you may find it difficult to eat right out of bed, but this aversion is mostly mental. Get used to taking in food of some sort early every day and it will be much easier on race day. You may find that a liquid meal is the best option if you dislike eating early in the morning.

- **Restock carbohydrate stores depleted by the overnight fast.** During the night, as you slept, your body was busy repairing and replacing tissues in an ongoing maintenance routine it has been engaged in since your conception. And, of course, there were energy demands throughout the night simply related to being alive—breathing, cardiac activity, movement, digestion, and other life-sustaining functions. All of this takes energy, and one of the most available fuel sources for this activity is the carbohydrate stored in your muscles as glycogen. So when you awake after several hours of sleep, your carbohydrate stores may be depleted by as much as 140 to 260 calories, depending on your body size and fat free mass (muscles, bones, hair, fingernails, organs—everything other than fat). Replacing these expended calories is very important to your immediate athletic performance, and the longer the race or workout session, the more critical this becomes.

- **Reestablish normal body fluid levels.** Besides using up energy as you slept, your body also lost water in your breath, through your pores, and during any bathroom visits. First thing in the morning, your body may be down 20 ounces (700 milliliters) from normal hydration levels. Failing to replenish right away sets you up for dehydration and a disastrous race or workout.

- **Optimize performance.** This is a big one. Other than simply restoring your fuel and fluid levels, proper preexercise nutrition can have a lot to do with how you perform. Certain nutrients have been shown to boost performance for some types of events. We'll examine these possibilities later in this chapter.

- **Prepare the body to recover quickly postexercise.** The better your hydration and fuel levels are going into the race or workout, the faster you'll recover, assuming you refuel and rehydrate adequately during exercise. But if you start with a low tank, even if you eat and drink as you should during activity, recovery may well be delayed. This means it will take you longer to return to a high level of training in subsequent days. It's even more critical if you are doing two- or three-times-a-day workouts and if you are stage racing.

Preexercise Eating

There is little doubt that preexercise nutrient intake can help your athletic performance. The big question has to do with what you should eat and drink. We can offer several guidelines that come not only from the research but also from our personal experiences as athletes and from coaching hundreds of others in several sports over the past 30 years. In a nutshell, here are the guidelines that will help you make decisions about what to take in before starting a race or workout.

- **Consume 200 to 300 calories per hour prior to exercise.** The amount you need is determined by your body size, how much you ate the night before, at what time that meal was eaten, and your experience with eating before exercise. We recommend eating no less than 2 hours before the race or workout. Three hours is usually better, especially if you tend to have a nervous stomach on race days. If you eat 2 hours before, take in 400 to 600 calories. If eating 3 hours before, you could eat 600 to 900 calories.
- **Take in mostly carbohydrate.** As was explained in the previous section, during the multihour fast of your night's sleep, your body's stores of glycogen were reduced. The fastest, most efficient way to restore this vital fuel source is by eating carbohydrate.

If chosen wisely, carbohydrate also has the advantage of digesting fairly quickly so that you won't be carrying a load of undigested foodstuffs early in the training session or race.

- **Reduce the glycemic index of the meal the more time you have before the start of the race or workout.** The glycemic index of a food indicates how quickly a carbohydrate's sugar gets into the blood. A quick release of sugar from the meal triggers the release of the hormone insulin by the pancreas. This results in a rapid decrease in the blood sugar level, followed quickly by increased hunger shortly before the race begins. That's not what you want to happen. But by eating a lower glycemic index food 2 or more hours before starting, your gut will have time to digest it and slowly replenish glycogen stores. Fruit, for example, is a good choice because its sugar, fructose, is slow to digest.

- **Keep the meal low in fiber.** There are several ways to reduce the glycemic index of a food. One of the most effective is the addition of fiber. But this may be too effective for a preexercise meal; the fiber in some foods, such as coarse, whole grain cereals, is so dense that it could well sit in your gut for several hours, soaking up fluids and swelling. That's not a good feeling to have at the start of a race or hard workout.

- **Include protein, especially the branched-chain amino acids.** Amino acids are the building blocks of protein. Certain amino acids, the "essential" ones, are critical for your health and fitness and must be in the foods you eat because the body can't produce them. Recent research out of the lab of Peter Lemon, PhD, at the University of Western Ontario reveals that three of these essential amino acids, those called branched-chain amino acids (BCAA), have benefits for performance when taken before aerobic exercise. (If you study protein for athletes, you're sure to come across Dr. Lemon's name often, as he is considered one of the leading authorities in the world on this topic.) In this study, cyclists were given 6 grams of BCAA or 6 grams of gelatin

1 hour before an exhaustive session on a bicycle. Compared with the gelatin feeding, the BCAA significantly improved time to exhaustion and maximum power output, while lowering heart rate at submaximum efforts. Blood sugar and lactate levels did not differ between the two trials.

Other research has revealed that a mixture of the essential amino acids and carbohydrate taken before strenuous exercise effectively stimulates protein synthesis after exercise. This is great news for the serious endurance athlete, as time to recovery is critical for performance. The faster you recover, the sooner you can do another quality workout; the more quality workouts in a given period of training, the better your subsequent performances in races.

Finally, an additional benefit of adding protein to a preexercise meal is that this lowers the glycemic index of the carbohydrate ingested along with it. A lowered glycemic index means a longer, slower release of sugar into the bloodstream during the subsequent exercise session, thus delaying the onset of fatigue.

- **Hydrate well.** You can prevent the onset of dehydration during exercise by making sure that you are well hydrated before starting. Furthermore, research has shown that consuming adequate fluids relative to thirst reduces protein breakdown during exercise. Anything you can do to spare protein or prevent its use as a fuel during a race or workout benefits both performance and recovery. You don't want to use muscle tissue to fuel exercise. Drinking well before exercise is one simple way to help ensure this doesn't happen.

- **Take in water only in the last hour.** The purpose here is to prevent a rapid influx of sugar to the blood, followed by the release of insulin to control it. Such a sugar-insulin (hypoglycemic) reaction is likely to leave you low on blood sugar at the start—just the opposite of what you intended—so you feel slightly dizzy and light-headed within a few minutes of exercise.

The exception to this guideline is that in the last 10 minutes prior to exercise, high glycemic index fluids may be consumed. This is explained in greater detail below.

Preexercise Food Choices

Foods to eat before exercise should be those that can be found in grocery stores, no matter where you are racing, or easily be carried while traveling. The following are examples of such food sources to eat prior to the last hour before starting exercise. You should select those that appeal to you in the morning while being well tolerated by your body. Try them on the days of race-simulation workouts and priority C races, well before the targeted priority A event for which you intend to use them. You may want to combine two or more of these to create some variety in your preexercise meal.

- **Fruit with eggs.** Eggs are loaded with protein and easily digested by most people. Boiled eggs may be taken to a race venue if they are kept chilled, or you can order scrambled eggs at a restaurant. One large, whole egg contains about 6 grams of protein and 1.5 grams of BCAA. Combine this with fresh fruit, especially fruit that is low in fiber, such as bananas, peaches, cantaloupe, honeydew, and watermelon. Fibrous fruits to avoid include apples, berries, dates, figs, grapes, pears, mango, papaya, and pineapple.
- **Applesauce mixed with protein powder.** Look for unsweetened applesauce. This is low in fiber and has a low glycemic index primarily due to its fructose content, and it's well tolerated by most people. Stir in 2 or 3 tablespoons of powdered egg or whey protein to further slow the glycemic reaction and to add BCAA. The BCAA content of protein powders varies with source and manufacturer, but they contain roughly 2.2 grams per tablespoon. Carry protein powder in a plastic bag when traveling to races.

- **Baby food, including animal products.** Chopped and pureed baby food can be found anywhere and is easily digested by the human gut at any age. Good choices are fruits or vegetables, along with chopped meats such as turkey, fish, or chicken.
- **Liquid meals.** If you tend to have a very nervous stomach prior to races, blending foods may produce a liquid you can more easily digest. Blend low-fiber fruit, such as those listed above, with fruit juice and 2 or 3 tablespoons of protein powder. Commercial drinks, although not optimal, are an option when you are away from home and don't have access to a blender. Look for products with added protein, such as Ensure High Protein. It's best to avoid those that use dairy as a base. Be aware that these drinks are becoming so popular with endurance athletes that stores in the vicinity of races often sell out days in advance. Bring your own or shop early.
- **Sports bar with protein.** This is the least attractive of the options, but it'll work in a pinch. Protein bars, sometimes called meal-replacement bars, are easily carried and available almost everywhere. While primarily a carbohydrate-based food source, they contain just enough protein to slow the glycemic reaction and add some BCAA to the meal. Be sure to drink lots of water with these because they are dry and might otherwise draw fluids from your body into the gut to assist with digestion, leaving you dehydrated.
- **Drink fluids including water.** You may also use coffee or tea, which have the benefits associated with caffeine, as described in Chapter 6. However, be aware that there are potential downsides with caffeine, such as upset stomach and increased nervousness. Fruit and vegetables juices may also be taken, but be sure to experiment with these during training sessions. Good choices are tomato, apple, and orange. Tomato juice often has added sodium, which may be beneficial if your race or workout is long and in the heat.

10 Minutes before Start

Taking in carbohydrate within the last hour or so, not including the final 10 minutes before starting, may cause hypoglycemia (low blood sugar) during the first several minutes of exercise in some people who are especially sensitive to sugar. For them, carbohydrate, especially a high glycemic load source, causes an almost immediate increase in blood insulin levels to reduce the blood's sugar level, resulting in hypoglycemia. Many athletes may well experience light-headedness or dizziness in the ensuing exercise because of this reaction. Why doesn't this happen when high glycemic index carbohydrate is taken in during the final 10 minutes before starting? The answer is that there just isn't enough time for the body to respond by pumping out insulin. By the time exercise occurs, the body immediately begins to down-regulate its need for insulin. During exercise, sugar intake produces smaller increases of this hormone because the muscles become more sensitive to insulin and permeable to glucose, reducing the need for large amounts of insulin that normally are required to escort the sugar into the muscle.

Taking in 100 to 200 calories from a few ounces of sports drink or gel, followed by 6 to 8 ounces of water, may well give you the energy boost needed right before starting without any negative effects. This is especially beneficial for those early-morning workouts when you get out of bed within an hour of heading out the door. It may also prove helpful to the athlete who just can't eat first thing in the morning.

Just as with the preexercise meal examples offered above, the purpose of this 10-minute topping off is to replenish glycogen stores while ensuring adequate hydration levels.

Chapter 3

STAGE II: EATING DURING EXERCISE

Eating during exercise is a learned skill that requires consider-able planning and testing, which includes discovering tasty nutrient sources along with the amounts and timing that work best for you. This demands careful trial and error and meticulous attention to detail. Don't assume that just because certain sources work well for someone else, they will also work well for you. Tolerance for food during exercise is an individual matter.

FOOD TOLERANCE DURING EXERCISE

The workouts that are the best indicators of what you can or cannot eat are the ones that most closely simulate the event for which you are training, including the expected race duration, intensity, terrain, and weather. You will find that your body's toler-ances for food and fluid change as conditions vary. The least important priority C races on your schedule that mimic the con-ditions of the priority A events serve as even better tests for nutri-tion because these also place psychological demands on you. The ultimate test is the goal race. From this experience, you can draw even better conclusions for future races.

The intensity of exercise has a great deal to do with how well the stomach tolerates food and drink. At very high intensities, such as above 85 percent max VO_2 (approximately at anaerobic threshold), the gastrointestinal system essentially stops functioning as blood is shunted to the hardworking muscles and to the skin for cooling. Conversely, at low intensities, such as when racing in an ultramarathon event that takes many hours to complete, many athletes experience an as-yet-unexplained mechanism that produces nausea. Fortunately, if the event for which you are training is short and intense, such as a 5-K run or bicycle criterium, there is no need to take in additional fuel. You have plenty on board already.

If, on the other hand, your event is long and not a steady effort but, rather, punctuated by high-intensity efforts that determine the outcome, such as a bicycle road race, then eating and drinking must occur at times when the intensity is low. The nausea associated with very long events, such as Ironman triathlons or ultramarathons, isn't as simple. Among the possible reasons for the queasiness:

- **Poor pacing.** This is the most common cause of nausea early in a long, steady race. Going too fast in the early stages—perhaps because of nervous energy and a poor pacing strategy while simultaneously taking in food, whether solid or liquid—causes the digestive tract to fill excessively. Due to the high intensity, the gut doesn't process what's taken in. Continuing to consume calories even after the intensity has settled at a more conservative level just exacerbates the problem. Slowing down dramatically and temporarily stopping food intake are the only solutions.
- **Excessive fluids.** Another possible cause of nausea in long-duration events is overdrinking. The stomach can hold roughly 32 ounces and empties at a rate of approximately 30 to 42 ounces per hour, depending on body size and exercise intensity.

If the stomach's reservoir capacity is exceeded, as can be the case with poor race-nutrition planning and a lack of refueling rehearsal, it has no choice but to remove the excess by vomiting.

- **Excessive nutrients.** Related to the last cause is another: taking in food or drink that is excessively concentrated with nutrients. The greater the fuel's nutrient content, the slower the stomach processes it. While physiology textbooks say that, on average, the stomach empties about 6 calories per minute, or 360 calories per hour, most long-distance athletes know it is possible to handle far more than that—perhaps as much as 600 calories per hour (and maybe even more in some large athletes). There seems to be a lot of variation in individual tolerance for food volume. Whatever your limit, slightly exceeding it for several hours will eventually lead to the stomach overfilling, with but one solution—puking.

- **Dehydration.** Dehydration in the heat may also contribute to nausea. If fluid intake is well below one's sweat rate for a long period of time, body fluids are shunted away from the digestive system to the skin (for cooling) and muscles (for work production). When that happens, the processing of fuel and fluids is reduced. In other words, the stomach's emptying rate falls and whatever is taken in accumulates until the excess triggers nausea. So, while it may seem contradictory, it is possible to be dehydrated and have a stomach full of fluid at the same time.

- **Salt water ingestion.** In ocean-swim events, such as Ironman-distance triathlons or long-distance swimming, swallowing seawater may set up the athlete for nausea later in the event. "Seawater poisoning" occurs when the high-sodium content of ocean water causes the stomach to shut down until the gut's sodium content is diluted, preferably by drinking plain water. If the athlete does not gradually take in water to dilute the sodium, or if he or she takes in fuel in any form (including liquid), the body will make its own adjustments by pulling water from the blood and intracellular space into the stomach. This can cause dehydration, further compounding the problem.

- **None of the above.** Your gut's displeasure during a given event could be due to several of the above scenarios—or it could be caused by something altogether different, such as nervous excitement, food poisoning, exhaustion, or extreme heat. It may also be that your body, while in good shape, is not yet fully prepared for a long-distance event. An extreme event relative to your fitness level may simply overwhelm your body's ability to cope.

The good news is that once you vomit, it's likely that you'll start feeling better. But don't get carried away by the newfound relief—the problem could soon come back to haunt you. At this point, slow down if you haven't already, and begin sipping water to see how that is accepted. If your stomach seems to handle that for 10 to 20 minutes or so, progress to a diluted drink by mixing water and a sports beverage. Take in only 2 to 3 ounces over 10 to 20 minutes. Again, if that stays down, try a normally concentrated sports drink. At some point, you will know that the conservative approach is working and you can resume a greater intensity, but be cautious; your stomach may still be upset. Even though this may "cost" you time, it is better to finish than to make the DNF (did not finish) list.

HYDRATION DURING EXERCISE

Keep in mind that hydration is at least as important as nutrient intake. It's easier to recover from a caloric deficiency than from dehydration. And because liquid empties from the stomach faster than solids and is less likely to cause gastric distress, it's best that most of your calories come from liquid sources during exercise. The shorter the event, the more important this is. But if you sense that dehydration is imminent, water or sports drinks should be the primary choice—not concentrated liquid calories. Liquid fuel sources other than sports drinks or water, while contributing to fluid intake, should not be considered your primary fluid source.

When trying to establish your fluid-intake needs during exercise, it's helpful to know your optimally hydrated body weight. To determine this, weigh yourself in the morning, before breakfast and after drinking a few ounces of water to satisfy your thirst, after 3 or 4 days of rest and greatly reduced training. (Be aware that a spring-loaded bathroom scale may easily vary by 1 or more pounds either way each time you step on it. Using a quality balance scale for this procedure is highly recommended.) The number on the scale will serve as a reference point for future comparisons after workouts. You will probably find that your body weight has increased about 1 to 3 percent during the rest period. This is because when fully hydrated and glycogen loaded, you carry "extra" fluid. This excess is due to the muscles being loaded with glycogen due to reduced training. For every gram of glycogen stored in the muscles, 2.6 grams of water are stored with it. During exercise, this glycogen is used as fuel; as it is expended, the stored water is released and can be used by the body to hydrate the cellular spaces. This is obviously helpful for the exercising body, although the benefits are minimized by total fluid losses from all sources, especially sweat.

Within a couple of hours of starting exercise, the extra glycogen and water are gone and your body is back to its preloaded weight. But what is important to realize here is that your body weight should never be allowed to dip below that depleted level as a result of acute exercise. By noting your body weight before exercise when rested and glycogen loaded, before exercise when not rested and loaded, and after exercise in various conditions of heat and humidity, you'll get a sense of what your various "normal" levels of hydration are. Your optimal training body weight lies between your fully rested and postexercise body weights. Your goal following exercise should be to return to that optimally hydrated state quickly, well before the next training session.

The key to preventing further losses of weight and directly associated hydration levels is to drink during exercise. Because a pint of water weighs about 1 pound, you can estimate your fluid needs based on your postworkout body weight in various combinations of exercise intensity and duration under varying heat conditions. For example, a 2-pound loss after a workout means you experienced a deficit of approximately 2 pints (960 milliliters) of water. Keeping a record of postworkout fluid losses relative to these variables will give you an idea of how much you should drink under various conditions to prevent dehydration. You'll discover that your fluid needs are not always the same but vary proportionally with intensity and weather conditions, especially temperature, and with the season. The more intense the exercise and the higher the temperature, the more fluids you'll need to take in during exercise. For example, in the spring, when the weather starts to warm up, you will require more fluids than are needed after you are fully adapted to heat. Duration also plays a role: For very short races— say, lasting just a few minutes—no water is required because you can't lose enough body fluid to dip below your lower safety limit.

HYPONATREMIA

Just as taking in too little fluid can cause performance-diminishing and even life-threatening conditions, drinking too much water can impair race outcomes or raise the risk of death by inducing a condition known as hyponatremia. The longer your events and workouts and the lower your intensity, the greater the threat of this happening. In recent years there have been two reported deaths in marathons related to overhydration-induced hyponatremia. Both were back-of-the-pack runners who had been on the road for several hours.

Hyponatremia occurs when the sodium concentration of the blood is reduced to dangerous levels. It can result from prolonged vomiting or diarrhea or from taking diuretics; but in endurance athletics, it's most commonly seen with excessive intake of fluid, especially water, during long events. Hyponatremia is extremely rare in events lasting less than 4 hours, but it's common in competitions taking 8 or more hours to complete. In studies at the New Zealand and Hawaii Ironman Triathlons, events that take 8 to 17 hours to complete, researchers found that up to 30 percent of finishers experienced mild to severe hyponatremia.

How does this happen? In a mistaken belief that one cannot take in too much water during exercise, the athlete overhydrates and may even gain weight during the event. The problem is most common with slower participants because they have greater opportunity and more time to drink. (The fastest athletes are more prone to dehydration than to hyponatremia; they find it more difficult to take in fluids at their level of competitiveness, plus they spend less time on the course.)

It can be difficult to determine if you are experiencing hyponatremia because the signs come on slowly. Early symptoms include headache in the forehead, nausea, muscle cramps, lethargy, confusion, disorientation, reduced coordination, and tunnel vision. One sure sign of hyponatremia is bloating. Look for puffiness and tightness around rings, watches, sock bands, and elastic waistbands. In extreme cases, the athlete may experience convulsions, unconsciousness, respiratory distress, or cardiac arrest. Because urination is greatly reduced or stops altogether when blood sodium concentrations are low, hyponatremia is often misdiagnosed as dehydration—and that can be a fatal error. If water intake is increased without additional sodium in a mistaken attempt to rehydrate the athlete, the condition worsens.

There is no doubt that you lose sodium during extensive exercise; the white blotches on your skin and clothes are visible signs of this. The key to preventing hyponatremia is balancing fluid and sodium intakes. Since you can now determine your fluid intake to offset sweat and other fluid losses during exercise by observing body weight, as described above, you can estimate how much sodium was lost and, therefore, how much needs to be replaced. Figure that a pint of sweat, or about 1 pound of body weight lost with exercise, contains about 500 milligrams of sodium. So for every 16 ounces (480 milliliters) of fluid you take in, you may also need to take in up to 500 milligrams of sodium. This can be in the form of naturally salty food and drink, salt added to food and drink, or sodium-supplement capsules. Sports drinks alone are not enough (their concentration is less than half of that in sweat) and, if the exercise is long enough, will eventually produce hyponatremia if used without any other sodium sources.

While this appears quite precise and scientific, there is one caveat: It appears that as you adapt to heat, less sodium is excreted with sweat. This could mean a 60 percent reduction from what was needed before. So in late-summer training and racing, you may not need as much sodium because you have likely adapted to heat. Experience is still the key to getting this right. But if in doubt, use the higher sodium level; the potential downside is not as great as getting too little.

Early in the heat-adaptation process, as when training or racing for the first few times in the early weeks of summer, your blood plasma will increase by as much as 10 percent during recovery periods. And since an increase in plasma dilutes sodium concentrations, you need to ingest more sodium at a similarly increased rate of 10 percent during your 4-hour-or-longer exercise sessions. When training volume is high while adapting to warmer weather conditions in early summer, it is wise to add a little extra salt to your food, especially immediately before and after exercise. (At other times of the year, you probably get adequate sodium in your diet, even if you watch sodium intake closely.) Once acclimated to the heat, your body will recalibrate and lose less sodium in sweat. That may take 2 to 4 weeks, depending on your exposure.

You can easily determine how much sodium is in the food and sports drinks you use because this information is required on food labels. Sports drinks, for example, run about 200 to 250 milligrams per pint (480 milliliters). Once you have subtracted the total amounts taken in from fluids, the balance reveals how much you'll need to increase your sodium intake. If you add salt to your food and drink, figure that 1 teaspoon of table salt (sodium chloride) is about 40 percent sodium. And since a teaspoon of salt weighs about 6 grams, you get about 2.4 grams (2,400 milligrams) of sodium per level teaspoon of salt. The simplest method for sodium supplementation and one used by many athletes is using sodium supplements. The sodium content of each will be printed on the package.

Let's now examine the unique nutritional characteristics of workouts and races of various duration ranges.

EATING DURING 2- TO 90-MINUTE EVENTS

These are the shortest exercise sessions that qualify as endurance activities and include 800-meter through about half-marathon runs, sprint-distance multisport races, bicycle criteriums and time trials, most mountain bike races, 5-K to about 30-K cross-country ski races, and most rowing events.

What sets such events apart from longer-distance racing is the high intensity. At the pace the athlete is traveling, taking in solid food is out of the question and, thankfully, not necessary. The focus of nutrition when training or racing for these events, regardless of one's speed, is on preventing dehydration, which becomes a risk as duration increases up to 90 minutes and as the heat index rises.

Assuming adequate nutrition in the days and hours preceding

a 2- to 90-minute session, the athlete's body is well prepared with glycogen stores. The risk of bonking is quite low for experienced athletes. Novices and weekend warriors may need to assume their cutoff for taking in carbohydrate is 60 minutes because they don't store as much glycogen in their muscles.

With this in mind, the greatest nutritional need at this duration is water. Drink up to 4 ounces (130 milliliters) per 10-minute block of time, depending on body size and sweat rate. For the shortest events—about 15 minutes or less—you probably won't need any water during exercise, even in the heat, as dehydration is a remote possibility. But it's still a good idea to be properly hydrated before the session begins.

That said, there is some evidence that a carbohydrate drink improves performance in a 1-hour event, but the mechanism isn't understood and the research is contradictory. There is no harm in taking in a sports drink for these events, but it's best to avoid solid foods and even gels, which will not be as effective as a sports drink and may well contribute to dehydration.

EATING DURING 90-MINUTE TO 4-HOUR EVENTS

Examples of race events in this range are half- to full-marathon runs, Olympic- to half-Ironman-distance multisport races, bicycle criteriums and road races, and 30-K to 100-K cross-country ski events. Longer workouts at a more leisurely effort are also included here.

At this duration, inadequate nutrition and environmental stresses on the body begin to take a toll on performance. The athlete is at risk for depleted muscle glycogen stores and dehydration, so nutritional goals must begin with taking in adequate fluids and carbohydrate. It is best to use a sports drink that replaces both carbohydrate and sodium. Take in up to 24 ounces (800 milliliters) per hour, depending on your body size and sweat rate. The longer the event, the more important it is to follow this guideline, as dehydration is a real threat not only to your performance but also to your health.

From the outset of the exercise session, replace some of the expended glycogen to delay the onset of fatigue while maintaining power. Do not wait until the latter stages of the workout or race to take in carbohydrate, as that may well set you up for a poor performance or even a bonk. The carbohydrate at this duration is best in a liquid form. Sports drinks are optimal, but gels with water as a chaser are also acceptable. Just be sure to drink 6 to 8 ounces of water—not sports drink—with every 100 calories consumed. Taking in less than that amount of water may lead to dehydration, as the gut will pull water from blood plasma and surrounding fluids to digest the highly concentrated gel. For the same reason, don't use solid foods. Assuming a good nutritional intake before the event and the consumption of a sports drink throughout, carbohydrate in solid form will have no marked advantage, but the potential downside is significant.

Especially for longer events in this range, using sports drinks instead of water has the added advantage of limiting muscle damage. For high-intensity exercise sessions, the body will turn to protein for a fuel source as glycogen stores run low. Much of that protein will come from muscle. Failing to get adequate carbohydrate during intense exercise in this duration range can result in muscle wasting.

In studies comparing the effects of carbohydrate and water on perceived exertion during intense exercise at this duration, carbohydrate was the clear winner. This means that even though your heart rate and blood acidosis levels may be the same whether you drink water or a sports drink, the effort will feel lower with the sports drink, especially if you add protein to it. A 4:1 ratio of carbohydrate to protein (primarily the branched-chain amino acids, described in Chapter 4) may actually enhance performance and postexercise recovery, while helping to prevent the transport of excessive amounts of serotonin to the brain. Serotonin is a chemical that can cause the onset of central nervous system fatigue, accompanied by increased sensations of exertion and even sleepiness. And, of course, taking in carbohydrate will delay fatigue

Lactic Acid's Bad Rap

For the better part of a century, athletes and physiologists alike have considered lactic acid a primary cause of fatigue during high-intensity exercise and referred to it as a "waste product" of muscle metabolism. But now this way of thinking is being challenged, as scientists have learned that this substance we produce in large quantities during exercise is not a cause of fatigue and actually helps to prevent it.

The former misrepresentation started with British physiologist and Nobel laureate Archibald V. Hill, who in 1929 flexed frog muscles to fatigue in his lab and noted that lactic acid accumulated when muscular failure occurred. He concluded that the lactic acid caused the fatigue associated with repeated muscle contractions. What he didn't know, and what we've only recently learned, is that when the muscle is part of a complete biological system instead of being examined in isolation from the rest of the body, lactic acid is processed and converted to

fuel to help keep the muscles going. It does not cause fatigue.

Nor does lactic acid cause muscle soreness the day after hard exercise. This myth has been around for decades and refuses to go away, despite evidence to the contrary over the past 20 years. Soreness is more likely the result of damaged muscle cells resulting from excessive usage.

So if lactic acid is not the villain we've made it out to be, what does cause fatigue and the burning sensation in the muscles during short, intense exercise bouts, such as intervals or races lasting just a few minutes? To get at the answer, it's necessary to understand the pH scale, which tells us how acidic or alkaline (base) the body's fluids are in a range of 1 to 14, as hydrogen ions increase or decrease. On this scale, hydrogen readings dropping below neutral 7 indicate increasing acidity, while those rising above 7 indicate escalating alkalinity. Examples of acidic fluids are hydrochloric acid (pH = 1) and due to the glycogen depletion that occurs normally with extended exercise.

When exercising at maximum intensity for this duration, take in up to 200 to 300 calories per hour in an equal distribution every

vinegar (pH = 3), while milk of magnesia (pH = 10.5) and ammonia (pH = 11.7) are alkaline.

At rest, the pH of your blood is around 7.4—slightly alkaline. In terms of your blood, small absolute changes in acid-base balance have major consequences. For example, during a 2- to 3-minute all-out effort, your blood's pH may drop as low as 6.4. In biochemical terms, this is a huge acidic swing, producing a burning sensation in the working muscles and their inability to continue contracting. Fatigue has set in.

If lactic acid didn't cause the drop in pH, what did? The answer has to do with our sources of fuel during such short exercise bouts—glycogen and glucose. Both are carbohydrates, but they have slightly different chemical compositions. Glycogen is stored inside the muscle, where it can be quickly broken down to produce energy. Glucose, which is stored in the liver and floats around in the bloodstream, is called on to produce en-

ergy for exercise when glycogen stores can no longer keep up with the demand or are running low. As glycogen is broken down to produce energy, it releases one unit of hydrogen. But if glucose must be used for fuel, such as when the intensity of the exercise exceeds glycogen's ability to keep up, two units of hydrogen are released. This rapid doubling of hydrogen ions in the system lowers the blood's pH, causing the burning and fatigue associated with acidosis. The same amount of lactic acid is released no matter which fuel is used.

Far from being an evildoer, lactic acid is an ally during intense exercise. It does a great deal to keep the body going when the going gets hard. Besides being converted back into a fuel source, when hydrogen begins to accumulate, lactate transports it out of the working muscle cells and helps to buffer or offset its negative consequences.

After nearly 80 years, lactic acid's bad boy reputation has been lifted.

10 to 20 minutes, primarily from liquid sources. The minimum intake is 1 calorie of carbohydrate per pound of body weight per hour. Consider adding a quarter gram of protein per pound of body weight. As of this writing, there is only one commercial sports drink available with this ratio of carbohydrate to protein—Accelerade, produced and marketed by Pacific Health (www.accelerade.com).

Drink 16 to 24 ounces (500 to 800 milliliters) of fluid per hour, depending on body size, sweat rate, and how hot the day is. High glycemic index drinks with much greater maltodextrin or glucose than fructose content are preferred, as some athletes experience gastrointestinal distress from even a moderate amount of fructose. Most commercial drinks include at least some fructose. Let experience be your guide.

Consider using a caffeinated sports drink or gel; this has been shown to enhance the utilization of the glucose in sports drinks. The mechanism here is not fully understood, and research in this area is limited. In the only study on this topic, conducted at University Hospital, Maastricht, Netherlands, there was no difference in the stomach-acid levels of the people using drinks with caffeine and those who didn't use caffeine.

As for electrolytes, replenish primarily sodium during exercise in the heat. The total replacement of the other common electrolytes (chloride, calcium, potassium, and magnesium) at this duration is not necessary. This, again, is best accomplished with a sports drink containing sodium. No additional supplementation is necessary because the risk of hyponatremia is low, although still possible with excessive intake of plain water.

EATING DURING 4- TO 12-HOUR EVENTS

At this duration we are moving into events in which the athlete's health and well-being during exercise cannot be taken for granted. Hyponatremia, as described earlier, is now a real threat, and nutritional planning is critical in ways other than simply performance.

Races in this range include marathon and ultramarathon running, half-Ironman- to Ironman-distance events, bicycle road races and century rides, and ultramarathon cross-country ski and rowing events.

At such durations the intensity of exercise is quite low, with the effort seldom, if ever, approaching the anaerobic threshold in most sports. The fuel source is now very heavily weighted in favor of fat, with carbohydrate playing a smaller, but no less important, role. There is an old saying in exercise science that "fat burns in a carbohydrate fire." In the real world of endurance athletics, this means that if carbohydrate stored as muscle glycogen runs low, the body will gradually lose its capacity to produce energy from fat. In other words, a bonk is highly likely during events in this category if carbohydrate ingestion is neglected for even a little while. Once an athlete is well behind the carbohydrate intake versus expenditure curve, catching up is difficult and may be accomplished only by slowing dramatically or stopping exercise altogether. This is the dreaded "death march" so commonly found late in these events.

Carbohydrate must be taken in right from the beginning of these sessions in order to stay close to the expenditure rate, delaying the onset of fatigue while maintaining power. Although replacing most of the expended glycogen is the goal for this duration, it's doubtful you will be able to restock all of it. At the highest intensities, the fastest athletes expend about 1,000 calories per hour, with perhaps up to 60 percent of that coming from carbohydrate-based glycogen. It's unlikely that all but the largest athletes consume that much carbohydrate. In fact, you don't need to replace it at all if you did a good job of eating quality carbohydrate in the 24 hours leading up to the race or workout. If you did, you have probably stored 1,500 to 2,000 calories as carbohydrate in your muscles and liver, depending on your body size. By keeping the hourly deficit at less than 100 calories, even the elite athletes in the longest of these events— those who are likely to burn the most calories—can avoid

(continued on page 44)

What Causes Muscle Cramps?

We've all had it happen. The race is going great—then all of a sudden, from out of nowhere, a muscle begins to feel "twitchy" and seizes up. You slow down, hoping it will go away. It does, but as soon as you start pouring on the power, it comes back. The promise of a stellar race is gone.

There is no more perplexing problem for athletes than cramps. Muscles seem to knot up at the worst possible times—seldom in training, but frequently in races.

The real problem is that no one knows what causes cramps. There are theories, the most popular being that muscle cramps result from dehydration or electrolyte imbalances. These arguments seem to make sense—at least on the surface. Cramps are most common in the heat of summer, when low body-fluid levels and decreases in body salts due to sweating are likely to occur.

But the research doesn't always support these explanations. For example, in the mid-1980s, 82 male runners were tested before and after a marathon for certain blood parameters considered to be likely causes of muscle cramps. Fifteen of the runners experienced cramps after 18 miles. There was no difference, either before or after the race, in terms of blood levels of sodium, potassium, bicarbonate, hemoglobin, or hematocrit. There was also no difference in blood volume between the crampers and the noncrampers, nor were there significant differences in the way the two groups trained.

For very long events—those lasting more than about 4 hours—a bit more is known. A few studies have linked these cramps to hyponatremia, or low sodium levels, which may result from drinking large volumes of fluids that are low in sodium and may be aggravated by starting the event at a sodium deficit. The day before and the morning of a long race, it may be a good idea to use salt to increase the body's levels. The sports drink used for the race should also provide adequate levels of sodium. For long races, eating salty foods may help prevent not only cramping but the life-threatening symptoms of hyponatremia.

It's interesting to note that athletes are not the only people who experience muscle cramping. Workers in occupations that require chronic use of a muscle, especially one that crosses two joints, but who don't sweat profusely (as athletes do), are also susceptible. A good example is musicians, who cramp in the hands and arms.

So if dehydration or electrolyte imbalance doesn't cause cramping, what does? Other theories are emerging. Some researchers blame poor posture or inefficient biomechanics. Poor movement patterns may cause a disturbance in the activity of the Golgi tendon organs—"strain gauges" built into the tendon to prevent muscle tears. When activated, these organs cause the threatened muscle to relax while stimulating the antagonistic muscle—the one that moves the joint in the opposite way—to fire. There may be some quirk of body mechanics that upsets a Golgi device and sets off the cramping pattern. If that is the cause, prevention may involve improving biomechanics and regularly stretching and strengthening muscles that

seem to cramp along with their antagonistic muscles.

Another theory is that cramps result from burning protein for fuel in the absence of readily available carbohydrate. In fact, one study supports such a notion: Muscle cramps occurred in exercising subjects who reached the highest levels of ammonia release, indicating that protein is being used to fuel the muscles during exercise. This suggests a need for greater carbohydrate stores before, and replacement of those stores during, intense and long-lasting exercise.

When you feel a cramp coming on, there are two ways to deal with it. One is to reduce your intensity and slow down—not a popular option in an important race. Another is to alternately stretch and relax the affected muscle group while continuing to move. This is difficult if not impossible to do in some sports, such as running, and with certain muscles.

Actually, there is a third option that some athletes swear by: pinching the upper lip. Who knows—it may work for you the next time a cramp strikes.

bonking. Slower athletes can keep the deficit even smaller, but that isn't particularly a problem because their burn rate is lower.

In such events, get about 300 to 600 calories per hour in an equal distribution every 10 to 20 minutes, primarily from liquid sources with a minimum of 0.5 calorie of carbohydrate per pound of body weight per hour. At the upper end of this race-duration range, around 12 hours, sports bars or even solid foods may be used as desired, but they should be considered a secondary source of energy. Solid foods must be of moderate to high glycemic index, low in fiber, and easily digested. Be sure to take in 6 to 8 ounces of water (not sports drink) for every 100 calories consumed.

Some athletes have success when using commercial meal-replacement drinks at durations of about 8 hours or more. If you decide to experiment with these, it's best to avoid those that use dairy products as the primary source. Unfortunately, most drinks in this category are largely cow's milk. One exception: Ensure.

Otherwise, the guidelines for carbohydrate fuel replacement are the same as in the previous section, including the possible use of a caffeinated drink with added protein. As with the 90-minute to 4-hour events, taking in some protein along with four times as much carbohydrate may help prevent the onset of central nervous system fatigue, which is marked by general malaise and even yawning—even though you're consuming adequate carbohydrate and aren't particularly bored.

The elite athlete's greatest concern at this distance is dehydration. Slower athletes should be able to easily avoid this calamity by taking in 16 to 24 ounces (500 to 800 milliliters) of fluid per hour, depending on body size and sweat rate, but they need to watch out for hyponatremia, as described above. Overhydrating with water by as little as 2 percent can bring on this dreaded condition.

Hand in hand with this concern for drinking too much is the need to replace sodium by taking in sports drinks, supplements, or solid food. The latter is more likely to be needed only during the longest events in this range, although some athletes continue to use only liquid sources of fuel even when approaching 12 hours.

As the duration of the event is extended, the need to replace electrolytes, especially sodium, becomes more important. The other electrolytes—chloride, magnesium, potassium, and calcium—are lost in such minute amounts during exercise that they don't become critical until the longest of ultraendurance events, such as those taking in the neighborhood of a full day to complete or conducted in long stages over several consecutive days.

For sodium, the most critical of the electrolytes, the upper intake level may be around 1,000 milligrams per hour in hot conditions. It could even be higher than that under certain conditions. One study of cyclists found the average loss of sodium during 6 hours of exercise in warm conditions (86°F and 30 percent humidity) was 2 grams, or about 2,000 milligrams, per hour. Since 1 pint of sweat weighs approximately 1 pound and contains about 500 milligrams of sodium, we could conclude from this study that these athletes were losing as much as a half gallon (2 liters) of fluid per hour. That's a whopping 4 pounds (1.8 kilograms) of body weight lost every hour if no fluid is taken in. At this rate, dehydration is imminent. Such extreme conditions must be respected.

Supplements, in addition to food and liquid sources of electrolytes, may be necessary because changing weather conditions, especially heat, may adjust the body's need for these salts more dramatically than for calories or fluids. So in hot weather, electrolyte intake should be considered a separate matter from nutrient intake and hydration.

EATING DURING 12- TO 18-HOUR EVENTS

Events in this duration include the Ironman-distance triathlon, double-century bike ride, and ultramarathons in such sports as running, mountain biking, cross-country skiing, swimming, and kayaking. The stresses placed on the athlete can be extreme, with fatigue, heat, humidity, hills, wind, and currents taking their toll and gradually reducing performance. Nutrition is critical for these events.

Much of what was said in the previous section remains true here. The caveats are that solid foods now become a necessity, and hunger may well dictate what you decide to use for fuel. This might include bananas, cookies, jelly sandwiches, fruit juices, and soup. All of the foods selected should be toward the high end of the glycemic index. Otherwise, intakes of carbohydrate, protein (especially branched-chain amino acids), and caffeine, as described above, may be continued, along with the intake of electrolyte-bearing fluids, especially those containing sodium.

EATING DURING EVENTS LONGER THAN 18 HOURS

These are the true "ultra" events of the world of endurance sports: the Race Across America (RAAM) and Paris-Brest-Paris bike races, double-Ironman-distance triathlon, Western States 100-mile run, and multiday bicycle racing tours such as the grueling Tour de France, Vuelta a España, and the Giro d'Italia. It can be very difficult to take in adequate food and water, but for events done in daily stages, such as the Tour de France, daily nutritional intake between stages is often the difference between finishing and dropping out.

The longer the event, the more crucial it is that caloric needs be met by balancing nutrient intake with expenditure. Unsupported events require the athlete to carry nutrients or purchase them along the route, which makes planning all the more critical—the preferred sources must be light or generally available at convenience stores. Plan on taking in at least 6,000 calories daily—and that's conservative. RAAM riders who spend at least 5 days riding across the United States, from the west to the east coast, typically report 10,000-calorie days.

The longer the event, the lower the intensity, diminishing the relative amount of carbohydrate used as fuel. Whereas carbohydrate may account for 80 percent of the expended calories in events that last less than 90 minutes, it may contribute only about 50 percent of the total energy used in ultraevents. This means that the carbohydrate content of your fuel need not be as carbohydrate-rich as for shorter events. Conversely, protein intake becomes more important and should make up 5 to 15 percent of your fuel, so your nutritional source should reflect this demand. Not getting enough protein may well result in muscle wasting. That's not conducive to good performance.

Fat also becomes more important in events of this duration. You'll burn a lot of it, so it's okay to take in a considerable amount—a fifth to a third of your fuel source—during the activity. In fact, ultramarathoners often report a craving for fat during their events. Fat tends to present fewer gut problems during exercise than carbohydrate does, but that doesn't mean it won't affect your stomach at all. Before the event, be sure to experiment to discover the mix and types of fuels that work best for you.

Nutritional Goals

Given the importance of refueling in events of this duration, it's a good idea to closely examine all aspects of nutrition in great detail. Let's start by considering the nutritional goals for the ultramarathon athlete.

- **Replace all of the expended carbohydrate.** Even at relatively slow velocities, a considerable amount of dietary carbohydrate is needed to delay the onset of fatigue while maintaining power. Carbohydrate should be taken in from the outset of exercise, using predominantly high glycemic index sources. It's generally best that the sports drinks you choose have greater maltodextrin or glucose sources than fructose.

  What changes from the previous discussions, however, is that the demand for carbohydrate relative to time is reduced. You'll be burning fewer calories from carbohydrate sources and more from fat, so the total replacement of carbohydrate is not as difficult as in shorter, faster events.

- **Prevent dehydration while avoiding hyponatremia.** Staying adequately hydrated for such events is critical. Once dehydrated, it is difficult to get fluid levels back to normal. Hyponatremia is a threat to all athletes, including the faster ones, in events of this duration. The key, as described above, is to ensure that adequate sodium is ingested.

- **Prevent central nervous system fatigue.** Low levels of branched-chain amino acids in the blood during these long events can allow serotonin to enter the brain, causing the central nervous system to fatigue even though the other systems of the body are doing well. (See "What Is Fatigue?" on page 122.)

- **Prevent muscle wasting.** It is not unusual for athletes in ultra-distance events, such as the Tour de France, to lose several pounds, mostly from muscle. A study of trekkers in the Andes found that those who supplemented their diet with branched-chain amino acids gained muscle mass over 21 days, while their placebo-supplemented companions who otherwise ate the same diet lost muscle. Without adequate protein intake, the trekkers' bodies were "cannibalizing" themselves. This helps us understand why, after ultramarathon events, the athletes look so gaunt. To prevent muscle catabolism, it is critical that the athlete take in a 4:1 ratio of carbohydrate to protein during the race.

- **Prevent hunger.** You will become quite hungry if you go 18 hours or longer with nothing more than sports drinks and gels. Foods including solid sources are a necessity, as they are more energy dense than liquid sources. You'll also find that after several hours, you become very tired of sweets and crave fat. Follow your desires and eat what sounds appealing, but consider these treats rather than main sources of fuel. The typical warnings still stand: Keep these foods low in fiber, and try them in workouts before using them in races.

Nutritional Guidelines

The guidelines for including fat and protein (primarily branched-chain amino acids) now shift toward fat and protein and slightly away from carbohydrate. Taking in your 300 to 600 calories hourly for carbohydrate, fat, and protein should be broken down, respectively, as 60 to 70 percent, 20 to 30 percent, and 10 to 15 percent. This proportion may enhance performance and recovery, while helping to prevent the serotonin buildup that can cause central nervous system fatigue and higher ratings of exertion.

Besides taking in more fat, the other significant change concerns electrolytes. Sweat contains large amounts of sodium and chloride but little potassium, calcium, and magnesium. It's critical that sodium be replaced, as discussed earlier in this chapter. But of the remaining electrolytes, there may be a need for only potassium and perhaps magnesium intake at these durations. The potassium and magnesium lost through sweat is negligible but, over several hours of sweating, can become significant and affect performance, especially under hot environmental conditions. Fortunately, replenishment is as simple as eating an occasional banana.

The body's need for potassium during extensive endurance exercise is quite small, on the order of 50 to 60 milligrams per hour, while magnesium needs may range from 2 to 10 milligrams per hour. Some sports drinks contain both of these electrolytes in addition to sodium and chloride. A single banana contains about 250 milligrams of potassium and 33 milligrams of magnesium, so eating one every 3 to 5 hours or so over the course of an ultraevent will maintain electrolyte status. Races of this distance often provide or allow support in the form of aid stations, feed zones, or even following support vehicles.

Good sources of energy now are fruit and vegetable juices, sports drink with protein added, and gels with water. An assortment of foods such as rice, potatoes, vegetables, turkey sandwiches, fresh fruits, soup, cookies, sports bars, and meal-replacement drinks will also provide carbohydrate, fat, and protein.

Chapter 4

STAGES III, IV, AND V: EATING AFTER EXERCISE

Immediately after a race or workout ends, it's time to start thinking about recovery. This should be your highest priority. The higher your athletic goals, the more important recovery becomes. If you aspire to achieve at your peak levels, then both the quantity and quality of training are crucial for success. The sooner you can do another key workout, the faster you will get into race shape and the better your results will be.

If everything was done right nutritionally, both before and during the exercise session, then you're well on your way to accomplishing this result. Following exercise, your objective must be to return your body to its preexercise levels of hydration, glycogen storage, and muscle protein status as quickly as possible. Diet is the critical component in this process.

There are three stages in this process: 30 minutes postexercise (Stage III); short-term postexercise, lasting as long as the exercise session (Stage IV); and long-term postexercise (Stage V), lasting until the next Stage I. Let's examine the details of each stage of recovery.

STAGE III: EATING 30 MINUTES POSTEXERCISE

This is the most critical phase because, at this point, your body is better prepared to receive and store carbohydrate than at any other time during the day. Get nutrition right now, and you are well on your way to the next key workout. Blow it, and you're certain to delay recovery.

Timing is a critical component for this stage. At no other time in your entire day is your body as receptive as it is now to nutrient intake. Research shows that the restocking of the muscles' carbohydrate stores is two to three times as rapid immediately after exercise as it is a few hours later. In the same way, other research reveals that the repair of muscles damaged during exercise is more effective if protein is consumed immediately after exercise. Don't delay. Begin refueling as soon as possible after your cooldown.

There are five goals for this brief but critical window of opportunity.

- **Goal #1: Replace expended carbohydrate stores.** During exercise, especially if it lasted longer than about 1 hour, you used up much of your carbohydrate-based energy sources. These can best be restored by taking in carbohydrates that are high on the glycemic load scale for quick replenishment of expended glycogen stores, along with sources that are lower on the scale to provide for a steady release of carbohydrates into the blood. Glucose, the sugar in starchy foods such as potatoes, rice, and grains, is a good source for quick recovery; while fructose, the sugar in fruit and fruit juices, provides a steady, slowly released level of sugar into the bloodstream. Take in at least three-fourths of a gram of carbohydrate per pound of body weight from such sources. This recovery "meal" is best taken in liquid rather than solid form, partly because solid foods often aren't very appealing at this time. A liquid meal is also absorbed more quickly and begins the rehydration process. Good sources are commercially produced recovery drinks. Or you can make your own "home-brew" recovery drink, which is much cheaper and exactly designed to suit your tastes. (See Table 4.5 on page 58.)

One of the highest glycemic load carbohydrates is glucose. By adding glucose to the homebrew, you replace the body's expended carbohydrate stores more quickly than by eating fruit and drinking fruit juice alone because these foods are rich in fructose, which the body takes much longer to digest. Pure glucose is difficult to find, although it is typically in commercial sports and recovery drinks. You can purchase glucose from various sources on the Internet, such as bulkfoods.com, sausage stuffer.com, spokanespice.com, and sportquestdirect.com.

- **Goal #2: Rehydrate.** Chances are good that you are experiencing some level of dehydration following a long or hard workout or race. At the greatest sweat rates, an athlete may lose around a half gallon (1,800 milliliters) of sweat per hour. Among the highest sweat rates ever reported in the research literature was about 1 gallon per hour in one of America's best all-time marathoners, 147-pound Alberto Salazar. Replacing such high rates of fluid loss during exercise is difficult, if not impossible, potentially leaving the athlete in a dehydrated state as the post-exercise stage of recovery begins.

  To replenish fluid levels, begin taking in 16 ounces (500 milliliters) of liquid for every pound lost during exercise. You may not be able to accomplish this in 30 minutes, so plan on continuing throughout the next few hours. You may need to take in 150 percent of what your weight indicates you lost just to keep up with your body's ongoing need for fluids in the hours following the workout or race. This is another reason for using a recovery drink rather than solid food right now.

- **Goal #3: Provide amino acids for resynthesis of protein that may have been damaged during exercise.** In an intense 1-hour workout, it's possible to use 30 grams (1 ounce) of muscle protein for fuel. With even longer exercise sessions, the protein cost of fueling the body is likely to rise, especially because carbohydrate is depleted in the working muscles as the body begins to break down protein structures within the muscle cells to create more glycogen.

Protein, particularly sources that are rich in the branched-chain amino acids (leucine, isoleucine, and valine), should be taken in at a carb-to-protein ratio of between 4:1 and 5:1 over the 30-minute recovery period. If using a protein powder to mix a recovery drink, the best source of protein is egg or whey products, which contain all of the essential amino acids and a healthy dose of branched-chain amino acids, as can be seen in Table 4.1.

Table 4.2 on page 54 provides a breakdown by body weight of the caloric components of a recovery drink with a 4:1 or 5:1 ratio of carbohydrate to protein. You may feel the need to take in more or fewer calories, depending on how hard or long the

TABLE 4.1

Branched-Chain Amino Acid Content of Selected Foods

SOURCE (100-CALORIE SAMPLE)	ISOLEUCINE (MG)	LEUCINE (MG)	VALINE (MG)	TOTAL BCAA (MG)
Egg white, powder	1,200	1,791	1,352	4,343
Egg white, raw	1,188	1,774	1,340	4,302
Whey protein	922	1,719	896	3,537
Meats	928	1,474	967	3,369
Soy protein	886	1,481	923	3,290
Seafood	744	1,285	803	2,832
Hard-boiled egg	389	442	494	1,325
Milk	323	524	358	1,205
Beans	319	524	349	1,192
Vegetables	238	287	245	770
Grains	130	303	172	605
Nuts and seeds	111	198	149	458
Starchy root vegetables	45	66	58	169
Fruits	20	31	29	80

TABLE 4.2

Recovery Drink Calories by Body Weight

WEIGHT (LB)	CARBOHYDRATE CALORIES (MINIMUM)	PROTEIN CALORIES	TOTAL CALORIES
100	300	60–75	360–375
110	330	66–83	396–413
120	360	72–90	432–450
130	390	78–98	468–488
140	420	84–105	504–525
150	450	90–113	540–563
160	480	96–120	576–600
170	510	102–128	612–638
180	540	108–135	648–675
190	570	114–143	684–713
200	600	120–150	720–750
210	630	126–158	756–788

workout was and how good eating sounds to you at this time. Even if you don't feel up to taking in this much immediately after finishing, at least begin to sip the drink and spread its intake over a longer period. The workout or race conditions may also influence how much you take in. For example, heat increases the need for both carbohydrate and protein.

- **Goal #4: Begin replacing electrolytes.** Electrolytes are the salts sodium, chloride, potassium, calcium, and magnesium, which are found either within the body's cells or in extracellular fluids, including blood. Dissolved in the body fluids as ions, they conduct an electric current and are critical for muscle contraction and relaxation and for maintaining fluid levels. During exercise, the body loses a small portion of these salts, primarily through sweat. The loss is typically not critical in events shorter than 4 hours or in cool weather, when the sweat rate is low. But after longer events or exercise in extreme heat, replacement is of greater significance, especially for sodium and possibly potassium.

Most of the electrolytes are found in abundance in natural food, which makes their replacement fairly easy. Drinking juice or eating fruit will easily replace nearly all of the electrolytes expended during exercise—with the exception of sodium, which is not naturally abundant in fruits and juices. Sodium is also the electrolyte most likely to need replenishment. Two or three pinches of table salt must be added to a postexercise recovery drink. Table 4.3 lists good juice and fruit sources to use in a Stage III postworkout drink.

TABLE 4.3
Electrolytes in Fruits and Juices Used during Recovery

	SODIUM (MG)	MAGNESIUM (MG)	CALCIUM (MG)	POTASSIUM (MG)
Juice (12 oz)				
Apple, frozen	26	18	21	450
Grape, frozen	7	16	12	80
Grapefruit, frozen	3	45	33	505
Orange, fresh	3	41	41	744
Pineapple, frozen	4	35	42	510
Fruit				
Apple, 1 medium, raw	1	6	10	159
Banana, 1 medium, raw	1	33	7	451
Blackberries, 1 c, frozen	2	33	44	211
Blueberries, 1 c, raw	9	7	9	129
Cantaloupe, 1½ c, raw	21	25	25	741
Grapes, 1½ c, raw	3	8	20	264
Orange, 1 large, raw	2	22	84	375
Papaya, 1 medium, raw	8	31	72	780
Peaches, 3 medium, raw	0	18	15	513
Pineapple, 1½ c, raw	2	32	17	262
Raspberries, 1½ c, raw	0	33	40	280
Strawberries, 2 c, raw	4	32	42	494
Watermelon, 2 c, raw	6	34	26	372

- **Goal #5: Reduce the acidity of body fluids.** During exercise, body fluids shift increasingly toward an acidic state. There is also evidence indicating that as we age, our blood and other body fluids become increasingly acidic. The cumulative effect is a disturbingly lowered pH (increased acidity). But regardless of age, if this acidic state following exercise is allowed to persist for some period of time, the risk of nitrogen and calcium loss is greatly increased. The reason for this is that the body attempts to reduce the acidity by releasing minerals into the blood and other body fluids that have a net alkaline-enhancing effect, thus counteracting the increased acidity. Calcium from the bones and nitrogen from the muscles meet this need.

  The problem is that in neutralizing the acid this way, we give up valuable structural resources. You're essentially peeing off bone and muscle as the acidity of your blood stays high. While cannibalizing tissue is necessary from a strictly biological perspective, this is an expensive solution from an athletic perspective. While body fluids may be chemically balanced by the process, future performance and even health may well be jeopardized as muscle and bone are compromised.

  Research has shown that fruits and vegetables are the only foods that have a net alkaline-enhancing effect. Table 4.4 demonstrates the acid- and alkaline-enhancing effects of various foods. The foods with a plus sign (+) indicate increased acidity; the greater the plus value, the higher the acid effect. Those foods with a minus sign (-) decrease the acid of the body fluids in direct proportion to their magnitude. So by preparing a recovery drink with fruits and juices that have a net alkaline-enhancing effect (they reduce acidity), you are doing more than merely replacing carbohydrate stores; you're also potentially sparing bone and muscle.

TABLE 4.4
Acid/Base Values of Food (100 g portions)

ACID FOODS (+)		ALKALINE FOODS (-)	
Grains		**Fruits**	
Brown rice	+12.5	Raisins	-21.0
Rolled oats	+10.7	Black currants	-6.5
Whole wheat bread	+ 8.2	Bananas	-5.5
Spaghetti	+ 7.3	Apricots	-4.8
Corn flakes	+ 6.0	Kiwifruit	-4.1
White rice	+ 4.6	Cherries	-3.6
Rye bread	+ 4.1	Pears	-2.9
White bread	+ 3.7	Pineapple	-2.7
		Peaches	-2.4
Dairy		Apples	-2.2
Parmesan cheese	+34.2	Watermelon	-1.9
Processed cheese	+28.7		
Hard cheese	+19.2	**Vegetables**	
Gouda cheese	+18.6	Spinach	-14.0
Cottage cheese	+ 8.7	Celery	-5.2
Whole milk	+ 0.7	Carrots	-4.9
		Zucchini	-4.6
Legumes		Cauliflower	-4.0
Peanuts	+8.3	Potatoes	-4.0
Lentils	+3.5	Radishes	-3.7
Peas	+1.2	Eggplant	-3.4
		Tomatoes	-3.1
Meats, Fish, Eggs		Lettuce	-2.5
Trout	+10.8	Chicory	-2.0
Turkey	+9.9	Leeks	-1.8
Chicken	+8.7	Onions	-1.5
Eggs	+8.1	Mushrooms	-1.4
Pork	+7.9	Green peppers	-1.4
Beef	+7.8	Broccoli	-1.2
Cod	+7.1	Cucumber	-0.8
Herring	+7.0		

Reprinted from the *Journal of the American Dietetic Association,* V95(7), Thomas Remer and Friedrich Manz, "Potential renal acid load of foods and its influence on urine pH," pp. 791–97, 1995, with permission from the American Dietetic Association.

HOMEBREW RECIPES

Based on all of the above, then, here's what you want in a home-made recovery drink: fruits and juices (to provide fluids and slow-releasing carbohydrate with electrolytes while reducing blood acidity), glucose (a quickly absorbed energy source), protein (to replace what was used in exercise and prevent further muscle breakdown during recovery), and sodium (because fruits and juices are low in this electrolyte). Using ingredients that are mostly found in your own kitchen, you can make a smoothie that fulfills all those requirements.

Start by filling a blender with about 12 to 24 ounces of fruit juice, based on your body weight (see Table 4.5). Apple, grape, grapefruit, orange, and pineapple are good choices due to their relatively high glycemic loads and electrolyte contents. Next, add a fruit from the list in Table 4.3 (see page 55) and glucose, also known as dextrose (see Table 4.5). Then, with the blender still

TABLE 4.5

Recipes for Homebrew Recovery Drink (by body weight)

BODY WEIGHT IN POUNDS (KG)	FRUIT JUICE (OZ)	GLUCOSE (TBSP)	PROTEIN POWDER (TBSP)	TOTAL CALORIES (APPROX.)
100 (45.5)	12	2	1½–2	390–415
110 (50)	12	2	1½–2	390–415
120 (54.5)	12	3	2	445
130 (59.1)	12	4	2–2½	470–495
140 (63.6)	16	4	2½–3	550–575
150 (68.2)	16	4	2½–3	550–575
160 (72.7)	16	5	2½–3	580–605
170 (77.3)	20	5	3–3½	660–685
180 (81.8)	20	5	3–3½	660–685
190 (86.4)	24	5	3–3½	720–740
200 (90.9)	24	5	3–3½	720–740
210 (95.5)	24	6	3–4	750–790

Each recipe also includes one fruit and two or three pinches of table salt.

running, add protein powder from either egg or whey sources (see Table 4.1 on page 53). Sprinkle in two or three pinches of table salt. If you didn't use frozen berries, add a handful of ice. There you have it—a fairly inexpensive drink that has all of the ingredients needed for immediate recovery.

You don't need to use this type of recovery drink after every workout, just those that include a significant amount of intensity or last at least 60 to 90 minutes. In fact, avoid using this drink when you don't need it, as the high glycemic load is likely to add unwanted pounds of body fat. After short and low-intensity workouts, you can make a homebrew without the glucose.

STAGE IV: SHORT-TERM POSTEXERCISE

For very intense, short workouts or those longer than about 60 to 90 minutes, recovery needs to continue beyond the initial 30-minute window. Although there is no research supporting this, we have had success in coaching athletes to continue to focus on recovery for the same amount of time that the workout or race took. So if you exercised for 2 hours, the initial 30-minute recovery period would be followed by an additional 90 minutes. That 2-hour total focuses on "macrolevel" recovery, meaning the emphasis is primarily on the intake of carbohydrate and protein.

As your body returns to a normal state, sensations of hunger will emerge. After not taking in any substantial food sources for perhaps several hours, the body begins to cry out for complete nutrition. How long it takes for hunger to appear depends on how long and intense the preceding exercise was. The foods you eat now should emphasize moderate to high glycemic load carbohydrates.

Short-Term Recovery Guidelines

The focus of this period is similar to that of the 30-minute window preceding it. The difference is that now there is a shift toward taking in more solid foods, although continued fluid consumption is also important. Here are guidelines for eating during this extended recovery period.

Carbohydrate remains very important at this stage of recovery, but the shift is toward solid foods, especially starchy vegetables that are high on the glycemic load scale while having a net alkaline-enhancing effect on body fluids. Good choices include potatoes, yams, and sweet potatoes, as well as dried fruits, especially raisins. These are excellent to snack on during Stage IV recovery because they have the greatest alkaline-enhancing effect of any food studied while also having a high glycemic load. That means a great amount of carbohydrate is delivered to the muscles quickly, which is more valuable at this time than having a high glycemic index. Table 4.6 lists the glycemic loads of various alkaline-enhancing fruits, juices, and vegetables. Notice that while some foods, such as watermelon, have a high glycemic index, their glycemic loads are low; the lower the load, the more of the food you will need to eat. Glycemic load is a measure of not only how quickly a food's sugar gets into your blood, but also how much carbohydrate is delivered. The foods listed first are preferred, but all are good choices. You may also select grains such as corn, bread, a bagel, rice, and cereal to continue the rapid replacement of carbohydrate stores. While these foods have a very high glycemic load, they have a net acid-enhancing effect, so be certain to include plenty of vegetables, fruits, and fruit juices to counteract the negative consequence.

During this extended recovery stage, continue taking in carbohydrate at the rate of at least 0.75 gram per pound of body weight per hour. Otherwise, your appetite may serve as a guide as to how much to eat. After especially long or intense exercise, you may find liquids more appealing than solids. If so, continue using a recovery drink, just as in the first 30 minutes post-exercise.

TABLE 4.6

Glycemic Load and Index of Selected Alkaline-Enhancing Foods
(100 g serving)

FOOD	GLYCEMIC LOAD	GLYCEMIC INDEX
Raisins	48.8	64
Potato, plain	18.4	85
Sweet potato	13.1	54
Banana	12.1	53
Yam	11.5	51
Pineapple	8.2	66
Grapes	7.7	43
Kiwifruit	7.4	52
Carrots	7.2	71
Apple	6.0	39
Pineapple juice	5.9	46
Pear	5.4	36
Cantaloupe	5.4	65
Watermelon	5.2	72
Orange juice	5.1	50
Orange	5.1	43
Apple juice	4.9	40
Peach	3.1	28
Strawberries	2.8	40

At this time you must also maintain your lean protein intake, using the same 4:1 or 5:1 ratio with carbohydrate. The purpose, as before, is to continue providing amino acids for the resynthesis of muscle protein and maintenance of other physiological structures that rely on amino acids, such as the nervous system. Animal products are the best sources of this protein because they're rich in essential amino acids, including the branched-chain amino acids that we now know to be critical to the recovery process. Fish, shellfish, egg whites, and turkey breast are excellent choices. It is best to avoid farm-bred fish and feedlot-raised animals, and not just at this time but throughout the day. The physical composition of their meat, especially the oils, is dramatically different from that of wild game and free-ranging animals.

If you continue eating fruits and vegetables now, you will also restock electrolytes that may be necessary for recovery, depending on how long the exercise session and how hot the weather. Also, there may be a need to add a small amount of table salt to food after exercise in the heat, especially if you're not heat adapted, and following long or intense sessions.

It's still important to drink at least 16 ounces (500 milliliters) for every pound of body weight lost during exercise. Because you will continue losing fluids during this extended recovery period, you will need to drink more than the amount lost during exercise. Fruit juices are an excellent choice because they also bolster carbohydrate stores and are rich in most electrolytes.

STAGE V: LONG-TERM POSTEXERCISE

You've gotten yourself through a grueling workout and refueled as you should in Stages I to IV of recovery. You're back at work or in class, spending time with the family, maintaining your house and landscaping—whatever it is you do when you're not training or racing. This part of your day may look ordinary to the rest of the world, but it really isn't. You're still focused on nutrition for long-term recovery.

This is the time when many athletes get sloppy with their diets. The most common mistake is to continue eating a high glycemic load diet that is low in nutrient value and marked by the high starch and sugar intake common in Stages III and IV, but doing this compromises development as an athlete. It's a shame to spend hours training, only to squander a portion of the potential fitness gains by eating less than optimal foods.

What are optimal foods? These are the categories of foods that have been eaten by our Paleolithic ancestors for 2.6 million years; the ones to which we are fully adapted through an inheritance of genes from the countless generations that preceded us here on Earth: fruits, vegetables, and lean protein from animal sources. Optimal foods also include nuts, seeds, and berries. These are also the most nutrient-dense foods available to us—they're rich in vitamins, minerals, and other trace elements necessary for health, growth, and recovery. Table 4.7 on page 64 compares the vitamin and mineral density of several foods. The three highest in each column are in bold print. Notice that vegetables especially provide an abundant level of vitamins and minerals; most other foods pale by comparison.

Stage V Recovery Guidelines

In terms of athletic performance, the nutritional goals and guidelines for this stage of recovery are as follows.

* **Maintain glycogen stores.** For some time prior to this stage of recovery, you intently focused your diet around carbohydrate, especially high glycemic load sources such as the sugars in starchy foods. While these foods are excellent for restocking the body's glycogen stores, they are not nutrient dense (see Table 4.7 on page 64). There is no longer a need to eat large quantities of such foods; in fact, they will diminish your potential for recovery. Every calorie eaten from a less than optimal food means a lost opportunity to take in much larger amounts of nutrients from vegetables, fruits, and lean animal protein. The more serious you are about your athletic performance, the more important this is.

  Furthermore, one of the beauties of the human body is that, regardless of which system or function we are talking about, it takes less concentrated effort to maintain than to rebuild. This means that by eating prodigious quantities of high glycemic load carbohydrates in the previous stages, you've rebuilt your body's glycogen stores, and now less carbohydrate is required to maintain that level. Low glycemic fruits and vegetables will accomplish that while also providing the micronutrients needed for the last stage of recovery.

TABLE 4.7

Comparison of Vitamin and Mineral Density of Selected Foods

FOOD (per 100 calories)	A	C	B₁	B₂	NIA (NIACIN)	B₆	B₁₂	FOLIC ACID	PANT (PANTOTHENE)
Vegetables									
Asparagus	341	**82**	**0.4**	**0.5**	4	**0.6**	0	**400**	0.7
Broccoli	**478**	**213**	**0.3**	**0.7**	0.3	**0.7**	0	**234**	**1**
Cauliflower	6	**226**	**0.3**	0.2	2	**0.9**	0	213	0.5
Spinach	**3,509**	43	**0.4**	**1**	**5**	0.5	0	**624**	0.6
Fruits									
Apple	9	10	0.02	0.02	0.1	0.1	0	5	0.1
Banana	9	10	0.04	0.1	0.6	0.6	0	21	0.3
Peach	127	16	0.1	0.1	2	0.1	0	8	0.4
Pear	3	7	0.03	0.1	0.2	0.03	0	12	0.1
Meats									
Salmon	214	*	0.2	0.2	**7**	0.2	**6**	*	*
T-bone steak	*	0	0.04	0.1	2	0.2	**1**	3	0.1
Tuna	**1,364**	*	0.2	0.2	**6**	0.3	**6**	*	*
Turkey	0	0	**0.4**	0.08	4	0.3	0.2	4	0.4
Grains									
Bagel	*	0	0.1	0.1	1	0.01	0	8	0.1
Long-grain rice	*	0.7	0.1	0.01	2	0.01	0.01	2	0.09
Whole wheat bread	*	0	0.1	0.08	2	0.08	0	23	0.3
Yellow corn	20	6	0.2	0.07	1	0.06	0	43	**0.8**
Dairy									
American cheese	*	0	0.01	0.1	0	0.04	0.4	2	0.3
Fat-free milk	173	2	0.1	0.4	0.02	0.1	**1**	15	**1**
Low-fat yogurt	25	1	0.07	0.3	0.2	0.08	**0.9**	17	0.9
Swiss cheese	*	0	0	0.1	0	*	0.7	*	0.2
Legumes									
Baked beans	18	*	0.2	0.06	0.5	0.1	0	26	0.1
Broadbeans	2	0.5	0.1	0.1	0.6	0.1	0	95	0.1
Peanuts	0	0	0.1	0.02	2	0.04	0	25	0.2
Soybeans	0.7	1	0.1	0.2	0.2	0.1	0	31	0.1
Nuts									
Almonds	0	0	0.04	0.1	0.6	0.2	0	10	0.1
Cashews	0	0	0.04	0.04	0.2	0.04	0	12	0.2
Macadamia nuts	*	0	0.04	0.02	0.4	0.03	0	36	0.04
Walnuts	2	1	0.06	0.02	0.2	0.09	0	10	0.1

The three highest vitamin and mineral contents in each column are indicated by a bold listing.
* No information available

NA (SODIUM)	K (POTASSIUM)	CA (CALCIUM)	P (PHOSPHORUS)	MG (MAGNESIUM)	FE (IRON)	ZN (ZINC)	CU (COPPER)	MN (MANGANESE)
18	**1,268**	100	**245**	77	3	2	**0.4**	**0.8**
34	552	**386**	160	**204**	3	0.5	0.2	**0.8**
26	**1,333**	113	147	47	2	1	0.04	0.7
300	**1,995**	**581**	238	**376**	**15**	**3**	**0.7**	**4**
1	196	12	12	7	0.3	0.06	0.07	0.08
1	430	7	21	31	0.3	0.2	0.1	0.2
0	462	14	30	16	0.3	0.3	0.2	0.1
1	208	19	18	9	0.4	0.2	0.2	0.1
67	384	7	**282**	31	0.6	0.5	0.07	*
28	158	4	83	11	1	**2**	0.06	0.006
27	175	*	*	*	0.7	0.4	0.05	*
41	194	12	139	18	0.9	1	0.03	0.01
121	25	14	23	7	1	0.2	0.03	*
0	27	9	17	7	1	0.2	0.03	*
261	72	30	107	38	1	0.7	0.1	1
16	229	2	94	29	0.6	0.4	0.05	0.2
291	110	150	120	9	0.3	1	*	*
147	472	**351**	**287**	33	0.1	1	*	*
110	369	288	226	28	0.1	1	*	*
478	88	223	162	9	0.2	1	*	*
429	320	54	112	35	0.3	1	0.2	0.4
4	245	33	114	39	1	1	0.2	0.4
139	112	9	61	30	0.4	0.6	0.1	0.4
0.3	297	59	141	50	3	0.7	0.2	0.5
2	125	45	89	50	0.6	0.5	0.2	0.4
2	98	8	85	45	1	1	**0.4**	*
61	39	11	63	15	0.4	0.3	0.2	*
2	78	15	49	26	0.4	0.4	0.2	0.5

- **Rebuild muscle tissues.** Despite your best efforts to take in amino acids in recovery Stages I and II, if the workout was sufficiently intense, you will have suffered some muscle cell damage. If you could use an electron microscope to look into the muscles used in hard training today, it would look like a war zone, albeit a very tiny one. You would see tattered cell membranes and leaking fluids. The body would be mobilizing its "triage services" to repair the damage as quickly as possible. To do this, the body needs amino acids in rather large quantities. Most needed are the branched-chain amino acids (BCAA) you read about earlier. Without them, the body is forced to cannibalize other protein cells to find sufficient amounts of the right amino acids to complete the job. Also needed are the essential amino acids, those that the body cannot produce and must come from food.

  BCAA and essential amino acids are most abundant in animal products. If you're hesitant to eat red meat from feedlot-raised animals, we don't blame you. The common beef products you buy in supermarkets are a poor source of food. While certainly rich in BCAA, meats from feedlot-raised animals are also packed with saturated and omega-6 polyunsaturated fats and are best avoided.

  So what should you eat to provide BCAA and the essential amino acids for your rebuilding muscles? The best possible source would be meat from game animals such as deer, elk, and buffalo. Of course, chances are that you don't have the time to go hunting, given your workout and career choices. (For our ancestors, hunting was exercise and career all rolled into one activity.) No, it's unlikely that you will find game meat outside your back door, and it can't be sold in supermarkets, either. But there are other readily available choices that are almost as good.

  Ocean- or stream-caught fish and shellfish are among the best protein sources; they are, after all, wild game. It's best, however, to avoid farm-raised fish, which is essentially the same as feedlot-raised cattle. Another good choice is turkey breast. It comes as close to providing the lean protein and fat makeup of game animals as any domestic meat available. It's still a good idea to seek out meat from turkeys that were allowed to range in search of food. The same goes for any meat you may choose. Free-ranging animals have not only exercised but also have more likely eaten foods that are optimal for their health. This means that saturated fat levels are low and omega-6 and omega-3 polyunsaturated fats are in better balance. You'll find that choosing such meats is more expensive than eating the more common meats of penned-up animals. It's just like so much in life: Quality costs more. You get what you pay for.

In Stage V, continue to take in 0.6 gram to 1 gram of protein per pound of body weight relative to your training load. The longer or more intense your exercise was, the more protein you should take in, as shown in Table 4.8.

- **Maintain a healthy pH.** In our discussion of Stage III, we told you about the acid- and base-enhancing properties of foods, demonstrated by Table 4.4 on page 57. The great need to lower the acidity of body fluids, including blood, continues in this stage, to reduce the risk of losing nitrogen and calcium. As explained earlier, nitrogen is an essential component of muscle, and calcium is crucial for bone health. Fortunately, the very

TABLE 4.8

Suggested Daily Protein Intake per Pound of Body Weight

TRAINING VOLUME (HOURS/WEEK)	PROTEIN (G)/DAY
<5	0.6–0.7
5–10	0.7–0.8
10–15	0.8–0.9
15–20	0.9–1
>20	1

foods that are the most nutrient dense are also the ones—the only ones—that reduce blood acidity: fruits and vegetables. Any fruit will do now, so eat whichever appeal to you. As for vegetables, it's best to choose those of vibrant colors—red, yellow, green, and orange—while avoiding white ones. Be aware that beans, although often categorized as vegetables, are net acid enhancing and best avoided.

- **Prevent or reduce inflammation.** All athletes are susceptible to inflammation of muscles and tendons—it comes with the territory. You may have a tendon that is a persistent problem for you following high-effort workouts and sometimes flares up, causing pain and discomfort. Muscle tissue damaged during an intense workout may also result in inflammation. If allowed to go unchecked, nagging inflammation can become a full-blown injury, causing you to miss training and lose fitness. Omega-3 polyunsaturated fat supplements have been shown to reduce inflammation by lowering the ratio of omega-6 to omega-3 fatty acids, which should be approximately two parts omega-6 to one part omega-3. Due to the high intake of omega-6 from snacks and other packaged foods that are abundant in our society, the average American diet has a 10:1 ratio of omega-6 to omega-3. In fact, avoiding omega-6 is quite a challenge in Western society. By consuming foods that are rich in omega-3— cold-water fish, leafy vegetables, macadamia nuts and walnuts, eggs enriched with omega-3, and liver—you can lower this ratio and reduce your inflammation risk. We recommend that to improve the odds of accomplishing this, you take an omega-3 supplement, such as fish oil or flaxseed oil. The details of this supplementation are found in Chapter 6.

- **Optimize body weight.** For most endurance sports, maintaining a low body mass translates into better performances. Yet, even with a lot of daily exercise to burn calories, avoiding weight gain can be a struggle for many endurance athletes. We think you will find that by eating a Stage V diet made up primarily of fruits, vegetables, and lean protein, weight control will not be a problem. It's when we eat less-than-optimal foods that we tend to add body fat.

STAGE V AND CARBOHYDRATE

On a conventional Stone Age nutrition plan, such as the one described in *The Paleo Diet,* a person would be eating much more protein and less carbohydrate than the diet we suggest here for athletes. The shift toward more carbohydrate is due to the need to quickly recover from strenuous exercise, a need that the average, sedentary person does not have—nor did our Stone Age ancestors. For the athlete who trains more than one time per day, as is common with many elite athletes, the absolute carbohydrate intake is even higher because the need to recover increases as the number of training hours rises.

For example, an athlete training once a day for 90 minutes may burn 600 calories from carbohydrate during exercise and needs to take in at least that much during Stages I, II, III, and IV of recovery. This athlete may be eating around 3,000 total calories daily. If he gets 50 percent of daily calories from carbohydrate, he would take in an additional 900 calories in carbs that day in Stage V, above and beyond the carbohydrate consumed in the earlier stages of the day. Of course, this carbohydrate should primarily come from fruits and especially vegetables, so calories aren't wasted by eating foods lacking in micronutrients.

The high-volume athlete may do two of these 90-minute exercise sessions a day, thus doubling the total requirement for carbohydrate to 1,200 calories during the first four stages that day. This shift toward greater volume of training also should be accompanied by an increase in total calories consumed daily. Say 3,600 calories are taken in on such a day; if the athlete is also eating a half-carbohydrate diet, he will need another 600 calories from carbohydrate sources this day in Stage V. This illustrates how the absolute carbohydrate intake varies with the training load of the athlete, despite the percentage of intake being the same.

STAGE V AND PROTEIN

Getting too little carbohydrate in the diet is seldom a problem for athletes; it's abundant in grocery stores, inexpensive, and enjoyable to eat. No, the real stumbling block is protein intake. When we do dietary assessments of athletes, we typically find that they aren't eating enough protein. Why? Because protein is not abundant in stores, it's relatively expensive, and it's not as enjoyable to eat as a sweet or starchy food. Protein in the form of meat has also gotten a bad rap in the last few decades. We've been taught that animal meat is bad for us as it contributes to heart disease, cancer, and assorted other evils. The problem with this conclusion is that it doesn't isolate the true causes of these diseases. It's not protein that is to blame for Western society's health woes but, rather, the saturated fats that often accompany it. Protein does not cause heart disease.

Let's not throw the baby out with the bathwater. Saturated fat should be greatly reduced in your diet, but not lean protein. Fish, shellfish, and turkey breast are excellent sources of lean protein and rich in essential and branched-chain amino acids. For now, the take-home message is that athletes need an abundance of amino acids daily, and these are best found in lean animal sources.

Since protein is so important to your total recovery, this is a good place to begin deciding what to eat at meals in Stage V. The first concept to understand is that the amount of protein you need is related to how much you train. For the average person on the street who does little or no exercise, the level of protein intake stays much the same from day to day, as physical activity is usually quite limited. It's different for the athlete who often pushes his or her body to near its limits and, in the process, potentially damages a lot of muscle tissue while using some protein as fuel. The greater your training volume or intensity, the greater the likelihood such cellular harm will occur. A considerable amount of amino acids from lean protein sources is needed in the hours following Stage IV recovery to repair this tissue and prevent the body from seeking amino acids from internal sources, such as other muscles or the immune system. Without adequate protein, the risk of a compromised immune system increases and the possibility of muscle wasting rises.

Table 4.8 on page 67 provides general guidelines for how much protein to eat with regard to your weekly training volume. Intensity of training is much harder to quantify, but you may also assume that when doing a lot of interval training, hill work, resistance training, or other high-effort exercise, you probably need to increase your protein intake to the next level in the table.

The next matter is deciding where you will get this lean protein. You may be aware that you can obtain all of the essential amino acids by mixing grains and legumes within a meal. Each of those food categories is lacking in one or more of the essential amino acids, but by eating them in combination, the meal becomes more balanced (although plant-based diets will always be lacking in the essential amino acids lysine and tryptophan). What is not generally explained, however, is that the volume of plant-based foods one has to eat to get adequate daily protein (see Table 4.9 on page 72) requires eating considerable amounts of grains and beans because these foods are nutritionally poor. In addition, they contribute to blood acidity levels (see Table 4.4 on page 57). A serious athlete attempting to get nearly a gram of protein per pound of body weight would need to eat all day long—and have a gut that can process a significant amount of fiber. Even if he or she could do this, blood acidity levels would stay high, and antinutrients would prevent the absorption of much of the limited micronutrients these foods have.

TABLE 4.9

rotein and Essential Amino Acid Content of Common Foods

FOOD (PER 100 CALORIES)	PROTEIN CONTENT (G)	ESSENTIAL AMINO ACID CONTENT (G)
Animal		
Cod (3.4 oz)	22	8.7
Shrimp (3.6 oz)	21	8.2
Lobster (3.6 oz)	21	8.1
Halibut (2.5 oz)	19	7.5
Chicken (2 oz)	18	6.8
Turkey breast (2 oz)	17	6.9
Tuna (1.9 oz)	16	6.3
Tenderloin steak (1.75 oz)	14	5.1
Egg, whole (1.25 oz)	7.7	3.4
Legumes		
Tofu (½ c)	10	3.6
Kidney beans (½ c)	7	2.8
Navy beans (⅓ c)	6	1.9
Red beans (½ c)	5	2.5
Peanut butter (1 Tbsp)	4.6	1.4
Grains		
Bagel (½ bagel)	3.8	1.1
Corn (¾ cup)	3.7	1.4
Whole wheat bread (1½ slices)	3	0.8
Brown rice (½ cup)	2.1	0.7

A 150-pound athlete training 15 hours a week would need to take in about 135 grams of protein a day (150 × 0.9), according to Table 4.8 on page 67. Assuming 20 percent of that comes from assorted vegetables, fruits, fruit juices, and sports bars and drinks consumed throughout the day, another 108 grams of protein would be needed that day. To get that from animal sources, he could eat:

4 ounces of cod
6 ounces of turkey breast
4 ounces of chicken

Those foods would provide all of the additional protein and contain 44.5 grams of the all-important essential amino acids for our theoretical athlete. The total energy eaten to get these nutrients would be 454 calories. To get the same amount of protein by combining grains and beans, he would have to eat *all* of the following in one day:

1 cup of tofu
1 cup of kidney beans
6 slices of whole wheat bread
1 cup of navy beans
1½ cups of corn
1 cup of red beans
1 cup of brown rice
2 bagels
2 tablespoons of peanut butter

Our athlete had better like beans and have a huge appetite! The above requires eating an additional 2,300 calories that day—more than five times as much as when eating animal products—just to get 108 grams of protein. Eating grains and legumes to get daily protein is not only very inefficient, but, far worse, the vegetarian athlete will come up short on essential amino acids—even if he or she can stomach all those beans and grains.

STAGE V AND FAT

Just as there are good and bad sources of carbohydrate and protein, there are fats and oils you should pursue in your daily diet and certain others to avoid. The desirables include omega-3 polyunsaturated and monounsaturated types. As described earlier in this chapter, lowering the ratio of omega-6 to omega-3 has positive implications for reducing the likelihood of inflammation, a persistent problem for athletes. Omega-6s, while necessary for health, are more than abundant in our modern diet. This fat is common in vegetable oils such as soybean, peanut, cottonseed, safflower, sunflower, sesame, and corn. Most snack foods and many grain products, including breads and bagels, rely heavily on vegetable oils due to their low cost.

Monounsaturated fats should also be included in the athlete's diet because of their health benefits, including lowering cholesterol and triglyceride levels, thinning the blood, preventing fatal heartbeat irregularities, and reducing the risk of breast cancer. Remember that health always comes before fitness. Good sources of monounsaturated fat are avocados, nuts, and olive oil.

Avoid the saturated fats found in abundance in whole dairy foods and feedlot-raised animals, especially beef, and trans fat found in many of the foods in our grocery stores—not only snack foods but also many bread products, peanut butter, margarine, and packaged meals. Steer clear of trans fat, referred to as partially hydrogenated oil on food labels, whenever possible. While saturated fat causes an increase in LDL (the "bad" cholesterol associated with heart disease), trans fat not only increases LDL but also decreases your body's production of HDL (the "good" cholesterol linked with a low incidence of heart disease). That's a double whammy best avoided. To give you some idea of how bad this stuff is, some countries are considering banning it, and Denmark has tightly restricted its use. As of this writing, the United States and Canada are considering better labeling to identify products containing trans fat.

PERIODIZATION OF STAGE V DIET

In working with athletes from novices to elites, we have found that varying the Stage V diet in parallel with training volume and intensity produces the best performances. By varying the macronutrient intake, it is possible to enhance the benefits sought in different types of training at certain points in the season. For example, if a purpose of the base (general preparation) period is to train the athlete's body to preferentially use fat for fuel, thus sparing carbohydrate, and we know that eating a diet higher in fat and lower in carbohydrate also promotes such a metabolic shift, then it seems reasonable to have the athlete eat more fat and less carbohydrate at this time in the season. We have used this strategy with athletes and observed changes in respiratory quotients (a laboratory measurement of how much fat versus carbohydrate is used for energy) indicating that glycogen, the muscle's storage form of carbohydrate, was being spared, compared with pretests in which carbohydrate was relatively high and fat low in the diet. Although there is no research in this area of sports nutrition, our experience supports the notion that aerobic training, along with a greater intake of fat, produces increased benefits in the form of glycogen sparing.

In the same way, when the intensity of training increases while volume stabilizes or decreases slightly in the build (specific preparation) period, the athlete uses more carbohydrate for fuel. During this period, which occurs about 6 to 12 weeks before priority A races, it is wise to increase the carbohydrate content of the diet slightly, while decreasing fat intake. Protein stays stable relative to the total training workload throughout the season.

Before going into more detail on this subject, it is important that we explain some basic tenets of periodization. Periodization is a system in which the endurance athlete's training program is designed so that a high level of fitness is typically achieved two or three times in a season. This system of training, largely developed by Eastern bloc countries in the 1960s, has been prevalent in Western countries since the 1970s and is widely employed by serious athletes around the world. In periodization, the season is divided into periods that may be 1 to 12 weeks in duration; each has a purpose and a unique method of training associated with it.

In the classic periodization model, the training year begins with general preparation made up of the preparation and base periods. The purpose of training for endurance athletes in this period is to produce gains in the areas of general aerobic fitness, strength, and sport skills.

Following this is specific preparation during the build and peak periods, when training becomes increasingly specific to the demands of the coming event. This is usually marked by a shift in emphasis from general endurance to higher-intensity training, although this is determined by the targeted race's characteristics. For example, for very long events, workout intensity is quite low, and long, slow endurance training continues much as in general preparation—although there may be race-specific training adjustments made relative to terrain, weather conditions, and equipment used. In the 1- to 2-week peak period, it is common for the athlete to significantly reduce the training volume while completing a "dress rehearsal" workout every 72 to 96 hours. During these periods, the gains made in the general preparation period are maintained, with reduced frequency of training for endurance, strength, and skills.

Next comes the competition or race period. This is what you've trained for. It's when the all-important priority A races are scheduled. For most athletes, the race period is best kept quite short—no more than 1 week. A few athletes—most likely elites, who have more latitude when it comes to devoting themselves to proper training and recovery—may be able to hold a peak of fitness for 2 to 3 weeks. Attempting to maintain a peaked level of fitness for too long will result in a gradual erosion of endurance due to the emphasis on rest at this period in the season.

The race period is followed by the transition period, when physical and mental rejuvenation is the goal. This may last from a few days at midseason to a few weeks at the end of the race season.

Just as the duration, frequency, and intensity of training are adjusted throughout the season, so must the types of foods and when they are eaten, as well the amount of calories consumed, be fine-tuned. Table 4.10 summarizes these objectives and unique nutritional requirements. When the workload is the greatest in the base

and build periods, the volume of food eaten and subsequent calories consumed are also at the highest for the year. Using these as the
standard, or 100 percent level, the other periods will require fewer
calories since the recovery demands are not as great. As previously
explained, there should be a shift between carbohydrate and fat according to the demands of the training sessions and races. Protein
remains about the same throughout the year. Table 4.11 on page
78 demonstrates these caloric and macronutrient adjustments.

TABLE 4.10

Parallel Periodization of Training and Nutrition

PERIOD	DURATION	WORKLOAD	EXERCISE EMPHASIS	NUTRITION EMPHASIS
Preparation (general preparation)	2–6 weeks	Moderate	General aerobic, cross-training, general strength training	Fat increased, carbohydrate decreased, protein stable
Base (general preparation)	8–12 weeks	High	Increasing volume, low intensity, usually aerobic, skills emphasis, specific strength training	Fat increased, carbohydrate decreased, protein stable
Build (specific preparation)	6–8 weeks	High	Reduced volume, increasing intensity, race-specific, aerobic and strength maintenance	Fat decreased, carbohydrate increased, protein stable
Peak (specific preparation)	1–2 weeks	Moderate	Tapering volume, race simulation every 72–96 hours, aerobic and strength maintenance	Fat decreased, carbohydrate increased, protein stable
Race (competition)	1 week	Low	Reduce volume greatly while maintaining fitness (especially with intensity), rest, mental preparation	Maintain fat, carbohydrate, and protein as calorie consumption is reduced in parallel with training reduction
Transition	3 days–4 weeks	Very low	Mental and physical rejuvenation, general aerobic	Fat increased, carbohydrate decreased, protein stable

TABLE 4.11

Approximate Caloric Breakdown by Training Period

TRAINING PERIOD	CALORIES (% OF PEAK INTAKE)	CARBOHYDRATE CALORIES (%)	PROTEIN CALORIES (%)	FAT CALORIES (%)
Preparation	90	50	20	30
Base	100	50	20	30
Build	100	60	20	20
Peak	90	60	20	20
Race	80	60	20	20
Transition	80	50	20	30

Now that we've laid out the general outline for eating relative to exercise throughout the season, let's see what the menu might look like for a day in the life of a particular athlete. Table 4.12 provides a breakdown of calories by source and recovery stage. Table 4.13 provides further detail on this athlete's food choices on this same day.

As can be seen from the examples in these tables, our hypothetical athlete focuses on appropriate recovery foods throughout the day. Before, during, and in the 30 minutes immediately following exercise (Stages I, II, and III), his food choices are intended to replace carbohydrate used in exercise and provide protein to prevent loss of muscle. In Stages IV and V, he concentrates on

TABLE 4.12

Daily Caloric Breakdown during the Build Period

RECOVERY STAGE	CARBOHYDRATE CALORIES	PROTEIN CALORIES	FAT CALORIES	TOTAL CALORIES
Stage I	165	35	0	200
Stage II	240	60	0	300
Stage III	450	90	0	540
Stage IV	225	45	40	310
Stage V	730	370	550	1,650
Totals for day	1,930	480	590	3,000
% of Total Calories	64	16	20	100

Example is for a 150-pound athlete's intense 90-minute workout while training 15 hours per week.

TABLE 4.13

Food Choices for a Day in the Build Period

TIME	ROUTINE	FOOD CHOICES	TOTAL CALORIES
Stage I			
5:00–5:30 a.m.	Arise, stretch, preworkout snack (10 minutes prior)	2 gel packets	200
		12 oz water	0
Stage II			
5:30–7:00 a.m.	Exercise (intervals)	48 oz sports drink	300
Stage III			
7:00–7:30 a.m.	Stretch, recovery drink	16 oz homebrew drink	540
Stage IV			
7:30–8:30 a.m.	Shower, dress, breakfast	6 oz turkey breast	280
		1 apple	100
		6 oz grape juice	100
		1 c coffee	6
Stage V			
8:30–11:30 a.m.	Work, snack	2 oz dried fruit with nuts	300
11:30–12:30 p.m.	Lunch	4 oz cod	111
		1 c fruit salad	170
12:30–5:30 p.m.	Work, snack	2 carrots	62
		1 banana	100
5:30–9:00 p.m.	Family time, supper, bedtime snack	6 oz salmon	300
		1 c broccoli	30
		Small spinach salad w/dressing	200
		8 oz herbal tea	2
		1 oz dried fruit with nuts	150
		3½ oz wine	75
Total Calories			**3,026**

Example is for a 150-pound athlete's intense 90-minute workout while training 15 hours per week.

eating foods that shift blood pH levels toward greater alkalinity to preserve bone and muscle tissue, as well as foods, such as nuts and fish, that are rich in omega-3 oils to reduce the risk of inflammation, and protein for continuing muscle recovery.

PART II

NUTRITION 101:
UNDERSTANDING BASIC CONCEPTS

Chapter 5

FOOD AS FUEL DURING EXERCISE

DIETARY ORIGINS

Upon introduction to the Paleo Diet concept, many people assume that there was a single universal diet that all Stone Age people ate. Nothing could be further from the truth. In the 5 to 7 million years since the evolutionary split between apes and hominins (primates who walk upright on two feet), as many as 20 different species of hominins may have existed. Their diets varied by latitude, season, climate, and food availability. But there was one universal characteristic: They all ate minimally processed, wild plant and animal foods. In the Introduction, we told you all about the foods they couldn't have consumed; in Chapter 8, we will show you the evidence for the food that they ate. But in the meantime, it's important to understand how the current Western diet differs from theirs and how these differences may affect exercise performance.

If you contrast the average American diet to hunter-gatherer diets (even at their most extreme deviations), the standard American diet falls outside the hunter-gatherer range for certain crucial nutritional characteristics. By examining the diets of more than

200 hunter-gatherer societies, we have found that the typical Western diet varies from ancestral hunter-gatherer diets in these seven key features:

1. Macronutrient balance
2. Glycemic load
3. Fatty acid balance
4. Potassium/sodium balance
5. Acid/base balance
6. Fiber intake
7. Trace nutrient density

MACRONUTRIENT BALANCE AND GLYCEMIC LOAD

Figure 5.1 compares the macronutrient (protein, fat, carbohydrate) composition between hunter-gatherer and typical US diets. Note that protein is universally elevated at the expense of carbohydrate, while their diets usually contain more fat than what we get. However, the type of fat that they consumed was healthful omega-3 and monounsaturated fats, rather than the artery-clogging saturated fats that burden the typical US diet. But the im-

FIGURE 5.1

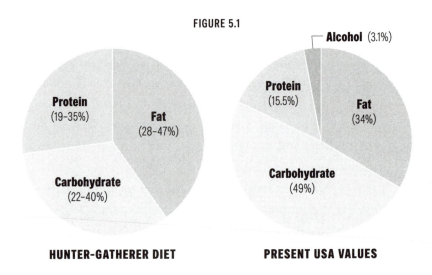

HUNTER-GATHERER DIET **PRESENT USA VALUES**

portant issue here for the athlete is the carbohydrate story. Not only was the carbohydrate content of their diet lower, but the quality of their carbs was worlds apart from what most of us eat.

Glycemic Index and Glycemic Load

The quality of any carbohydrate food can be determined by its glycemic index. The glycemic index, a scale that rates how much certain foods raise blood sugar levels compared with glucose, was developed by Dr. David Jenkins at the University of Toronto in 1981. Sometimes white bread, which has a glycemic index of 100, is used as the reference food rather than glucose. One of the short-comings of the original glycemic index was that it only compared equal quantities of carbohydrate (usually 50 grams) among foods to evaluate the blood glucose response. It didn't take into account the total amount of carbohydrate in a typical serving. This limitation has created quite a bit of confusion. For instance, watermelon has a glycemic index (GI) of 72, while a milk chocolate candy bar tops out with a GI of only 43. Does that mean we should eat candy bars rather than fruit? Of course not! The candy bar is a much more concentrated source of carbohydrate (sugar) than watermelon is. You have to eat only 3 ounces of the chocolate to get 50 grams of carbohydrate, whereas you would have to eat 1½ pounds of watermelon to get 50 grams of carbs. To overcome this limitation, scientists at Harvard University in 1997 proposed using a new scale called the glycemic load, defined as the GI multiplied by the carbohydrate content in a typical serving. The glycemic load effectively equalized the playing field and made real-world food comparisons possible.

Almost all processed foods made from refined grains and sugars have quite high glycemic loads, whereas virtually all fresh fruits and veggies have very low glycemic loads (see Table 5.1 on page 86). The Web site www.glycemicindex.com helps you determine the GI and glycemic load of almost any food.

TABLE 5.1

Comparison of Glycemic Load and Index of Refined and Unrefined Foods (100 g portions)

WESTERN REFINED FOODS			UNREFINED TRADITIONAL FOODS		
Food	Glycemic Index	Glycemic Load	Food	Glycemic Index	Glycemic Load
Crisped rice cereal	88	77.3	Parsnips	97	19.5
Jelly beans	80	74.5	Baked potato	85	18.4
Cornflakes	84	72.7	Boiled millet	71	16.8
Lifesavers	70	67.9	Boiled broad beans	79	15.5
Rice cakes	82	66.9	Boiled couscous	65	15.1
Table sugar (sucrose)	65	64.9	Boiled sweet potato	54	13.1
Shredded wheat cereal	69	57.0	Boiled brown rice	55	12.6
Graham crackers	74	56.8	Banana	53	12.1
Grape-Nuts cereal	67	54.3	Boiled yam	51	11.5
Cheerios cereal	74	54.2	Boiled garbanzo beans	33	9
Rye crisp bread	65	53.4	Pineapple	66	8.2
Vanilla wafers	77	49.7	Grapes	43	7.7
Corn chips	73	46.3	Kiwifruit	52	7.4
Mars bar	68	42.2	Carrots	71	7.2
Shortbread cookies	64	41.9	Boiled beets	64	6.3
Granola bar	61	39.3	Boiled kidney beans	27	6.2
Angel food cake	67	38.7	Apple	39	6.0
Bagel	72	38.4	Boiled lentils	29	5.8
Doughnut	76	37.8	Pear	36	5.4
White bread	70	34.7	Watermelon	72	5.2
Waffles	76	34.2	Orange	43	5.1
100% bran cereal	42	32.5	Cherries	22	3.7
Whole wheat bread	69	31.8	Peach	28	3.1
Croissant	67	31.2	Peanuts	14	2.6

Meat and seafood generally don't contain any carbohydrate and cause minimal rises in blood sugar and insulin levels (see Table 5.2).

Surprising—and somewhat alarming—is the paradoxically high insulin response of milk (90) and fermented milk (98) com-

TABLE 5.2

Blood Glucose and Insulin Responses (239-kcal sample)

FOOD	GLUCOSE	INSULIN
White bread	100	100
Eggs	42	31
Beef	21	51
Fish	28	59

The glycemic reference is white bread with a glucose and insulin response of 100.

pared with their low glycemic responses (30 and 15, respectively). A similar dissociation of the blood insulin and glucose response occurs in yogurt. Generally, however, the GI of most foods nicely parallels the insulin response or insulin index (II). Hence, high GI foods are almost always high II foods.

Because the carbohydrates in Paleolithic diets came from minimally processed, wild plants, and because hunter-gatherers ate no refined grains or sugars (except for seasonal honey), the glycemic loads of their diets would have been very low by modern standards. But remember, the fat and protein intake would have been higher. What are the implications of these dietary macronutrient patterns upon endurance performance?

Muscle Fuel Sources

When you are at rest and not exercising, about 60 percent of the energy needed to fuel your body is provided by fats. The balance is provided by carbohydrate because protein is a relatively minor source of energy. At rest, free fatty acids (FFA) circulating in the bloodstream provide the major source of fat to fuel metabolism. FFA in the blood comes from fat stored in cells in your belly, thighs, and any other place where you accumulate fat. At low exercise levels (25 percent of your aerobic capacity), fat provides 80 percent of the muscle's fuel, and the balance (about 20 percent) comes from carbohydrate. At 25 percent max VO_2, most of the fat fueling muscle contraction still comes from FFA in the blood, although a small amount is derived from stored fat droplets inside muscle cells—the intramuscular triglycerides (IMT). Twenty to 30 years ago, exercise scientists didn't pay much attention to IMT when it came to endurance performance; their sights were narrowly focused upon glycogen. Glycogen is made up of chains of glucose molecules, which is how carbs are stored inside muscle cells.

Let's continue with the tutorial on muscle fuel sources so you can eventually see how Paleolithic macronutrient patterns weren't necessarily a liability for performance. As exercise intensity increases, so does IMT usage by the muscles. At approximately 65 percent max VO_2, IMT stores are being maximally drawn on, so that energy contribution from fats and carbs is about 50:50. When exercise intensity increases to 85 percent max VO_2, IMT supplies only 25 percent of the energy needed for muscle contraction. Finally, as you continue to 100 percent of your aerobic capacity, glucose from muscle glycogen stores becomes the preferred and necessary fuel source. Why is that? Why isn't fat used to fuel very intense and high-level exercise?

If you look at the caloric density of fat, it is 9 calories per gram—more than twice as much as carbohydrate's 4 calories per gram. So, at least on the surface, it looks like fat would be the preferred fuel for high-level exercise because it's such a concentrated energy source. But there's another side to the story, and it's called fuel efficiency—a concept you know better as "miles per gallon." When you look at body fuel efficiency in terms of oxygen rather than energy density, the picture changes. It takes considerably more oxygen for muscles to burn fat than carbohydrate. Carbohydrate yields 5.05 calories per liter of oxygen, whereas fat gives only 4.69—a difference of 7 percent. During aerobic metabolism, this 7 percent caloric advantage for carbs translates into a threefold faster energy production in the muscles. The take-home message: Muscle stores of glycogen are absolutely essential in performing endurance exercise at or above 85 percent max VO_2 for any extended period.

But here's the problem: There is a limit to how much glycogen the muscles can store. Trained endurance athletes can store twice as much muscle glycogen as couch potatoes can. However, it's important to know that muscle glycogen stockpiles cannot be shifted from one muscle to another during exercise: Any glycogen in your arms will not help your legs and vice versa. The values for muscle glycogen in Table 5.3 represent whole-body muscle stores and obviously will be considerably lower for specific muscle groups.

Because the muscle's glycogen stores are limited, high-intensity endurance activity (> 85 percent max VO_2) can last only as long as the glycogen lasts. But there's a catch here, and if you are an experienced endurance athlete, you know it: You can drink athletic drinks containing glucose to slow the muscle's glycogen loss during exercise but, unfortunately, not fast enough. The maximum rate that ingested glucose can be metabolized during exercise is about 1 gram per minute—still not fast enough to replace what's being lost during hard exercise. As muscle glycogen stores become depleted, you're forced to slow down because the remaining fat stores require more oxygen to be burned. This reduced oxygen efficiency of fat compared with glucose is precisely why you must reduce your intensity once muscle glycogen reserves are severely depleted.

TABLE 5.3

Total Body Carbohydrate Stores in a Nontrained Person

SOURCE	AMOUNT (G)	CORRESPONDING CALORIES
Blood glucose	5	20
Liver glycogen	100	400
Muscle glycogen	400	1,600

There is still a way out of this bottleneck. You can slow muscle glycogen loss by increasing how efficiently you burn fats and by increasing your IMT stores. Fats play a key role in how well you will perform in ultraendurance events and bicycle road races. In long, moderate-intensity races such as these, not only do you deplete your carbohydrate reserves, you simply cannot metabolize ingested carbs (from drinks or energy bars) as fast as you are losing them. Accordingly, if you can maximize both your muscle IMT and glycogen before the race, you will be in a lot better shape during the race. Michael Vogt, PhD, and colleagues from the University of Bern in Switzerland recently showed that athletes consuming a 53 percent fat diet for 5 weeks were able to double their IMT stores without compromising muscle glycogen stockpiles. Further, the athletes' endurance performance at moderate to high intensities was maintained with a significantly larger contribution of fat to energy output.

Your individual dietary strategy will depend upon the length and intensity of your race. If ultraendurance events are your thing, then you may want to give a higher-fat diet a try—but make sure it contains healthy fats, not the lethal saturated and trans fats that are found in the standard American diet. Shorter, high-intensity races require more carbs and less fat, but it is still important that you try to maximize both IMT and muscle glycogen stores.

Now let's tie up the loose ends. Our ancestral dietary patterns couldn't have allowed us to restore muscle glycogen day in and day out. High-glycemic-load carbs on a year-round basis simply did not exist. Additionally, Stone Age people typically did not eat three meals a day. Contemporary studies of the Ache hunter-gatherers in Paraguay show that men usually ate only a single large meal in the evening. About 10 days a month they took breakfast, but they almost never had a midday meal. Women and children, on the other hand, stayed closer to camp and ate frequently throughout the day. In modern scientific experiments, the conditions the Ache men experienced (long fasting periods) have been shown to increase IMT, as have high-fat diets. Consequently, our Paleolithic relatives were much more reliant upon IMT when it came to running down animals or doing long, drawn-out, heavy work. You, on the other hand, have the luxury of adding performance-enhancing high-glycemic-load carbs to your diet whenever you want. But remember the take-home message that we emphasize throughout this book: moderation and quality. Avoid refined grains and sugars and replace them with better choices and at the right time, as outlined in Chapters 4 and 9.

Macronutrient Balance: Protein

One of the striking differences between ancestral and modern diets is the protein content. Protein makes up about 15 percent of the calories in the US diet, whereas in hunter-gatherers' diets it would have been between 19 and 35 percent of total energy. Compared with fat and carbohydrate, protein is a relatively negligible fuel source during rest. Even with moderate to strenuous exercise lasting up to 2 hours, protein accounts for less than 5 percent of the energy cost of the activity. However, during the end stages of prolonged endurance events, protein can contribute up to 15 percent of the total energy cost.

The building blocks of all proteins are smaller compounds called *amino acids*. Before proteins can be used to produce energy in muscles, they must first be broken down into their constituent amino acids. One of these amino acids, alanine, is then released into the bloodstream, where it travels to the liver and can be converted to glucose in a process known as *gluconeogenesis*. However, the conversion of alanine to glucose amounts to only about 4 grams per hour—just a trickle, compared with values as high as 3 grams of glucose per minute needed during very high-intensity exercise.

Does this mean that you should forget about protein and worry only about carbs and fat when it comes to improving performance? Absolutely not. As explained in Chapters 1, 2, and 9, upping your protein intake may positively influence the development of fatigue, muscle protein synthesis during recovery, and immune function. Also, don't forget that lean meats, fish, and seafood are rich sources of trace nutrients such as zinc, iron, and vitamin B_6—trace nutrients that will almost certainly be low if you are following a starch and refined carb diet.

FATTY ACID BALANCE

When you adopt the Paleo Diet for Athletes, you will want to get rid of the bad fats and concentrate on the health-promoting ones. As you have seen, increasing fat in your diet may not be a bad thing when it comes to endurance performance. Getting the right kinds of fat into your diet may also improve your immune system and help lower the risk of many inflammatory diseases, heart disease, certain autoimmune diseases, and some cancers.

Chemical Structure of Fats

Like any other specialty area, you have to take some time to master the language before you can get a handle on how things work. Most athletes are concerned with their diet and know a little bit about the three major types of dietary fats: saturated, monounsaturated, and polyunsaturated. Let's get into just a bit more detail.

Technically, all fats are called acylglycerols; each is composed of a glycerol molecule bound to 1, 2, or 3 acyl molecules. A more familiar term for an acyl molecule is "fatty acid." So if a saturated fatty acid is attached to a glycerol molecule, it can legitimately be called a fat. If the saturated fatty acid is not connected to glycerol, then it formally is not a fat but, rather, a free fatty acid. The same holds for monounsaturated and polyunsaturated fatty acids: If they are bound to glycerol, they are fats. If not, they are free fatty acids. All free fatty acids aren't really free; they must be linked to a protein molecule to travel in the blood.

If a single fatty acid is connected to a glycerol molecule, it is called a monoacylglycerol or monoglyceride. Two fatty acids connected to glycerol make a diacylglycerol (or diglyceride), and three fatty acids attached to glycerol are called a triacylglycerol or, more commonly, a triglyceride. Virtually all the fats you eat and almost all the fats you store in adipose (fat) tissue are triglycerides. Storage triglycerides in your fat cells can be used to fuel your muscles, but the fatty acids have to be first cleaved from the glycerol molecule and then bound to a protein molecule (albumin) to be transported in the bloodstream as free fatty acids.

Next, let's discuss the three major types of dietary fats, how they are labeled, how their structures vary, and how they affect your health and performance.

Saturated Fatty Acids

Saturated fatty acids are the simplest of the three major families of fatty acids because they contain no double bonds between carbon atoms in the backbone of the molecule. Consequently, each carbon atom is fully "saturated" with hydrogen atoms. Figure 5.2 is a schematic diagram of a saturated fatty acid called lauric acid, which is given the technical designation of 12:0; it contains 12 carbon atoms and 0 double bonds between the carbon atoms. It also has an omega end and a carboxyl end. (You'll see why knowing which end is which is important when we talk about differences between omega-6 and omega-3 fatty acids.)

FIGURE 5.2

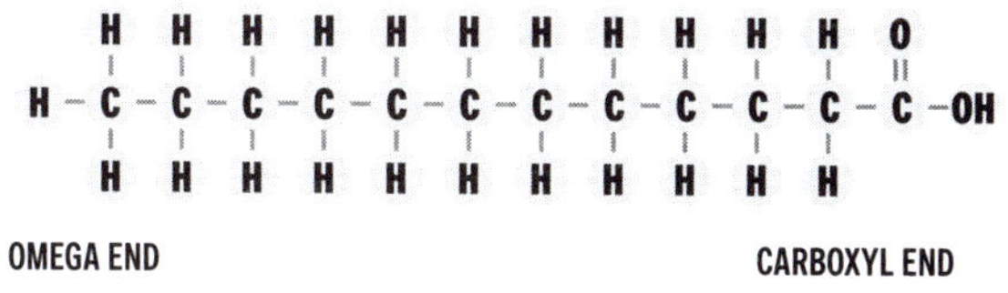

OMEGA END   CARBOXYL END

The other major dietary saturated fatty acids are 14:0 (myristic acid), 16:0 (palmitic acid), and 18:0 (stearic acid). Of all of these, 12:0, 14:0, and 16:0 raise blood cholesterol levels, whereas 18:0 is neutral. Both 12:0 and 14:0 are found in relatively small concentrations in fatty foods, so 16:0 is the real villain in butter, cheese, lard, bacon, salami, and other fatty meats responsible for clogging your arteries and promoting heart disease. Chapter 11 spells out just what foods are high in saturated fats and should be avoided.

Monounsaturated Fatty Acids

Compared with saturated fatty acids, monounsaturated fatty acids are good guys—they lower blood cholesterol levels. They are labeled "mono" unsaturated because there is a single double bond in their carbon backbone. Figure 5.3 is a diagram of oleic acid, also known as 18:1ω9. The "ω" symbol stands for "omega." Again, "18" means that there are 18 carbons in its backbone; the "1" means there is one double bond, which is located 9 carbon molecules down from the omega end. Monounsaturated fatty acids are found in nuts, avocados, olive oil, and other oils listed in Chapter 11. These are some of the healthful fatty foods you want to include in your diet if you decide to up your fat intake.

FIGURE 5.3

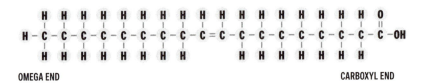

OMEGA END   CARBOXYL END

Polyunsaturated Fatty Acids (Omega-6s)

Polyunsaturated fatty acids are called "poly," meaning "many," because they contain two or more double bonds between the carbon atoms in their backbone. Figure 5.4 illustrates linoleic acid, or 18:2ω6. By now, you probably are getting the drift of this naming scheme: Linoleic acid contains 18 carbon atoms and 2 double bonds, and the last double bond is located 6 carbon atoms down from the omega end of the fatty acid backbone.

FIGURE 5.4

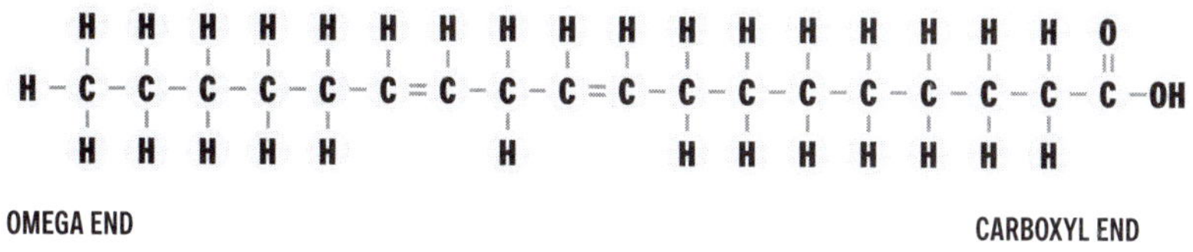

OMEGA END   CARBOXYL END

Linoleic acid is a member of the omega-6 family of polyunsaturated fatty acids and is found in high concentrations in corn oil, safflower oil, and other salad oils and processed foods made with vegetable oils. Excessive intake of omega-6 polyunsaturated fats may promote heart disease, inflammation, and certain cancers; and the typical American diet contains way too much of this fat. In Chapter 11, you'll learn how to achieve just the right balance of this fat on your menu.

Polyunsaturated Fatty Acids (Omega-3s)

Almost anyone who has an interest in diet and health has heard of omega-3 fatty acids, but most people really don't know what they are. This will change for you in about 2 seconds, now that you are becoming an accomplished lipid chemist with this tutorial. The simplest omega-3 polyunsaturated fatty acid is called alpha-linolenic acid (ALA), abbreviated 18:3ω3. If you have been following along, you know that ALA contains 18 carbon atoms in its backbone and 3 double bonds, the last of which is 3 carbon atoms down from the omega end. Figure 5.5 on page 96 shows a diagram of this fatty acid. These diagrams are helpful in understanding the structure and names of the various fats, but they don't tell you everything. The carbon-to-carbon bonds in their backbones are not straight (180 degrees) but form a 109-degree angle. Hence, their actual physical structures look different than these diagrammatic representations.

FIGURE 5.5

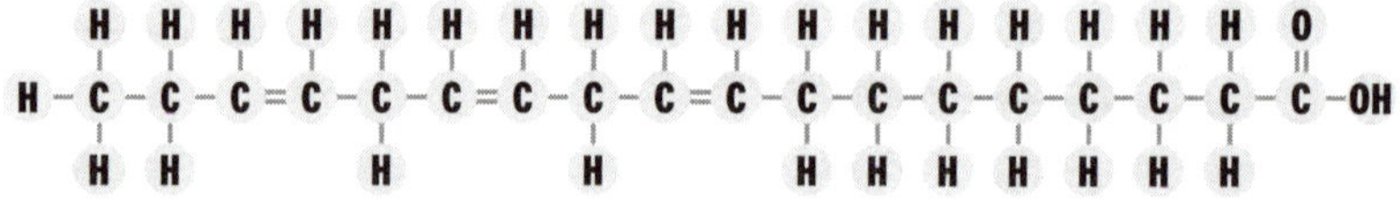

OMEGA END   CARBOXYL END

ALA is the simplest omega-3 fatty acid and is found in high concentrations in flaxseed and canola oils. In the body, the liver can turn ALA from flaxseed or canola oil into longer chain omega-3s such as eicosapentaenoic acid (EPA) or 20:5ω3 and docosahexaenoic acid (DHA) or 22:6ω3. However, this process is quite inefficient, and only about 4 percent of ALA is turned into DHA. Most of the beneficial biological effects of omega-3 fatty acids result from the long chain metabolites of ALA, which are EPA and DHA. You're better off getting your omega-3s from fish and seafood, which are rich sources of both EPA and DHA.

There's been very little research on how omega-3 fatty acids may affect exercise performance, but literally thousands of scientific experiments have shown that these fatty acids promote good health. Omega-3s are potent anti-inflammatory agents comparable or superior to aspirin. In one study of 10 elite endurance athletes, by Dr. Tim Mickleborough at Indiana University, dietary fish oil supplementation proved to be highly effective in reducing exercise-induced constriction of the airways leading to the lungs. This isn't of interest only to elite athletes: Exercise-induced asthma (EIA) is a real problem that may affect as much as 10 percent of the general population. If that includes you, then increasing your dietary intake of omega-3s not only makes sense but may be essential medicine. Even if you don't suffer symptoms of EIA, your long-term health will benefit in many ways if you get more of these highly therapeutic fatty acids into your diet.

Trans Fatty Acids

Trans fatty acids have been in the news lately, so you may know that they raise your blood cholesterol levels and, like saturated fats, may increase your risk for heart disease. Trans fatty acids most frequently are formed when vegetable oils are solidified into margarine or shortening by a process called hydrogenation. Consequently, hydrogenated or partially hydrogenated vegetable oils contain trans fatty acids. Recently, European scientists participating in a large clinical trial called the TransLinE Study showed that trans fatty acids can be formed when vegetable oils are deodorized. Careful deodorizing prevents the formation of trans fatty acids. So, when you buy vegetable oil, make sure the label guarantees that the product is trans fat free.

Trans fatty acids are isomers of normally occurring fatty acids—meaning that they have the same molecular weight as a normal fatty acid but a slightly different structure. We've already talked about oleic acid, a monounsaturated fat labeled 18:1ω9 or, more precisely, 18:1ω9 cis. That means the hydrogen atoms adjacent to the single double bond are on the same side (cis). Figure 5.6 shows a trans fatty acid designated 18:1ω9 trans. It is called a "trans" fatty acid because the hydrogen atoms about the double bond are on opposite sides. This specific trans fatty acid is also known as trans elaidic acid and is the bad guy responsible for the cholesterol-raising effects of trans fatty acids found in margarine and shortening. The deodorization of vegetable oils produces trans isomers of 18:3ω3 (ALA), which also negatively affect your blood lipid profile. Do yourself a favor and keep these nasty fats out of your diet.

FIGURE 5.6

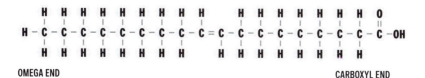

OMEGA END   CARBOXYL END

POTASSIUM/SODIUM BALANCE

In the typical US diet, we get almost 10 grams of salt per day. Because salt is made up of sodium and chloride, this translates into a daily intake of 3.5 grams of sodium and 6.5 grams of chloride. Most people know that the sodium part of salt is not good for health, particularly when we get too much of it. But few people have a clue that the chloride portion is also problematic (more on this later). Consider the ratio of potassium to sodium in the average American diet: Because our average daily potassium intake is a paltry 2.6 grams, the ratio (2.6:3.5) is 0.74. One of the reasons we have so little potassium in our diets is that in the United States we simply eat too few fruits and veggies, the richest sources of this element. Ninety-one percent of the US population does not meet the USDA recommendation of two to three daily servings of fruit and three to five daily servings of vegetables. In stark contrast, a modern-day Paleo Diet, like that outlined in Chapter 9, contains 9 grams of potassium and 0.7 gram of sodium, for a ratio of 12.5. From hundreds of computer simulations of modern-day Paleo diets, we have found the ratio of potassium to sodium is always greater than 5, whereas in the typical US diet, it is always less than 1.

This complete inversion of the Paleo potassium/sodium ratio may produce a number of potential health problems that may hurt your race-day performance. Similar to the effects of having too few omega-3 fatty acids in your diet, excessive sodium also worsens exercise-induced asthma symptoms. Experiments from our laboratory in both humans and animals show beyond a shadow of a doubt that reducing dietary salt for those with EIA is therapeutic. This strategy won't eliminate EIA, but it will vastly improve symptoms. Similarly, if you suffer from hypertension or osteoporosis, lowering the salt and upping the fruit and veggies in your diet may prove helpful. For athletes training or racing long distances in heat, we don't suggest eliminating salt completely but, rather, using it moderately and following the guidelines established in Chapters 2, 3, and 4.

ACID/BASE BALANCE

Most athletes and many nutrition experts alike are unaware of the concept of dietary acid/base balance and how it may affect health, well-being, and athletic performance. All foods after digestion report to the kidney as either acid or base (see Table 4.4 on page 57). If the diet produces a net metabolic acidosis, then the kidney must buffer this acid load with stored alkaline base. Ultimately, alkaline base can come from calcium salts in the bones. Alternatively, more acid can be excreted in the urine by having the muscles break down and release more of the amino acid glutamine. Over the long haul, both effects may hurt your performance. Accelerated bone mineral loss increases the likelihood of stress fractures—clearly a liability in your training schedule.

Accelerated glutamine loss from a net acid-producing diet may adversely affect exercise performance through a wide variety of mechanisms. Glutamine supplementation has been shown to increase growth hormone and help spare muscle mass in critically ill patients and in some animal experiments. Also, like alanine, glutamine can be converted to glucose in the liver and may provide an additional carbohydrate source during prolonged exercise. Finally, depleted blood glutamine levels in endurance athletes are a symptom of overtraining and increase the likelihood of infection and upper respiratory illness. Because most endurance athletes eat a net acid-producing diet similar to the typical American diet outlined in Table 5.4 on page 100, chances are good that glutamine reserves will be compromised. By following the Paleo Diet for Athletes, you will be getting plenty of glutamine from lean meats, fish, and seafood.

TABLE 5.4

Acid/Base Balance in Average US Diet

NET ACID-YIELDING FOODS

Cereal grains = 23.9% energy

Meats, fish = 15.7% energy

Dairy = 10.6% energy

Nuts, legumes = 3.1% energy

Eggs = 1.4% energy

Salt = 9.6 g/day

NET ALKALINE-YIELDING FOODS

Vegetables = 4.8% energy

Fruits = 3.3% energy

NEUTRAL (BUT DISPLACE ALKALINE FOODS)

Refined sugars = 18.6% energy

Refined oils = 17.9% energy

Values represent percentage of the total daily energy consumed.

FIBER INTAKE

The average person in the United States does not get enough fiber. Current intakes (15 grams per day) fall way short of recommended levels (about 25 to 35 grams per day). When you adopt the Paleo Diet for Athletes, fiber will become a nonissue because you will get it almost entirely from fresh fruits and vegetables. A common perception is that whole grains are excellent sources of fiber. Think again. Figure 5.7 shows this not to be the case in its depiction of the average total fiber content in a 1,000-calorie serving of 3 refined cereals, 8 whole grain cereals, 20 fresh fruits, and 20 nonstarchy vegetables. When it comes to soluble fiber, whole grains are lightweights compared with fruits and veggies.

Fiber has little influence upon exercise performance, but it helps to normalize bowel function and prevent constipation, and it may help to avert "runner's trots," which can be more embarrassing than detrimental to performance. Increased fiber con-

FIGURE 5.7

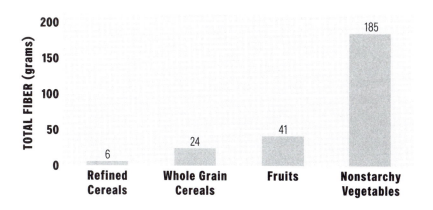

sumption may also slightly improve your blood chemistry and over the course of a lifetime may prevent varicose veins, hemorrhoids, hiatal hernia, and other illnesses associated with the gastrointestinal tract.

TRACE NUTRIENT DENSITY

Chapter 1 revealed what a nutritional lightweight the USDA Food Pyramid diet is, compared with the Paleo Diet for Athletes, particularly when we get down to the issue of vitamins and minerals. Most people in the United States would be lucky to eat as well as the USDA Pyramid designers would like us to eat. In fact, we don't do very well at all. Table 5.5 on page 102 shows that more than half of the US population gets insufficient vitamin B_6, vitamin A, magnesium, calcium, and zinc. The problem comes not only from our avoidance of fruits and veggies but also our consumption of so many empty calories in the form of refined sugars and grains. Refined sugars make up 18 percent of our daily calories yet have absolutely zero vitamins and minerals. Grains compose 24 percent of our daily food intake, but, unfortunately, 85 percent of the grains consumed in America are taken as refined grains. Figures 5.8 and 5.9 (see pages 102 and 103)

TABLE 5.5

US Individuals Age 2 and Older Meeting RDAs

NUTRIENT	PERCENTAGE
Vitamin B_{12}	82.8
Protein	79.5
Vitamin B_3	74.1
Vitamin B_2	70
Vitamin B_1	69.8
Folate	66.8
Vitamin C	62
Iron	60.9
Vitamin B_6	46.4
Vitamin A	43. 8
Magnesium	38.4
Calcium	34.9
Zinc	26.7

These are the 13 nutrients most lacking in the US diet (1994–96), according to 1989 RDAs.

FIGURE 5.8

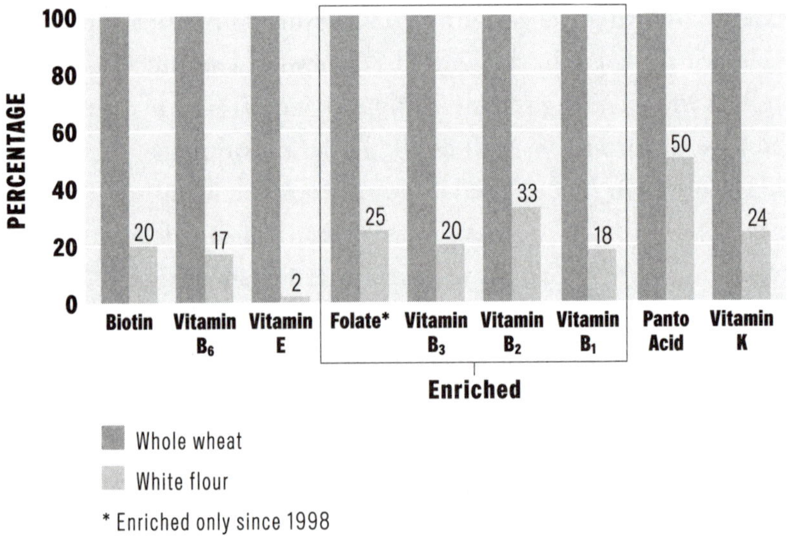

Whole wheat
White flour
* Enriched only since 1998

FIGURE 5.9

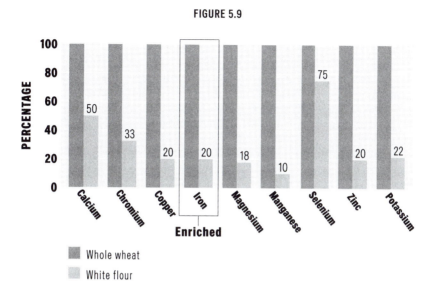

show how the refining process strips whole wheat of most of its vitamins and minerals.

These figures give you a pretty good idea that white flour is a nutrient-depleted mess! Even governmental agencies understand that white flour isn't such a good thing. Starting shortly after World War II, all white flour was required by law to be enriched with vitamins B_1, B_2, B_3, and iron. It's almost inconceivable to call this stuff "enriched" when at least 18 vitamins and minerals are severely depleted during the refining process, yet only 4 are added back. Wait, make that 5. In 1998, legislation required further supplementation of white flour with folic acid. Within 3 years after the folic acid fortification program began, the incidence of spina bifida (a major birth defect) declined by 19 percent.

Based on the above, it would appear that you would be a whole lot better off eating whole grains to get calcium, iron, magnesium, and zinc. Wrong! Whole grains contain numerous substances called antinutrients that can impair nutrient absorption or adversely affect health in a wide variety of ways. Phytic acid, otherwise known as phytate, is an antinutrient found in all whole grains and legumes that binds calcium, iron, magnesium, and zinc and severely inhibits their absorption. Whether whole or refined, grains are an inferior food when it comes to vitamins and minerals. Do yourself a favor and get the bulk of your carbs from fresh fruits and veggies.

Chapter 6

BEYOND FOOD

Science has not yet come close to matching Mother Nature's nutritious produce. The foods that, as hominins, we have been eating for at least 2.6 million years—fruits, vegetables, and meats—are still the best sources for all our fitness and health needs. Labs have yet to produce anything that even approaches the various and rich nutritional values of, for example, spinach.

But for the serious athlete, there are a handful of products that can effectively supplement the Paleo Diet to enhance performance. Some of these supplements are referred to in sport science as ergogenic, from the Greek words *ergon* ("work") and *gennan* ("to produce"). Such products claim to directly improve performance by increasing stamina, strength, reaction times, or some other measurable component of sport execution. Other supplements may not be ergogenic but profess to speed recovery. The faster you recover, the sooner you can do another hard workout—and that, combined with rest, is what produces high fitness.

The most effective ergogenic aids are also the most common—the ones we accept as so basic to endurance sport that we seldom even think of them as supplements. These are sports drinks and gels. For events lasting longer than about 90 minutes, taking in some sort of supplemental energy source is a necessity if you are to perform at or near your potential. Sports drinks and gels are appropriately used immediately before, during, and immediately after workouts and races—but only at those times.

This chapter discusses supplements that we recommend besides sports drinks and gels, but there are also many that we do not recommend for athletes. During the past 25 years of our involvement with serious endurance athletes, we have seen unbelievable claims every year for some pill, powder, or potion "guaranteed" to make you stronger or faster or more enduring. These products come and go, and of the hundreds we have observed in all this time, only a small number have proven at all effective—and none have matched the marketing hype.

With few exceptions, even the most effective of these supplements should be considered simply as the icing on the cake, and a very small dab of icing at that. The performance benefits of most of the suggested products described in this chapter are minuscule when compared with exercise, sleep, and a nutritious diet.

When considering a supplement for use with your training, there are some concerns to keep in mind. Scientific research on most supplementary aids usually finds a great variability in results between study participants. Unfortunately, many—perhaps even most—of these studies have not used athletes; they have used sedentary, "normal" subjects. To further confuse the matter, most of these people are college students, so little is known about the effects on older athletes. These products may be less effective for highly trained athletes because the greater the fitness level, the smaller the margin for performance improvement. If a supplement sounds too good to be true, it probably is. Also, some supplements are marketed and hyped based solely on theoretical benefits. Some of these rely on limited animal studies and have no basis for recommending their use to humans.

Many athletes believe that if a supplement is sold over the counter in a health food store, it must be both safe and legal, but this mistaken assumption has cost some athletes their eligibility to compete because they wound up with tainted products. Others have used products that were not on the prohibited list, only to find out that banned ingredients were not listed on the label. When it comes to supplements, it is decidedly a market in which the buyer must beware.

Athletes tend to select supplements based on hopes for effectiveness, and most (but not all) are also concerned about safety. However, it's important to be aware that other substances or medications you use could have a reaction with an otherwise safe supplement. If in doubt about using any product, talk to your doctor.

SUPPLEMENTS TO AVOID

Let's first consider both prohibited substances and those that are legal but ineffective. We do not recommend using any of these supplements. Their purported performance benefits can be categorized into one or more of four categories:

* Potential energy source that increases the body's fuel supply
* Anabolic enhancement that stimulates muscle growth or increased muscle-to-mass ratio (fat loss)
* Cellular component that allows cells to function more effectively
* Recovery aid that promotes physical rejuvenation following exercise

The supplements in Table 6.1 on page 108 are banned by most US sports agencies and the International Olympic Committee because of their negative implications for health and also because their use is considered unethical. Table 6.2 on page 108 offers a partial list of products typically promoted to endurance athletes but that are generally ineffective. Some might be beneficial for an athlete with a particular deficiency, such as iron-deficiency anemia, but iron supplements, which can be toxic, should be taken only under a doctor's care. Never take supplements

TABLE 6.1

Partial List of Prohibited or Controlled Supplements

PRODUCT PROMOTED TO ENDURANCE ATHLETES	BENEFIT CLAIMS
Anabolic steroids	Anabolic enhancement, recovery aid
Clenbuterol	Anabolic enhancement, cellular component
Dehydroepiandrosterone (DHEA)	Anabolic enhancement
Ephedrine	Anabolic enhancement, cellular component
Erythropoietin (EPO)	Cellular component
Growth hormone (hGH)	Anabolic enhancement
Testosterone	Anabolic enhancement

These are prohibited by the International Olympic Committee and controlled by the World Anti-Doping Agency.

on a whim. Using a product when you don't have a deficiency is not only ineffective, it may also be risky for your health.

SUGGESTED SUPPLEMENTS

The following discussion of supplements includes a short list of those that we suggest all athletes—and nonathletes—use. With very few exceptions, everyone should supplement their diet with antioxidants and fish oil capsules, and some should also use vitamin D supplements. These are not ergogenic aids; in other words,

TABLE 6.2

Nonprohibited but Generally Ineffective Supplements

PRODUCT PROMOTED TO ENDURANCE ATHLETES	BENEFIT CLAIMS
Bee pollen	Potential energy source
Carnitine (L-Carnitine)	Cellular component
Chromium	Anabolic enhancement
Coenzyme Q10 (CoQ10)	Cellular component
Ginseng	Cellular component
Iron	Cellular component
Multivitamin/mineral supplement	Recovery aid, cellular component
Yohimbine	Anabolic enhancement

the suggested supplements listed below will not produce immediate results in terms of athletic performance. They will, however, benefit postexercise recovery when it is viewed as a long-term endeavor involving weeks and months. Using these supplements regularly over a long period of time enhances your potential for recovery following hard workouts and races if you are also eating a nutritious diet and getting plenty of sleep.

Antioxidants

As your body uses oxygen to produce energy for living and, especially, for exercise, chemically reactive molecules called free radicals are released. These free radicals damage otherwise healthy cells and delay recovery. Even worse, they have been implicated in diseases such as cancer and heart disease. The longer or more intense the exercise, the greater the number of free radicals produced and the greater the risk of damage to muscle cells. Air pollution also contributes to free radical production, so if you exercise near traffic or where industrial pollution is high, you are at even greater risk.

The good news is that the more fit you are and the more consistently you train, the lower your risk of damage from free radicals. It should also be noted that taking it easy on recovery days inhibits free radical production. This is yet another good reason to make your easy days truly easy by staying below 70 percent of your max VO_2 (about 75 percent of maximum heart rate).

Considerable scientific evidence suggests that supplementing an athlete's diet with vitamins C and E reduces the negative effects of free radicals. For example, in one study conducted at the Nagoya Institute of Technology in Japan, runners increased their training for 6 days. Some took 1,200 international units of vitamin E daily, while others received a placebo. Those taking the vitamin E experienced significantly less damage to their muscle cells. In a similar study conducted at Miami University, taking 1 gram of vitamin C the day before a 30-minute bout of exercise reduced oxidative stress from 32 percent to 5.8 percent, compared with a placebo. Vitamin C has also been shown to reduce the risk of catching a cold following exhaustive exercise, when the immune system is compromised. A review of three studies involving extensive skiing, military training, and a 90-K run showed that most participants taking 0.6 to 1 gram of vitamin C per day avoided upper respiratory infections, compared with those taking a placebo.

Some studies suggest that older athletes may benefit even more from antioxidant supplementation than young athletes do because the potential for systemic injury and breakdown becomes greater with age.

The Paleo Diet for Athletes is rich in antioxidants. By eating lots of fresh fruits and vegetables, you'll be getting more than 500 milligrams of vitamin C and more than 25 international units of vitamin E daily. But our experience, as supported by the scientific evidence, leads us to believe that, as an athlete, you will benefit from C and E supplements as well. This is because we are exposed to many more toxic substances in the environment and in our food than our Stone Age ancestors could ever have encountered. We recommend that you take 1 gram of C and 400 international units of E daily. Food alone won't provide these high levels.

Another antioxidant that is associated with a lowered incidence of cancer and shows promise for oxidative stress in athletes is the mineral selenium. There is a considerable variation in the selenium content in the diet, depending on the soil in which the food was grown. To be on the safe side, take 150 to 300 micrograms of selenium daily.

Fish Oil Capsules

Humans evolved on a diet with about a 2:1 ratio of omega-6 to omega-3 fatty acids. Today the ratio for the American diet is about 10:1. We get a tremendous amount of omega-6 in our diet because it is prevalent in the vegetable oils used in so many of our processed foods, from bread to salad dressings to potato chips to meat from feedlot-raised animals. The oils with the highest ratio are safflower and peanut oils, but others used extensively by the food industry include soybean, cottonseed, sunflower, sesame, and corn oils. Oil that is high in omega-6 has been shown to be harmful to our health because it promotes the development of heart disease, skin cancer, and diabetes, and it contributes to inflammatory conditions such as arthritis and asthma. Omega-6 may also prolong or even contribute to the muscle and tendon inflammations prevalent with athletics.

Omega-3 fatty acid, on the other hand, counteracts the negative health consequences of omega-6. For the athlete, the benefits are a greater release of growth hormone during sleep as well as improved aerobic metabolism. Omega-3 may also reduce muscle soreness and speed recovery.

Both plant and animal foods contain omega-3 fatty acid. The amount in plants is small and must be chemically altered by the liver to make it usable. Animal foods, however, provide a more readily available source of omega-3 because its structure and availability in animal tissues, especially in the oils of cold-water fish (such as salmon, mackerel, herring, halibut, cod, and tuna), need no further modification in the human body.

Two active ingredients in omega-3 are responsible for its beneficial effects: eicosapentaenoic acid (EPA) and docosahexaenoic acid (DHA). You should consume 2 to 3 grams of EPA and 1 to 2 grams of DHA daily. Three ounces of oily fish contain about 1 gram of omega-3, so if your diet is extremely rich in such seafood—that is, you eat it at every meal—you may not need to supplement at all. Otherwise, you can purchase fish oil capsules and take what you need in conjunction with your daily intake of fish. Check the label for the EPA and DHA content of each capsule.

If you find that fish oil supplements cause fishy-smelling

burps, try freezing the capsules or taking them with meals. If you regularly use aspirin or other blood-thinning medications, be aware that fish oil can increase your risk of bleeding.

Vitamin D

Most endurance athletes don't need vitamin D supplements; the body requires only about 15 minutes of sun exposure a day to create adequate levels. But those few who spend a good deal of time exercising indoors during the winter months, when training outside can be difficult, may need to supplement their diets with D. The same goes for those in northern regions, where the winter sky is overcast for days at a time and the athlete is clothed from head to toe to stay warm. This suggestion assumes that dairy and margarine have been eliminated from the diet, because these foods are fortified with vitamin D (and have been since the 1950s). D deficiency is associated with diseases such as rickets and cancers of the breast, prostate, and colon, so this is one supplement intended for health purposes rather than performance.

On days when you are not getting adequate sun exposure, between 400 and 800 international units is a reasonable level of supplementation. Do not take more than that because vitamin D is fat soluble, which means that it can accumulate in the body and become toxic if you consume too much. The upper limit for adults is around 2,000 international units per day, so 800 is very safe—and it's cheap "insurance," considering the long-term health consequences.

On the other side of the coin, it is possible to get too much sun exposure and increase your risk of skin cancer. Keep these guidelines in mind:

• When the weather breaks at the end of the winter and you begin training outside more frequently, build up your sun time gradually.

- Use sunscreen to prevent sunburn early in the season.
- Reduce the sun protection factor (SPF) as your tan develops because sunscreen reduces the body's production of vitamin D and melanin.

OTHER EFFECTIVE SUPPLEMENTS

The supplements discussed below are generally shown to be safe and may be effective for you as ergogenic or recovery aids. Realize, however, that if you haven't mastered the major requirements of training—exercise, sleep, and nutrition—there is no reason to use any of these aids. In fact, it is not necessary to use them even if you are a successful, highly experienced athlete. Only a few of the hundreds of athletes we have coached and consulted with during the past 25 years have used such aids; the others—including pros in a variety of sports and whose livelihoods depended on race performance—did quite well without these products. Our experience has been that the better the athlete, the less likely he or she is to use supplemental performance aids. We discuss them here only so you will know which have held up under scientific scrutiny and so that you may be more wary of the marketing hype that accompanies this category of nutritional aids.

Should you decide to try any of the supplements discussed below, understand that each has distinct benefits that you may or may not fully realize because there is considerable difference in individual response. Supplements can also produce unwanted side effects that negate the benefits. Before using any of these in a race, be sure to first try them in training.

Sodium Bicarbonate (Baking Soda)

In short endurance events lasting about 7 minutes or less, one of the greatest challenges faced by the athlete is the buildup of acidity related to acid production by the muscles. As the blood and fluids surrounding the muscle cells become more acidic, their ability to function effectively is greatly reduced. Since the 1940s, sports scientists have been looking at sodium bicarbonate—the common baking soda in your kitchen—as a way of counteracting this acidity. Although the research is not without contradiction, generally, sodium bicarbonate has been shown to reduce blood and muscle acidity by neutralizing hydrogen ions associated with very high-intensity efforts. A review of 29 such studies, by L. G. Matson and Z. V. Tran, examined time to exhaustion in short events and found an average 27 percent increase in exercise duration with sodium bicarbonate compared with a placebo.

It's both inexpensive and easy to make a baking soda supplement to use if you compete in short races or engage in intensive interval training at or above your aerobic capacity. All it takes is about 300 milligrams per kilogram of body weight—roughly 4 to 7 teaspoons of baking soda, depending on your size, mixed into approximately 32 ounces of sports drink or water (see Table 6.3). Drink this mix 1 to 2 hours prior to your race start.

TABLE 6.3

A Precompetition Drink for Short Races

BODY WEIGHT IN POUNDS (KG)	BAKING SODA (TSP) (MIX WITH 32 OZ FLUID)
100 (45.5)	3½
110 (50)	3¾
120 (54.5)	4
130 (59)	4½
140 (63.6)	4¾
150 (68.2)	5
160 (72.7)	5½
170 (77.3)	5¾
180 (81.8)	6
190 (86.4)	6½
200 (90.9)	6¾
210 (95.5)	7

Use for events of 7 minutes or less duration.

Caffeine

Caffeine is classified as a stimulant and is the most commonly taken drug in the world. It is also often used as an ergogenic aid by athletes in a wide variety of sports and has been shown to be effective in many research studies. For example, one study showed that relatively low doses of caffeine may improve 40-K time trial performance in novice to elite athletes by 55 to 84 seconds—approximately 2 percent. That's a considerable improvement, just for drinking coffee before racing.

How does caffeine work its magic? It is still not fully understood, despite numerous studies over the past few decades. What has been shown is that it has the potential to improve concentration, reduce fatigue, boost muscular power, and enhance alertness. For the endurance athlete, caffeine may improve performance by allowing more fat to enter the bloodstream to be used for fuel, thereby sparing carbohydrate stores for use later in the race or training session. But the endurance benefits may well be related to other physiological effects seen in the research—or to something not yet discovered. Nevertheless, caffeine is considered by most sports scientists to be an effective ergogenic aid.

Be aware, however, that just as with all drugs, caffeine use may have a downside. Potential side effects of using caffeine to improve performance include stomach upset, headache, nervous jitters, increased heart rate, anxiety, and sleeping difficulties. It is also a diuretic that will moderately increase your urine volume (although at least one study has found this not to be the case during exercise), though it has been shown not to have any negative consequences on electrolyte balances for athletes. Athletes with high blood pressure should consult their doctors before using large amounts of caffeine, even though it's considered a relatively safe supplement.

Some studies indicate that those who use caffeine regularly do not realize as great an endurance benefit as do those who generally abstain, taking it only before selected exercise sessions. So limiting your daily intake of caffeine and eliminating it from your diet in the 2 or 3 days preceding a race or important workout may increase its benefits. Some people, however, do not respond to caffeine as much as others, which is reflected in the many studies that have found no significant exercise benefits in some participants.

How much caffeine is needed to produce an ergogenic benefit? Perhaps less than previously thought, according to recent research. At least 6 milligrams per kilogram of body weight used to be considered necessary. Now studies show that half that amount produces an ergogenic benefit—perhaps as little as a few ounces of strong coffee. Table 6.4 shows the minimum amount of various caffeine-containing products needed to get 3 milligrams of caffeine. The most efficient way to take in caffeine before a race or hard workout is by drinking strongly brewed coffee. It takes nearly twice as much Red Bull and nearly three times as much tea to equal the caffeine in coffee. For races lasting less than 2 hours, it may be most effective to complete your intake of caffeine an hour or so before the start of exercise so the body has time to respond

TABLE 6.4

Ounces of Product Needed for 3 mg Caffeine

Body weight in pounds (kg)	Coffee, brewed	Red Bull	Tea	Mountain Dew	Diet Coke	Coca-Cola	Pepsi
100 (45.5)	8	14	22	30	35	37	45
110 (50)	9	16	24	33	39	40	49
120 (54.5)	10	17	27	36	42	44	53
130 (59)	11	19	29	39	46	48	58
140 (63.6)	12	20	31	42	49	51	62
150 (68.2)	13	21	33	45	53	55	67
160 (72.7)	13	23	35	48	56	59	71
170 (77.3)	14	24	37	51	60	62	76
180 (81.8)	15	26	40	54	63	66	80
190 (86.4)	16	27	42	57	67	70	85
200 (90.9)	17	28	44	60	70	73	89
210 (95.5)	17	30	46	63	74	77	93

to the performance-enhancing effects. For longer races, caffeine ingestion can continue right up to the start.

Also, a growing body of scientific evidence shows that taking in caffeine during competition or intense exercise can benefit performance. For example, replacing sports drinks with cola during the latter stages of exercise enhanced endurance performance in one study of cyclists. Taking in 1 to 1.5 milligrams of caffeine per kilogram of body weight every 20 minutes in events that last 2 hours or longer may be quite effective for you. This can be done by using gels that have added caffeine or with soft drinks such as colas. Such supplementation may be done in place of preexercise caffeine ingestion. Bear in mind that each gel packet contains about 100 calories and must be washed down with at least 6 ounces of water. Plan for no more than 6 such servings of caffeine products, or up to 2 hours of supplementation, during exercise.

Phosphatidylserine

Phosphatidylserine (PS) is a little-known substance that has been studied for 30 years in relation to many lifestyle abnormalities, such as schizophrenia, neurological disabilities in children, Alzheimer's disease, and Tourette's syndrome. It has also been studied extensively in regard to recovery after surgery and among those under severe emotional stress. Limited research also shows that PS promotes more rapid recovery following intense training for serious athletes.

PS is a phospholipid that is available in very small quantities, perhaps up to 80 milligrams a day, in the diet. It is found in the cell membranes of muscle tissue and in cells of the immune system, where it plays a key role in maintaining structural integrity. More important, from the perspective of athletic performance, it has been shown to reduce blood levels of cortisol, a hormone the body releases to break down muscle protein to be used for energy in times of stress, such as during heavy training or after very intense races. Reducing cortisol has the potential to maintain muscle mass, thus reducing the time necessary to recover after strenuous exercise. For example, a placebo-controlled study of nine healthy men who engaged in unusually difficult exercise after taking 800 milligrams of PS for 10 days found that cortisol levels were significantly reduced. The researchers concluded that this dosage counteracts the stress-induced release of cortisol.

There is reason to believe that simply taking 1 to 2 grams of PS immediately before or after intense exercise, rather than using it on a daily basis, will suppress cortisol secretion and promote muscle recovery. There are no known side effects from supplementing with PS, which may be purchased at stores that specialize in sports supplements.

Glutamine

One of the primary benefits of eating the Paleo Diet is that adequate protein is consumed, allowing muscles to recover quickly. When athletes eat the standard high-carbohydrate, low-protein diet that has been common since the 1980s, they do not get enough of the muscle-building amino acids. Not only does this paucity of protein compromise the muscular system, it also presents a challenge to the immune system, which relies heavily on amino acids to create the defenders that fight off infections. Without adequate dietary protein, hard-training endurance athletes experience muscle wasting and frequent upper respiratory infections. Athletes we have worked with over the years have experienced fewer colds and sore throats after switching to the Paleo Diet for Athletes. They also report needing less time to recover after challenging workouts and races.

For a few athletes, however, there are still times when the training workload is so great that even the Paleo Diet is not enough to keep them healthy while maintaining and quickly rebuilding muscle tissue. These are the few athletes who train in the range of 3 or more hours daily. For them, it may be helpful to supplement the diet with glutamine. The research generally supports its effectiveness in rebuilding muscle, boosting immune system function, and speeding recovery from workouts.

Glutamine is a conditionally essential amino acid, meaning that the body can produce it but occasionally needs dietary sources to meet the demand. When the body is under stress from heavy training, the level of glutamine in the muscles and blood decreases dramatically as the body produces more white blood cells to fight infection and repair damaged muscle tissue. If the body's stores of glutamine and capacity to produce it are inadequate to meet the demand, the risk of overtraining, discussed in Chapter 7, greatly increases.

Glutamine, the most abundant amino acid in the body, has been studied since the 1960s in the treatment of extensive burns and recovery from major surgery; less research has been done on its benefits for endurance athletes. Nevertheless, those studies show great promise for this supplement. Eric Newsholme, PhD, at Oxford University, has extensively studied glutamine use by athletes, and his work suggests that chronically overtrained athletes may experience low plasma glutamine levels. For example, in a study at Dr. Newsholme's lab, 151 rowers and runners completed intense 2-hour workouts while drinking either a glutamine-based sports drink or a placebo and were then monitored for their health over the ensuing week. Those who received the glutamine reported a 19 percent rate of infection. The athletes who drank the placebo reported a 51 percent infection rate.

The dosage relative to the volume of intensity and duration has not been well established, but it appears that supplementing with 1 to 10 grams on the days of very hard workouts and races may be beneficial. It is probably best to divide this into two or three doses, taken with meals. There is no known downside from taking in glutamine at this level, and any excess will be excreted in your urine.

Other Supplements

There are two other safe and nonprohibited supplements we have not discussed here—creatine and beta hydroxy-methyl-butyrate (HMB)—because they have been shown to increase muscle mass and are more appropriate for sports such as weight lifting and bodybuilding. No studies have conclusively shown these to be effective aids for endurance athletes, so we cannot recommend them.

Chapter 7

OVERTRAINING AND DIET

Recovery is one of the keys to high performance in sports but is little appreciated by most athletes. The commonly accepted road to success is hard workouts, and the more the better. That isn't entirely wrong, but without paying close attention to the recovery side of the training equation, hard workouts spaced closely together are not possible. If you recover quickly and more completely following hard training sessions, then your body is ready to go hard again sooner. That leads ultimately to peak performances.

As a highly motivated athlete who only pays lip service to recovery, you soon experience a deep and compelling fatigue. You wake up in the morning tired. You are unable to complete even the easiest workouts. Fatigue haunts your every step throughout the day. And this goes on relentlessly for days or even weeks. You're overtrained.

How could this situation have been avoided? The answer is recovery. Recovery has several components, the two most critical being rest and nutrition. What you eat plays as great a role in your day-to-day performance as anything else in your training arsenal does, yet many athletes get it wrong. Let's take a closer look at

(continued on page 124)

What Is Fatigue?

Fatigue is a primary limiter standing between you and better performance. If you could delay fatigue, you would go faster and last longer at a given effort level—the ultimate purpose of training. Yet we never rid ourselves of fatigue, which is actually a good thing because this prevents us from damaging our bodies. But understanding what brings on fatigue during a race or workout may point to strategies that could raise your fatigue threshold, allowing you to go faster or farther.

Fatigue or tiredness that causes a drop in power and performance varies according to the duration of the event. Fatigue during an 800-meter footrace is far different from that near the end of an ultramarathon run. The causes are also different. Other than overheating and dehydration, which can obviously limit performance, there are at least four common physiological reasons for fatigue during endurance events: increasing system acidity, depletion of glycogen and glucose, neuromuscular junction failure, and increased tryptophan in the brain.

Increasing system acidity. As described in "Lactic Acid's Bad Rap," on page 38, accumulating hydrogen ions in the blood and fluids surrounding muscle cells increase the body's acidity and are a cause of fatigue during short, high-intensity efforts. For example, while an athlete is going up a steep hill for several minutes during a bike race, acid levels may reach such a concentration that the athlete experiences heavy, labored breathing and a burning sensation in the legs, forcing him or her to slow down. But at the end of a marathon, acid levels are barely above the resting level, even though the athlete is fatigued. This form of fatigue is best kept at bay by training, especially that done frequently near or above the anaerobic threshold. To approximate your anaerobic threshold effort, pace, power, or heart rate, complete a 30-minute time trial at an all-out effort. Your average for the last 20 minutes will be close to your anaerobic threshold.

Depletion of glycogen and glucose. Glycogen is the carbohydrate form of fuel stored in the working muscles. During the early stages of endurance exercise, glycogen and fat are the primary sources used for energy production. For fat to be used as fuel, carbohydrate must be present in the muscle. As glycogen stores begin to run low after several minutes of exercise at above 70 percent of max VO_2, the body turns to the carbohydrate in the blood called glucose. Meanwhile, the liver continues to provide a steady stream of glucose to the blood from its storage reserves. Once the working muscles have expended their glycogen and the blood and liver have run out of glucose, the party's over. You "bonk," meaning that fatigue is like a heavy weight—you can't go on, despite the fact that you have thousands of calories of fuel stored as fat available. This depletion may take only 90 minutes or so, depending on how fast you are going and how fit you are. We each have a limit.

The only way to avoid this form of fatigue is to replace carbohydrate stores by taking in fuel, either liquid or solid, during exercise. This could be sports drinks, or gels or sports bars washed down with water. Fruit and vegetable juices are not as effective because their primary sugar is fructose, which requires a long processing time in the body and may not get to the muscles in a timely manner. It also has a tendency to upset some athletes' stomachs during exercise. If your event will last longer than about 90 minutes, carbohydrate replenishment should start right away.

Neuromuscular junction failure. The nervous system transmits electrochemical impulses from the spinal cord to the muscle fiber. The point at which the nerve axon meets the muscle fiber is where the muscle innervation occurs. For some unknown reason, this stimulation late in an exercise session may fail. When that happens, the athlete is unable to fully stimulate a muscle group to contract. The result may be called fatigue and may also be associated with cramping. Because this situation is not fully understood, avoiding it is somewhat of a mystery, but it might help to stay adequately hydrated, eat a diet rich in electrolytes, and have a high level of fitness relative to the race in which you are competing.

Increase of tryptophan in the brain. We don't know a lot about this fatigue factor, either. Here's what is known: In long-duration events, usually about 3 hours or more, some changes take place in the blood amino acid levels, leading to subtle chemical reactions in the brain that make you feel sleepy. You may yawn, feel like

(continued)

123

What Is Fatigue? *(cont.)*

lying down, and even have trouble keeping your eyes open. Merely finishing becomes a struggle.

In 1988, researchers found that blood levels of an amino acid tryptophan more than doubled during long-distance events. That was curious because the other amino acids are reduced during exercise. The interesting thing is, certain types of tryptophan and the branched-chain amino acids (BCAA) compete to get into the brain on the same blood "carrier"—albumin. Usually the BCAAs win this competition and get into the brain in larger quantities than the tryptophan does. But as the BCAAs are depleted, more tryptophan finds its way into the brain, where it is converted into a chemical known as serotonin. Serotonin is what helps you fall asleep at night.

If you tend to suffer from such a condition near the end of long races, it may be worth your while to experiment with BCAA supplementation prior to racing. Since BCAAs are a normal part of the foods you eat, the likelihood of any long- or short-term health problems from including them in your prerace meal is low. Still, it's advisable to try this in training before trying it in a race.

Unfortunately, no standard dosage has been established. Some studies had success administering up to as much as 14 grams (14,000 milligrams) of total BCAA prior to exercise. It's probably best to ingest this no less than 1 hour before the start. This is why including protein in your prerace meal is suggested in Chapter 2.

overtraining and how food choices impact your capacity for quick recovery.

BEYOND FATIGUE

Effective training is more than workouts. It is a carefully balanced state of well-being between stress and rest. When this balance is achieved, your fitness improves at a steady rate. When rest exceeds stress (a rare occasion for serious athletes), the body quickly achieves a high level of readiness to race. This takes only a few days and is referred to as tapering or peaking. Go beyond these few days and fitness erodes. You may have experienced the latter situation if you were injured or sick and couldn't work out.

When stress only just exceeds rest for a few days, the body adapts and becomes more fit. This is the purpose of training: Overload the body with the right amount of stress, then allow it to rest. During rest, the body's adaptive processes take place—muscles grow stronger, enzymes become more abundant, the heart increases its ability to pump blood, and other seminal physiological and psychological changes occur. This is the ultimate goal of the endurance athlete.

On a more sinister note, when stress greatly exceeds rest for more than a few days, the athlete begins to experience unrelenting fatigue and exhaustion. The body's capacity to adapt is compromised, and the defense mechanisms intended to prevent death are initiated. This is overtraining.

Overtraining may not result simply from too much exercise and too little rest. The stress component could also be related to work, school, relationships, finances, relocating, or a myriad of other stressors that make up your nonathletic life. Such stress when combined with what even may be a perfectly appropriate level of exercise will produce overtraining if rest is inadequate, just as surely as too much exercise produces overtraining. In this case, you are "overliving" rather than overtraining. Regardless, the body experiences much the same result.

All of this is not to say that you shouldn't push yourself in training or that you should never experience fatigue. In order to grow as an athlete, you must regularly flirt with overtraining. You will have days when you are tired and even some when you can't (or at least know you shouldn't) complete the workout. This state of fatigue is called overreaching and is an early point on the path to overtraining. The difference between overreaching and overtraining is that when you are overreached, you quickly recover with rest. By paying close attention to the elements of recovery, especially rest and nutrition, you can avoid overtraining and steadily improve your fitness.

How long does it take to progress from being overreached to overtrained? The answer, as with most such questions, is "It depends." Many variables may influence the answer. Studies that have dramatically increased the training volume for 5, 7, and 10 days were unable to produce a significant decline in performance, although the athletes showed signs of overreaching. In other research, it took 15 days to produce verifiable overtraining in a group of cyclists who increased their volume by 50 percent. And in one study with young, highly fit rowers, it took 3 weeks to fully achieve overtraining. It may well be that youth and a high level of fitness provide some immunity from overtraining and delay its onset for up to 3 weeks. On the flip side, older or less fit athletes, including novices, may well achieve an overtrained state in 2 weeks or even less.

IF IT ISN'T OVERTRAINING, WHAT IS IT?

Some common signs of overtraining in endurance athletes are listed in Table 7.1. Note that not all of these signs will be present if you allow yourself to become overtrained, and some symptoms that you experience may not even be listed. Overtraining is a condition that is unique to individual circumstances, although certain characteristics are common, such as decreased performance and chronic fatigue.

It's also quite possible that some of these symptoms, including decreased performance and chronic fatigue, signal an illness such as mononucleosis or another viral infection. Even if you're certain your symptoms are caused by overtraining, it's wise to consult your physician just to be sure you don't have some other condition.

TABLE 7.1

Common Symptoms of Overtraining

PHYSIOLOGICAL
Decreased performance
Decreased strength
Decreased maximum work capacity
Changes in heart rate at rest, exercise,
    and recovery
Increased frequency of breathing
Insomnia
Loss of appetite
Increased aches and pains
Chronic fatigue

PSYCHOLOGICAL
Depression
Apathy
Decreased self-esteem
Emotional instability
Difficulty concentrating
Irritability

IMMUNOLOGICAL
Susceptibility to illness
Slow healing of minor scratches
Swollen lymph nodes

BIOCHEMICAL
Negative nitrogen balance
Flat glucose tolerance curves
Reduced muscle glycogen concentration
Delayed menarche
Decreased hemoglobin
Decreased serum iron
Lowered total iron-binding capacity
Mineral depletion
Elevated cortisol levels
Low free testosterone

OVERTRAINING AND DIET

Overreaching that spirals downward to overtraining often starts, in part, with diet. You train hard to achieve very high performance goals. Knowing that several hard workouts are needed weekly for success, you repeatedly push yourself to the limit. The vigorous exercise results in a decreased appetite for hours afterward. Combined with incomplete recovery, the reduced caloric intake leads to greater fatigue and lackluster training. Being highly motivated, you continue this pattern of hard workouts, less food, and inadequate recovery for 2 to 3 weeks—and you're overtrained. One consequence of the early stages of overtraining is even less appetite, which further exacerbates the all-too-common state of the overtraining syndrome you've managed to realize.

This lesson is driven home quite effectively in a study conducted by David Costill, PhD, and his colleagues at Ball State University. The researchers doubled the training workload of a group of competitive collegiate swimmers for 10 days. After a few days, about 30 percent of the swimmers experienced much greater difficulty in maintaining the quality of the training sessions than did the others. The scientists found that the swimmers who were merely muddling through with the high workload were eating almost 1,000 calories per day less than those who were successfully coping. The low-calorie swimmers were well along the path to overreaching in a matter of days. Had the study continued longer, there is little doubt that those taking in the fewest calories would eventually have wound up overtrained.

Besides intense exercise, other training factors that may contribute to a reduced appetite are high air temperatures and humidity. Emotions related to stress and mood may also produce this effect, as may acute exposure to training at altitude. Don't ignore a poor appetite when, following exercise, you experience fatigue that is not reduced after a day or more of complete rest or much lighter workouts. Be cautious with your training at this time, and carefully monitor your food intake to ensure that you are getting adequate calories and nutrients.

MACRONUTRIENTS AND OVERTRAINING

While many studies implicate nutrition in the process of becoming overtrained, none specifically addresses the dietary requirements of avoiding this condition. However, some research does suggest likely dietary scenarios associated with overtraining.

Carbohydrate

Depending on body size, a well-trained and properly fed endurance athlete may have up to about 2,000 calories stored away as carbohydrate. Most of this resides in the muscles as glycogen, with smaller amounts in the liver (glycogen) and blood (glucose). Compared with the potential energy available from fat and protein, glycogen and glucose are quite limited, representing only 1 to 2 percent of the body's total energy stores. Nevertheless, this fuel source is critical to success in endurance activities. As previously mentioned, there is an old saying in exercise physiology that illustrates this phenomenon: "Fat burns in a carbohydrate flame." As stored carbohydrate is depleted, the body can no longer efficiently use fat, the body's most abundant fuel, for energy; it must turn to protein to keep the fat-burning flame flickering. This is a time-consuming metabolic process associated with heavy fatigue and rapidly decreasing pace despite a high effort. Failure to maintain glycogen and glucose stores can easily lead to poor performance and perhaps to overtraining.

During intensive endurance exercise, the body shifts from primarily using glycogen to keep the flame burning to relying on blood glucose and, finally, on liver stores of glycogen as fuel slowly depletes. This process may take 60 to 90 minutes, depending on your fitness level and exercise intensity. The most common form of exhaustion in extensive endurance sports is closely related to this depletion of carbohydrate fuel. Carbohydrate intake both during and immediately following exercise is critical to success in endurance sports.

There is considerable research showing that consistently low carbohydrate intake during and following exercise may contribute to overreaching and eventually to overtraining. As the training intensity increases, this becomes even more critical. High glycemic load foods are a necessity in Stages II, III, and IV of recovery, as described in Chapters 3 and 4, in order to maintain glycogen and glucose stores and help prevent overtraining. Just a few days of inadequate eating at these critical times, when training intensity increases, can easily set you up for a disastrous season.

Fat

If carbohydrate is so important for avoiding overtraining, you might wonder why the Paleo Diet for Athletes suggests eating more fat and less carbohydrate during the base (general preparation) period of training—might not this set you up for overtraining? No, it won't. Plenty of research indicates that well-trained endurance athletes actually continue to have good results on a diet that is somewhat higher in fat and lower in carbohydrate than is typically recommended by nutritionists, especially when intensity is low, as in the base period.

A 1994 study reported in the prestigious journal *Medicine and Science in Sports and Exercise* used well-trained runners as subjects. The runners spent 7 days eating each of three diets, then tested at the end of each 7-day period for running time to exhaustion at a fixed intensity just below anaerobic threshold. On their "normal" diet, they ate 61 percent of their daily calories as carbohydrate and 24 percent fat. Their "fat" diet was made up of 50 percent carbohydrate and 38 percent fat—similar to the diet recommended here for your base period. The runners' "carbohydrate" diet included 73 percent carbohydrate and 15 percent fat. Protein stayed about the same (12 to 14 percent) in all three trials. The testing revealed that the fat diet produced the best average times to exhaustion (91.2 minutes), compared with the carbohydrate (75.8 minutes) and normal (63.7 minutes) diets.

In another, more recent study, 11 duathletes ate high-fat (53 percent fat) or high-carbohydrate (17 percent fat) diets for 5 weeks each. At the end of these periods, they completed a 20-minute time trial on a bicycle ergometer and ran a half marathon. There were no significant differences in performance between the two sets of test data, regardless of the diet. On the bikes there was a 1-watt difference, and for the run there was a 12-second difference in times.

The take-home lesson from these studies and others is that substituting fat for carbohydrate in the base period will not harm your training or promote overtraining, so long as you use the post-workout recovery methods in Chapter 4 to replenish carbohydrate stores. In fact, a higher-fat diet proves to be beneficial because the body becomes more efficient at burning fat for fuel while sparing glycogen, one of the same benefits we seek in doing long, slow endurance training in the base period. But as the intensity of training rises in the build (specific preparation) period, more carbohydrate is necessary to restock the significantly depleted glycogen stores in the muscles. Shifting your diet between carbohydrate and fat in the base and build periods of the season, with protein remaining relatively constant, will not cause overtraining and will boost your fitness.

Of course, as described in Chapter 4, the fat you add to the diet in Stage V of your daily recovery during the base period should be the "good" types—monounsaturated and polyunsaturated, especially omega-3. These fats are found in foods such as fish, avocados, nuts, eggs enriched with omega-3, leafy green vegetables, meat from free-ranging animals, and in olive, canola, and flaxseed oils.

Protein

Recovery following challenging workouts is essential for avoiding overtraining. If nutritional action is not taken after a hard training session, the body may not be ready to go by the next workout, leading to a gradual decline in performance over the course of a few days, followed by overreaching and, ultimately, overtraining. More and more research suggests that, besides consuming carbohydrate immediately after such sessions, taking in protein improves the recovery process. This enhancement is a result of greater glycogen stores that restock faster, along with quicker rebuilding of damaged muscle tissue. Adding protein to your postworkout drink, as described in Chapter 4, will go a long way in promoting recovery while helping to avoid overtraining.

In much the same way, taking in adequate protein throughout the day is quite beneficial to your physical well-being and capacity for training. It has been our experience that most endurance athletes get far too little protein; instead they concentrate their diets around carbohydrate, especially from starches and sugars. Such an amino acid–poor diet will eventually catch up with these athletes. Protein is necessary to repair muscle damage, maintain the immune system, manufacture hormones and enzymes, replace the red blood cells that carry oxygen to the muscles, and provide energy for exercise when carbohydrate stores are tapped. The following indicators of inadequate dietary protein overlap considerably with the markers of overtraining listed in Table 7.1 on page 127.

- Frequent colds and sore throats
- Slow recovery from workouts
- Irritability
- Poor response to training (slow to get in shape)
- Chronic fatigue
- Poor mental focus
- Sugar cravings
- Cessation of menstrual periods

The highest-quality protein is that which is most available to the body for absorption and includes large amounts of all of the essential amino acids. Animal products fit that definition and should be included in meals throughout the day. And the more you train, the more critical this is for avoiding overtraining.

Of the essential amino acids, four stand out as being critical to recovery: leucine, isoleucine, valine, and glutamine. The first three are the branched-chain amino acids (BCAA). During exercise, blood levels of BCAA and glutamine decline, contributing to a unique type of weariness called central fatigue—common in events lasting several hours. A training program that is challenging will likely leave you feeling chronically fatigued for days and may well be the result of inadequate protein intake.

Water

Many endurance athletes simply don't drink enough water throughout the day, leaving them in a nearly constant state of dehydration. When athletes are dehydrated, even if only slightly, recovery is compromised and the risk of overtraining increases. For such athletes, merely drinking more water between workouts is an effective way of boosting performance while helping to avoid overtraining.

Dehydration reduces all bodily fluids, including the blood's plasma. As plasma levels decline, the blood becomes thicker, forcing the heart to work harder to move it through the body. As little as 2 percent dehydration can slow the body's recovery from training dramatically. Thirst is a pretty good mechanism for avoiding this situation, so long as you pay attention to it.

Thirst is triggered by two conditions—a decrease in the fluids within and surrounding the cells and an increasing blood concentration of electrolytes, especially sodium. Drinking more fluid than your weight loss indicates you need, plus including some sodium when training heavily, will help you steer clear of dehydration.

One study at Loughborough University in the United Kingdom illustrates how critical it is for performance to know how much fluid you need. Well-trained runners completed two 90-minute exercise bouts, separated by 4 hours, at 70 percent of their aerobic capacities on two different occasions. During the 4 hours between runs, they drank a carbohydrate-electrolyte solution. On one occasion, they drank as much as they wanted, with no restrictions; the other time, they were weighed after the first run and drank sufficiently to replace the loss. Initially, the fluid intake was the same after the first run. But when drinking to replace weight loss, they drank more fluids in the 4th hour of recovery than when they used thirst as their only guideline. They also increased their times to exhaustion on the second run by 16 percent when fluid intake was linked to weight loss rather than merely to thirst. It's wise to know how much water to take in after exercise, then exceed it slightly—by perhaps as much as 20 percent—in the few hours after a workout. Every pound of weight lost in exercise should be replaced by 1.2 pints of fluid.

Adding sodium to your diet in recovery will also help replenish lost fluids more quickly and speed recovery in order to avoid over-training. For example, in another study, six people exercised in the heat for 90 to 110 minutes, losing an average of 2.3 percent of their body weight. Then, over a 3-hour period, they drank as much as they wanted of either plain water or water with sodium added. Drinking water only, they restored 68 percent of the water lost during exercise, whereas they restored 82 percent when salt was added. Additionally, urine volume was greater when plain water was consumed. The subjects retained 51 percent of the plain water but 71 percent of the water-sodium fluid. Adding a bit of salt to your Stage III and Stage IV food and fluids will allow you to take in, absorb, and retain more fluids. This is critical for recovery.

MICRONUTRIENTS AND OVERTRAINING

Many studies have reported that athletes make poor dietary choices, contributing to low vitamin and mineral status that is compounded by normal losses during periods of increased training. A study of Dutch elite athletes showed that the female swimmers had an inadequate iron intake, while cyclists were not getting enough vitamins B_1 and B_6. Similar research on women runners has shown repeatedly that due to restriction of calories, extremely high carbohydrate intake, or vegetarian eating patterns, these athletes are often low in iron, zinc, magnesium, and calcium. Among both male and female runners, dietary zinc and iron have been shown to be low. Inadequate iron intake has also been confirmed for cross-country skiers; 50 percent of Nordic women skiers in a Winter Olympics had prelatent iron deficiency, and 7 percent were anemic. In a study of 1,300 German athletes in various sports, 21 percent had low levels of serum magnesium, and 14 percent lacked iron. There is little doubt that many athletes do not meet their nutritional needs when it comes to micronutrients. Such deficiencies may well contribute to the onset of overtraining.

An athlete who is deficient in vitamins A, B_6, C, or E is at high risk for a weakened immune system and illness related to overreaching. In the same manner, deficiencies of the minerals zinc, magnesium, copper, and iron may result in impaired immunity. All of this once again underscores the importance of eating a diet that is rich in micronutrients once you are into Stage V of recovery. The most nutrient-dense foods are vegetables and lean meats, including fish and poultry. However, eating a lot of cereal grains negates the benefits because these foods contain high amounts of phytates, which decrease the body's absorption of minerals such as iron and zinc.

Just as eating an inadequate diet can set you up for overtraining, relying on supplements instead of nutrient-dense foods to provide micronutrients can also be detrimental. For example, excessive amounts of vitamin A, vitamin E, and zinc have been shown to weaken the immune system, thus contributing to overtraining symptoms. An excessive intake of iron promotes bacterial growth and can induce a zinc deficiency. The best way to ensure a balanced diet is to eat plenty of vegetables, fruits, and lean meats—not to take pills or eat lab-designed food products marketed to athletes. Science has yet to catch up with Mother Nature when it comes to producing food.

PREVENTION AND TREATMENT

There are no preliminary symptoms to warn you when you have gone too far with an imbalance between stress and rest. The progression from a normal and recurring state of overreaching to full-blown overtraining is so gradual that you won't recognize the impending doom. By the time you realize that you've pushed too hard, it's too late, and your only recourse is loss of fitness by greatly reducing the training stress. If you believe you may be overtrained, take 3 to 5 days of complete rest, and then do a short, low-intensity workout. If you feel normal, you were only in an advanced stage of overreaching and are free to gradually return to regular training (but do so cautiously). But if after several exercise-free days the test workout feels like a wearisome burden, you are probably overtrained or are sick and should see your doctor. Take another 3 to 5 days of complete rest before retesting your status as before. Continue this pattern until exercise becomes fun again, which may take weeks or even months. Throughout the process, be sure to eat a nutritious diet made up primarily of fruits, vegetables, and lean meats, including fish and poultry.

It is far better to prevent overtraining in the first place than to deal with it after the fact, especially when you consider that it can take weeks if not months to recover. So what must you do to avoid it?

At its essence, overtraining results from training mistakes, and two are particularly common. The first is an imbalance between stress and rest, which usually occurs when the athlete suddenly increases the training workload in either volume or intensity—or both. The second scenario involves cutting back on recovery by substituting more challenging workouts for easy ones. Athletes have even been known to do both: suddenly increase the workload and eliminate rest and recovery days. Given the work ethic, the motivation, and, in some serious endurance athletes, the obsession, this seems like a sure route to success. It is not; it is a sure route to failure.

The best way to avoid this pitfall is to follow a long-term, periodized training plan that schedules weekly rest and recovery days, monthly rest and recovery weeks, and annual rest and recovery months. This plan should also provide for a gradual progression in the training workload and fit your unique characteristics, including sport experience, age, susceptibility to illness and injury, and goals.

Nutrition often plays a role in the onset of overtraining. Even a suitably aggressive training regimen that leads to an acceptable level of overreaching may be undermined by a diet that does not encourage quick recovery. In our experience, such a diet is usually lacking in total calories, protein, or micronutrients. This is all too common for the serious endurance athlete who concentrates on sugar and starch, eats a vegetarian diet, or is concerned about body weight and reduces calories despite a high workload. Any one of these scenarios will diminish recovery in what might be an otherwise appropriate training program.

PART III

OUR
STONE-AGE
LEGACY

Chapter 8

WHY EAT LIKE A CAVEMAN?

MAKING SENSE OUT OF NUTRITIONAL CHAOS

As an athlete, you probably are aware that even small variations in your performance can significantly alter how well you place in any given race. However, you may never have considered how huge this effect can be.

Consider a 1 to 2 percent difference in your time for a 10,000-meter race. At first it sounds fairly insignificant. Whether you run 1 to 2 percent faster or slower in a 10-K race is immaterial, right? Wrong! At the US Outdoor Track and Field Championships in 2003, just 28.31 seconds (a mere 1.69 percent difference) separated the top 10 finishers in the men's 10-K final. Even more telling were the top three finishers' times. The winner, Alan Culpepper, beat the second-place finisher, Meb Keflezighi, by 2.23 seconds—in relative terms, a minuscule 0.13 percent difference in performance. The third-place finisher, Daniel Brown, was 8.12 seconds behind the winner. Eight seconds sounds like a lot, but in actuality it is only 0.48 percent slower than the champion's winning time. These numbers graphically illustrate how very small differences in performance can have an enormous impact on how well you place. But more important, they emphasize how crucial it is for you to optimize every factor that can possibly influence your race-day performance.

Your basic training foundation (intensity, frequency, and duration of exercise) clearly is of utmost importance in shaping how well you will perform. Over the long haul, how well and how fast you can recover from each and every workout will determine how hard you can train over the course of an entire season. Also, there is little doubt that staying healthy and free from injury and illness are essential in permitting you to train at higher intensities for longer periods, which in turn will benefit your race performance.

Now, let's go back to that crucial 1 to 2 percent difference in performance and have a look at Culpepper's top three race times for the 10-K during the 2003 season. The slowest of those (28:14:92) is 1.99 percent slower than his top time (27:41:90), whereas his second-best finish (27:55:36) is 0.81 percent slower than the top time. You can see that not only do small performance differences emerge between athletes, but they also appear within individuals. Given similar wind, weather, and altitude conditions, why might your performance vary by 1 to 2 percent? What factors might be responsible for these tiny but important performance differences? How about your muscle glycogen stores—might they be involved? Does the ability of your muscles to overcome fatigue from a previous race or workout play a role? What's the effect of a slight upper respiratory illness or lingering tendinitis? How about your ability to maintain quality workouts between races? Without a doubt, any or all of these issues have the potential to influence your race day performance by 1 to 2 percent—or even more.

Nutritionists, exercise physiologists, and physicians alike agree that athletic performance can go to hell in a handbasket very rapidly on a faulty diet. However, they have dogmatically argued for decades that a "balanced" diet is all that's needed to maximize athletic performance, provided an optimal training schedule is followed. But what exactly is a "balanced diet"? More precisely, what is the starting point for any athletic diet? Is it the same diet that optimizes your health and well-being? And what is the best diet to optimize immune function and prevent colds and upper respiratory illnesses or to speed recovery from—or even prevent—muscle strains or injuries? All of those questions beg a much larger and all-encompassing question, one that, when answered correctly, provides us with an elegant, grand organizing template that allows us to make sense out of all this nutritional and dietary confusion and chaos.

Nutrition is every bit as contentious as politics and religion. It seems like everybody's got an opinion about proper diet, including health agencies, the government, leading scientists, diet doctors, and popular nutritionists. From the consumer perspective, the study of nutrition appears jumbled and chaotic. One day you hear one thing; the next, the exact opposite. Margarine is good for your health; margarine contains trans fatty acids. Eggs increase your blood cholesterol; eggs don't increase your cholesterol levels. Fiber prevents colon cancer; fiber doesn't prevent colon cancer. Pizza is a healthful food; pizza is junk food.

The USDA Food Pyramid poster, espousing healthful eating, is found in almost every elementary school and hospital lunchroom in the country. Yet a recent article in the prestigious *Scientific American* magazine, written by scientists from the Harvard School of Public Health, loudly condemned the Pyramid's dietary recommendations. Thirty million Americans are now following Dr. Atkins's advice to eat more fat and meat to lose weight. In utter contrast, Dean Ornish tells us fat and meat cause cancer, heart disease, and obesity and that we would all be a lot healthier if we were strict vegetarians. Who's right and who's wrong? How in the world can anyone make any sense out of this apparent disarray of conflicting facts, opinions, and ideas?

In mature and well-developed scientific disciplines, universal paradigms guide researchers to fruitful end points as they design their experiments and hypotheses. For instance, in cosmology (the study of the universe), the guiding paradigm is the big bang concept, showing that the universe began with an enormous explosion and has been expanding ever since. In geology, the continental drift model established that all of the current continents at one time formed a continuous landmass that eventually drifted apart to form the present-day continents. These central concepts are not theories but indisputable facts, serving as orientation points for all other inquiry within each discipline. Scientists do not know everything about the nature of the universe, but it is unquestionable that it has been and is expanding. This central knowledge then serves as a template that allows scientists to make much more accurate and informed hypotheses about factors yet to be discovered.

The study of human nutrition has no such guiding template or organizing paradigm. Except for a few scientists and individuals who are privy to a new way of thinking about diet and nutrition, nutrition remains an immature discipline. Most of this field's leading scientists and major players are completely unaware of a very powerful idea that could bring order to the fog of disarray and chaos. So, you may ask, what is the larger and all-encompassing question that, when asked and answered correctly, can provide us with the template, the holy grail, the magical looking glass desperately needed to fill this void in nutritional theory?

The question is a very simple question—a child's question: "Why?" That's right; the "why" question. Why do we have nutritional requirements in the first place? Humans, most other primates, the guinea pig, and a few species of bats must obtain vitamin C from their diet, whereas all other mammals can synthesize vitamin C from glucose, a simple sugar found in the bloodstream of all mammals. Why in the world do humans have a dietary requirement for vitamin C when other mammals do not?

For that matter, why do we have dietary requirements for any nutrient? What we are looking for here is not the proximate (nearby) answer but, rather, the ultimate answer. Every registered dietitian worth his or her degree knows that without vitamin C, we get scurvy. A dietitian who can remember the metabolic pathways well enough may even be able to tell you why scurvy causes all of its symptoms. But that is merely the proximate answer to "Why?" Do you know the ultimate answer to why we have a dietary vitamin C requirement? By answering correctly, you will be staring directly at the holy grail of nutritional science. The correct answer to this question represents the guiding template and the organizational paradigm that nutrition is so dearly missing.

THE GIFT FROM THE PAST

The selection of appropriate food for wild animals in zoos is no hit-or-miss business. Zookeepers at state-of-the-art facilities like the San Diego Zoo's Wild Animal Park realized long ago that if they wanted animals to stay healthy and happy and even breed in captivity, they needed to replicate each animal's natural environment as closely as possible. That meant duplicating diet as well. When lions or any other purely carnivorous cats were fed only raw muscle meat, their health rapidly deteriorated, and they developed vitamin A deficiency and bone loss (osteoporosis) and eventually died. Careful observations of wild lions in their natural habitat revealed that they ate their prey's entire carcass, including the organs, liver (an excellent source of vitamin A), and calcium-rich ribs. Accordingly, both vitamin A deficiency and osteoporosis were averted when these wild animals ate the diet that they were genetically adapted to eat. Lions are not only endowed with sharp fangs and claws to take down their prey, but their digestive tracts are much shorter than those of herbivores (plant eaters), which accommodates their calorically dense food. Additionally, lions' livers and other metabolic machinery have become specifically modified to cope with an all-flesh diet. Pure carnivores like cats are literally genetically programmed to eat the flesh of other animals—it would make about as much sense to feed these animals cereal grains and berries as it would to feed antelope meat.

All species of animals—whether cats, antelope, or tropical fish—occupy and exploit specific ecological niches and are well suited to their place in the environment. Their genetic makeup reflects their adaptation to their ecological niche, including not only their outward appearance but also the foods they are genetically programmed to eat. When new and different foods are fed to these animals, it almost invariably results in ill health or disease. Zookeepers know that exotic species of South American monkeys can be kept alive on cereal-based chow, but these animals don't do well, are prone to disease, and will not reproduce under these conditions. Only when they are fed their normal diet of insects, leaves, and tropical fruit do they thrive and produce offspring in captivity. Similarly, successful tropical fish hobbyists understand the superiority of live food over dry flaked fish food for getting certain exotic fish to breed in their aquariums.

Human nutritional requirements were determined in the exact same manner as those for lions, exotic monkeys, and tropical fish. As a species, we are genetically well adapted to the foods and food types that we typically encountered in our original and natural ecological niche. What, then, is the native human niche, and what foods and food types are typically encountered?

HOW WE KNOW WHAT PALEOLITHIC PEOPLE ATE

You likely realize by now that the original and natural human ecological niche was that of a hunter-gatherer, and you probably deduce that hunter-gatherers ate wild plant and animal foods. Well, right you are! However, the essence of the question—what did hunter-gatherers eat?—lies in the precise details. The Introduction discussed the foods and food types that couldn't have been eaten by our Stone Age ancestors, but now let's talk about what they ate—and how we know this.

Except for certain rare bits and pieces of tangible evidence, such as fossilized human feces (coprolites) and a few isolated cases of mummified bodies found with stomach contents intact, almost all estimates of Stone Age diets must be inferred from circumstantial evidence. The four main sources of circumstantial evidence include: (1) studies of other primate diets; (2) studies of fossils; (3) anthropological accounts of modern-day hunter-gatherers, called ethnographic studies; and (4) examination of our own, present-day biochemical and metabolic pathways.

Before we look at these four lines of circumstantial evidence, it is important to make it clear from the outset that there was no single, standardized Stone Age diet. The Paleolithic Age (Old Stone Age) began with the manufacture of the first crude stone tools, some 2.6 million years ago in Africa, and ended 10,000 years ago with the development of agriculture in the Middle East. The Stone Age ended a little later (5,000 to 8,000 years ago) for most Europeans and Asians, as agriculture spread from its origins in the Middle East. For some isolated hunter-gatherers, the Stone Age literally ended only within the last century. During the Paleolithic Age, perhaps as many as 20 distinctive species of the human tribe existed (see Figure 8.1 on page 149). The best available information tells us that their diets were as varied as the environments they inhabited. However, of utmost importance to us are the universal dietary characteristics that transcend time, geographic locale, and even species. These worldwide dietary similarities established the range and limits of foods that shaped our modern genome and represent the range and limits of foods to which we are now genetically adapted.

1. Other Primate Diets

By analyzing a special kind of DNA called mitochondrial DNA, found in all living primates, scientists have determined that our closest living relative is the chimpanzee. Even though our outward appearance is quite different from that of chimps, there actually is only about a 1.6 percent difference between our genome and theirs. A careful look at Figure 8.1 reveals that the earliest member of our tribe (*Sahelanthropus tchadensis*) lived between 6 and 7 million years ago in Africa. Scientists aren't completely sure if this primate was an ape or a hominin (a primate that walks upright on two legs). Nevertheless, it was during this time or slightly later that the "last common ancestor" existed before the evolutionary split between chimps and hominins. The important point here is that the anatomy and diet of the last common ancestor was probably quite similar to that of modern-day chimps.

From field observations of chimpanzee eating habits and analysis of their feces, anthropologists have a pretty good handle on what they eat. In the wild, a chimp's diet contains about 93 percent plant food, primarily ripe fruit. However, the wild fruit they eat would gag us. These fruits are tough, fibrous, and, by modern standards, definitely not sweet. Many contain substances that taste like turpentine. For wild chimps, a succulent apple or orange would be a candylike treat and voraciously gobbled up. You may be surprised to learn that wild chimps hunt, kill, and eat small monkeys and antelope. During the dry season in Africa, meat can account for almost 25 percent of a male chimp's diet.

If you have seen pictures of wild chimps, you may have noticed their large, protruding guts. A chimp has a big gut not because it is fat (like the average American couch potato) but because it needs a large, metabolically active gut to handle all of that tough, fibrous fruit. Chimps are relative geniuses in the animal world; however, their average brain size (400 cubic centimeters) is about a third the size of ours. The difference between their brains and

FIGURE 8.1

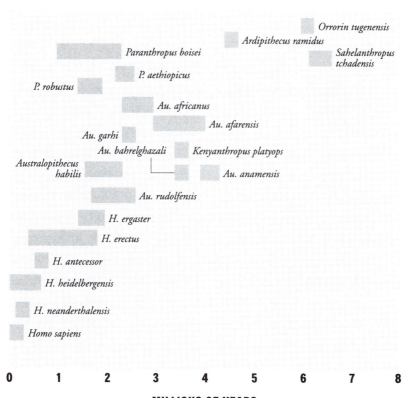

guts and ours—and the reason for it—forms one of the most eloquent ideas in all of evolutionary anthropology. It also gives us a good clue to the kind of diets we modern humans are genetically programmed to eat. Let's see how this works.

The brain is the most metabolically active organ in our bodies. In fact, at rest it uses nine times more energy than any other organ does. So, in order for us to have evolved a large brain, two possibilities exist: Either our overall metabolism increased, or the metabolism and size of another organ decreased. Think about it this way: If your entire body was made up of brains, it would have an overall metabolic rate nine times higher than it actually has. Of course, that's not the case, but we do have a body that contains three times more brain relative to our body size than a chimp does. It seems reasonable to conclude that the evolution of our large brains caused our overall metabolic rate to increase. Right? Wrong! Our net metabolic rate at rest is exactly as predicted for our body size. So the first possibility is out, leaving the second—that another organ got smaller. And, indeed, a human's gut is about half the size it should be, compared with a chimp's.

Anthropologists call this concept the expensive tissue hypothesis. This evolutionary brain/gut energy trade-off could have occurred only when the demands placed upon the gut to digest a bulky, fibrous, plant-based diet were reduced by the consumption of more energetically dense foods. Slightly before the fossil record shows brain size increasing, hominins began to manufacture the first stone tools that were used to butcher and dismember animal carcasses. Taken together, these facts verify that starting about 2.6 million years ago, hominins began to eat more and more animal food. It was this energetically dense food (meat, marrow, and organs) that allowed natural selection to relax the former selective pressure that had required a large, metabolically active gut. Literally, without meat, marrow, and organs in the diets of our ancient ancestors, we would not be here now. And the take-home message for you, the athlete, is that animal food (meat and organs) has been part of our ancestral diet from the get-go.

2. The Fossil Record

One of the most important clues we have in trying to piece together what our Stone Age ancestors ate is the fossil record. These are the items our prehistoric relatives left behind: their garbage, possessions, tools, weapons, and, less frequently, bones and teeth. Unfortunately, the fossil record is biased and will never allow us to peer into archaic diets with exacting precision. You don't have to be an archaeologist to figure this out. Animal remains such as hard teeth and bones resist decomposition in the soil and, thus, have a much greater chance of becoming fossilized than do soft plant remains. So when archaeologists dig up the remains of an ancient campsite, they rarely, if ever, find any evidence that plant foods were consumed. What they do find, typically, are bones of prey animals embellished with stone cut marks and sometimes the stone tools themselves. Does this mean that our Paleolithic relatives were total carnivores? Hardly. Our hunter-gatherer ancestors were opportunists: If it could be eaten, it probably was. But a few emerging themes play out in the fossil record, even with this preservation bias favoring animal remains.

The very earliest hominins that made stone tools were small (full-grown adults weighed 60 to 80 pounds and stood about 4½ feet tall) and probably not much more intelligent than chimps. Consequently, they probably weren't very good hunters of large animals. Many anthropologists believe that stone tool marks found on bones of large animals such as the zebra, wildebeest, and hippo came about from scavenging rather than hunting.

By about 1.7 to 2 million years ago, hominins had achieved modern-day body proportions from the neck down. A remarkable, nearly complete male skeleton found in Kenya and dated to 1.6 million years ago would have stood 6 feet tall when alive, with a slender body and narrow hips similar to the bodies of modern-day champion runners from Kenya. Slightly later, tool making became a bit more sophisticated, and medium to large prey animals became the preferred target. At one particularly amazing archaeological site in Kenya, called Olorgasailie, 400 stone hand axes were found along with the butchered remains of 65 extinct gorilla-size baboons. At another site in Germany, dated to 400,000 years ago, seven wooden spears were discovered with the butchered bones of more than 10 horses.

Just as in politics, there are smoking guns in the fossil record; these show beyond a shadow of a doubt what was going on. A few examples: In 1950, German anthropologists found an 8-foot thrusting spear, dated to 125,000 years ago, lodged between the ribs of an extinct straight-tusked elephant. How do you think that spear got there? A similar find was made in August 1951, when summer rains brought heavy flooding to the Greenbush Creek a mile northwest of Naco, Arizona. Erosion in the arroyo exposed part of a skull with teeth and the tusk of a large mammoth. Further excavation revealed eight razor-sharp stone spear points embedded between the animal's ribs. Because there were no stone cut marks on any of the mammoth's bones, anthropologists deduced that "this one got away."

How incredible would it be if we could have just a single photograph of our Paleolithic relatives going about their hunting and food collecting activities? We do have the next best thing—a highly detailed drawing, "The Shaft of the Dead Man," which you can see at the Web site www.culture.gouv.fr/culture/arcnat/lascaux/en/. This drawing, made 17,000 years ago in the famous Lascaux Cave in France, depicts a wounded European bison with its entrails spilling out and a spear stuck between its ribs. The enraged animal is in the process of goring a human armed with a spear-throwing device called an atlatl.

Now, why would our ancestors have risked life and limb to kill large, ferocious beasts to get meat? Couldn't they have gone after much less dangerous small prey like rabbits, partridges, clams, and fish? Why would anyone in their right mind lunge a flimsy wooden spear between the ribs of a 6- to 8-ton elephant? They did it because they had to. At the time, they were aware of no other alternative solution to survive. Why is that?

Believe it or not, you can get too much of a good thing, and protein is good for you only up to a certain point. You can include as much carbohydrate and fat in your diet as you like with no immediate ill effects, but the same can't be said for protein. In the typical US diet, protein makes up about 15 percent of our daily calories, whereas in hunter-gatherer diets, it would have been con-siderably higher, ranging from 25 to 40 percent of the daily energy intake. Laboratory studies in humans show that the maximum amount of protein we can ingest on a regular basis is about 40 per-cent of our daily calories. Anything above this and we get sick—a lesson our hunter-gatherers knew quite well. Early frontiersmen and explorers also knew exactly what happened when they were forced to eat only the lean meat of fat-depleted animals. They called this sickness "rabbit starvation." After eating enormous quantities of very lean meat, they would become nauseated and irritable, lose weight, develop diarrhea, and eventually die. They were better off starving than continuing to eat only lean meat. The only way around this situation: Get either fat or carbohydrate into the diet to dilute the protein level to below 40 percent.

In the modern world, it is easy to change the fat content of any food. Lobster is extremely lean (84 percent of its energy is protein) and would quickly cause protein poisoning if that's all you ate. Most of us prefer to dip our lobster in melted butter, which allows us to eat all we want and never develop symptoms of protein ex-cess. Hunter-gatherers weren't so lucky. Fat and protein came in a single packet—the animal's carcass. Either the animal had fat or it didn't. There was no such thing as adding fat to a food. Similarly, if you were to eat a carbohydrate source such as brown rice or potatoes along with the lobster, you'd dilute the protein below the crucial 40 percent protein ceiling and have no problems whatso-ever. However, until the development of agriculture and domesti-cation of cereal grains, hunter-gatherers, particularly those living at higher latitudes, had no reliable year-round source of carbohy-drate.

Now let's answer the question of why Stone Age hunters risked life and limb on a regular basis to kill large, unruly beasts. Large animals are fat animals. The larger a species, the more body fat it has. The average body fat content of a small animal like a squirrel

(1 pound) is 5.2 percent by weight, whereas a large animal such as a musk ox (900 pounds) has 20.5 percent body fat by weight. If we look at the squirrel's body fat by total calories rather than weight, it's clear why the sole consumption of squirrels would cause protein poisoning. A squirrel's entire body is 35 percent fat by energy (calories) and 65 percent protein—way over the 40 percent ceiling. In contrast, the musk ox's body is 73 percent fat and 27 percent protein. A carcass containing only 27 percent protein can easily be consumed in its entirety without even coming close to the protein ceiling.

The fossil record unmistakably tells us that ancestral humans have always included meat and animal foods in their diets, but there is tantalizingly little evidence showing how much meat was eaten. And there is even less evidence to reveal how much plant food was typically consumed. Fortunately, anthropologists have developed a clever procedure that can give us a rough approximation of the dietary ration of animal to plant by measuring stable isotopes in the fossilized bones and teeth of long-dead hominins. Stable isotopes are elements like carbon 13 and nitrogen 15 that vary slightly from the normal versions. Julia Lee-Thorp, PhD, and her colleagues from the University of Cape Town in South Africa have measured stable isotopes in many of the very first hominins that were living in Africa 1 to 3 million years ago, and she concluded that all ate significant quantities of both animal and plant foods. Using stable isotopes to examine the diets of Neanderthals living in Europe 30,000 years ago, Mike Richards, PhD, of the University of Bradford in the United Kingdom concluded, "The isotope evidence overwhelmingly points to the Neanderthals behaving as top-level carnivores." In a similar study of Stone Age people living in England 12,000 years ago, he summarized, "We were testing the hypothesis that these humans had a mainly hunting economy, and therefore a diet high in animal protein. We found this to be the case . . . "

Dr. Richards's isotopic data are interesting but come from very specialized groups of our ancestors, whose diets may have significantly varied from the mainstream. The Neanderthals generally lived in Europe during the Ice Age, when very little plant food would have been available on a year-round basis. Consequently, they may have had no choice but to eat animal food. Similarly, many anthropologists believe that modern humans living in Europe 12,000 to 40,000 years ago may have developed animal-based diet strategies because of the relative abundance of large game animals. There is another avenue available to us that can help to solve the riddle of how much plant and animal food was typically found in our ancestors' diets.

3. Ethnographic Studies

Hundreds, if not thousands, of descriptions of hunter-gatherers and what they ate have been written throughout historical times. These accounts were penned by explorers, sailors, trappers, frontiersmen, physicians, anthropologists, and others who encountered native peoples during their travels. Fortunately, an industrious anthropologist, George Murdock, PhD, took it upon himself to compile and organize historical accounts not only of hunter-gatherers but of all the world's cultures and how they lived. His enormous database included more than 100 specific data points for each society. In 1967, Dr. Murdock completed his life's work with the publication of a massive volume called the *Ethnographic Atlas*, a work that allows anybody to easily compare and contrast any society or culture on earth.

One year after the publication of Dr. Murdock's massive volume, a young anthropologist at Harvard, Richard Lee, PhD, utilized some of the hunter-gatherer data from the *Ethnographic Atlas* to establish the plant-to-animal composition in the average hunter-gatherer diet. Dr. Lee concluded that hunted animal foods composed 35 percent of the energy in the average hunter-gatherer diet and that plant foods made up the balance (65 percent). For the next 3 decades, Dr. Lee's conclusion became the unquestioned dogma in anthropological circles. Unfortunately, his analysis was flawed, and it wasn't corrected until 32 years later with our publication of a reanalysis of the *Ethnographic Atlas*'s hunter-gatherer data. Let me show you how I came to this conclusion.

It's pretty hard to overeat raw carrots and celery—in fact, most of us have had enough after one or two carrots or celery stalks. Can you imagine eating 65 percent of your daily calories from celery? An active man who takes in 3,000 calories a day would have to eat 27 pounds of celery to obtain 65 percent of his daily calories from this plant food. Okay, perhaps celery is an extreme example. How about tomatoes? Try 20 pounds! Cantaloupe, maybe? Twelve pounds! Perhaps potatoes would work: To get 65 percent of 3,000 calories (1,950 calories), you would have to eat 4 pounds. This is a doable situation. But the problem is that most wild tubers and roots bear little resemblance to today's thoroughly domesticated potatoes. Compared with their modern counterparts, wild tubers are smaller, usually more fibrous, less starchy, and, therefore, not nearly as calorically dense.

It became increasingly clear to me that only a very few wild plant foods could be consumed at quantities approaching 65 percent of the daily caloric intake. These were oily nuts and seeds, tubers, and cereal grains. Grains were out of the equation because they were rarely, if ever, consumed by hunter-gatherers, as explained in the Introduction. Also, when hunter-gatherers forage for food, they need to make some critical decisions. First, they must get more energy from the food they are hunting or gathering than the energy they expend to obtain it. It would be a losing proposition to run around all day using up 800 calories, only to bring back 500 calories. Second, hunter-gatherers prioritize food choices relative to their energy return rate. These are the foods that give them the most "bang for their foraging buck"—large animals are preferred over small, and animal foods are almost always preferred over plant foods. Anthropologists have dubbed these hunter-gatherer decisions "optimal foraging theory."

At any rate, all of this information made me suspicious. It seemed unlikely that plant foods could have made up the majority of daily calories in the typical hunter-gatherer diet. So I went back to the original *Ethnographic Atlas*, plugged all the data points for the 229 hunter-gatherer societies into a spreadsheet, and reanalyzed the whole kit and caboodle. I completed my analysis on Christmas Day 1997 and could not believe my eyes. Not only were the results different from Richard Lee's analysis, they were exactly reversed. Plant foods represented about 35 percent of the total calories, while animal foods stood out at 65 percent! How could this be? I carefully checked all of the more than 2,000 data points—no errors there. Hmm! What was going on?

At last I saw it. Dr. Lee had failed to include fished animal foods along with hunted animal foods in determining the overall animal-to-plant subsistence ratio.

One of the huge problems with ethnographic studies is that they are almost entirely subjective. We went back to some of the original studies that Dr. Murdock had used to estimate the subsistence ratios and were dumbfounded at how he did it. There were absolutely no concrete data in many of these accounts of hunter-gatherers to show how much meat or plant food was consumed. Using some of the accounts as a starting point, my research team and I rooted out each and every quantitative study in which the foods were weighed and the caloric content known. It turned out that 13 reports could be used. Two of them involved Eskimos, who have no choice but to eat animal food, so we were down to 11 reports. These more robust, quantitative studies were in agreement with our earlier analysis and once again demonstrated that animal foods made up two-thirds of the average energy intake in hunter-gatherer diets.

So, three separate lines of evidence (other primate diets, the fossil record, and ethnographic studies) now independently point to the notion that meat, organs, and animal foods have always been a significant part of the diet to which we are genetically adapted. But, as you'll see in Chapter 9, wild animals and domesticated, feedlot-produced animals are worlds apart nutritionally. Eating a modern diet with 65 percent of its energy coming from fatty meats produced from grain-fed animals is not even close to resembling our ancestral diet.

Let's take a brief look at a piece of the puzzle that has only recently surfaced, showing the types of foods Mother Nature intended for us.

4. Biochemical and Metabolic Pathways

Within our own body's biochemical machinery lie clues to the way in which diet has changed in the 5 to 7 million years since our evolutionary split from the apes. It may come as a surprise to you, but we humans have evolved a number of biochemical adaptations that are parallel to those found in pure carnivores. Obviously, we are not pure carnivores. We are omnivores that are genetically adapted to eating a mixed diet of both plant and animal foods. However, substantial biochemical evidence suggests that, during the past 2.6 million years, we have made a significant evolutionary shift that has brought us closer to a meat-based diet than to a plant-based diet.

Pure carnivores, such as cats, must obtain all of their nutrients from the flesh of other animals. Because of this they have evolved certain biochemical adaptations that demonstrate their total dietary dependence upon animal-based foods. Most of these adaptations involve either the loss or reduced activity of certain enzymes required to build essential nutrients. These losses occurred because the evolutionary selection pressure to maintain these enzymes and metabolic pathways was no longer needed. Let me give you a few examples and show you how humans have moved down a similar evolutionary pathway.

Taurine is an amino acid that is not found in any plant food and is an essential nutrient in all cells of the body. Herbivores, such as cows, are able to synthesize taurine from precursor amino acids found in plants, whereas cats have completely lost that ability. Since all animal foods (except cow's milk) are rich sources of taurine, cats have been able to relax the evolutionary selective pressure required for taurine synthesis because they obtain all they need from their exclusive meat-based diet.

Humans, unlike cats, still maintain the ability to synthesize taurine in the liver from precursor substances. However, this ability is limited and inefficient—so much so that infant formula must be supplemented with taurine. Without taurine supplementation in infant formula, bottle-fed babies are more susceptible to visual and hearing problems as they grow. Even adults don't fare much better if they stop eating meat. Studies show that vegan vegetarians have low levels of blood and urinary taurine—levels that indicate our poor ability to synthesize taurine from vegetable amino acids. Similar to cats, our inefficiency to build taurine from plant amino acids occurred because of our long reliance upon taurine-rich animal food.

A second example, similar to the taurine story, is the situation with long-chain fatty acids. Cats have almost completely lost the ability of the liver to convert 18-carbon to 20-carbon fatty acids. All cells in the bodies of mammals require 20-carbon fatty acids to make localized hormones called eicosanoids and prostaglandins. Herbivores have no choice but to synthesize 20-carbon fatty acids in the liver from plant-based 18-carbon fatty acids, since 20-carbon fatty acids occur only in animal food and are not found in any plant foods. Again, cats have nearly lost the ability to build 20-carbon fatty acids from their 18-carbon precursors because there was no need for it; they got all the preformed 20-carbon fatty acids they required from the flesh of their prey. Similarly, humans maintain very inefficient pathways to convert 18- to 20-carbon fatty acids because of our more than 2-million-year history of meat consumption.

In the Introduction, we discussed the foods that couldn't have been consumed by our Stone Age ancestors; in this chapter, we illustrated those that were eaten. By putting both of these pieces of the puzzle together, a much clearer picture emerges of the foods that we are genetically programmed to eat. These are the foods that provide us with optimal health and well-being. By mimicking the nutritional characteristics of the ancestral human diet with commonly available modern foods, it is entirely possible to eat a Stone Age diet in the 21st century. In the next chapter, we will explain how easily this can be accomplished.

Chapter 9

THE 21ST-CENTURY PALEO DIET

SPECIAL DIETARY NEEDS OF MODERN ATHLETES

As a serious athlete, you have a lifestyle and activity level that are far different from that of the average American. Chances are your training patterns also vary significantly from the daily activity patterns of our Paleolithic ancestors. They were unlikely to ever run 26.2 miles as fast as they could, nonstop. Nor would they work and run at high-intensity levels day after day, week after week. The only reason for doing so would be under extreme conditions in which their lives were continually at risk, and the only way to survive would be to run far and fast every day. Such situations would be rare. As you will see in the next chapter, the more typical manner of "exercise" for the Paleolithic athlete would have involved long, steady hunts and foraging expeditions conducted at a moderate pace until the kill was imminent or the gathered foods were hauled back to camp. At these times their effort would increase, but they would no doubt rest at every opportunity. Ceremonial dance would also provide nearly continuous "exercise," but the intensity would be relatively low.

What all of this means for you is that your diet must be

modified slightly to accommodate your "unusual" high-level training patterns that are a requisite for peak performance during competition. These modifications, as you are now well aware, involve exactly when and what you eat before, during, and immediately following exercise. These critical dietary nuances were discussed extensively in Chapters 2, 3, and 4.

Now let's get down to the crux of this chapter: What should you eat for the remainder of your day, from the time short-term recovery ends until just before the next workout begins? During this period, you should be eating in a manner similar to that of your Paleolithic ancestors. You'll quickly discover that your day-to-day recovery is greatly enhanced and, as a result, your performance will improve.

21ST-CENTURY DIETARY TWEAKS

Let's make it clear from the start: It would be nearly impossible for any athlete or fitness enthusiast living in a typical modern setting to exactly replicate a Paleolithic hunter-gatherer diet. Many of those foods are unavailable commercially, no longer exist, or are totally disgusting to modern tastes and cultural traditions. Do brains, marrow, tongue, and liver sound appealing to you? Probably not, but to hunter-gatherers, these organs were mouthwatering treats that were gobbled up every time an animal was killed. For hunter-gatherers, the least appetizing part of the carcass was the muscle tissue, which is about the only meat most of us ever eat.

Most of the familiar fruits and veggies that we find in the produce section of our supermarkets bear little resemblance to their wild counterparts. Large, succulent, orange carrots of today were nothing more than tiny, purple or yellow, fibrous roots 1,000 years ago. The numerous varieties of juicy, sweet apples that we enjoy would have resembled tiny, bitter crabapples a few thousand years ago. Thanks to thousands of years of selective breeding, irrigation, and, later, fertilizers and pesticides, we now eat domesticated fruits and veggies that are larger and sweeter, and have less fiber and more carbohydrate, than their wild versions. Does this mean that you need to go out and forage for wild plants and animals to stock your pantry for our lifetime nutritional plan? Absolutely not! Nearly all of the performance rewards and health benefits of the Paleo Diet for Athletes can easily be achieved from modern-day foods and food groups that had a counterpart in Stone Age diets.

The fundamental dietary principle for the Paleo Diet for Athletes is simplicity itself: unrestricted consumption of lean meats, poultry, seafood, fruits, and vegetables. Foods that are not part of the modern-day Paleolithic fare include cereal grains, dairy products, high-glycemic fruits and vegetables, legumes, alcohol, salty foods, high-fat meats, refined sugars, and nearly all processed foods.

The exceptions to these basic rules were fully outlined in Chapters 2, 3, and 4. For instance, immediately before, during, and after a workout or competition, certain nonoptimal foods may be eaten to encourage a quick recovery. During all other times, meals that closely follow the 21st-century Paleolithic diet described here will promote comprehensive long-term recovery and allow you to come within reach of your maximum performance potential.

ANIMAL AND PLANT FOOD BALANCE

A crucial aspect of the 21st-century Paleolithic diet is the proper balance of plant and animal foods. How much plant food and how much animal food were normally consumed in the diets of Stone Age hunter-gatherers? There is little doubt that whenever and wherever it was ecologically possible, hunter-gatherers preferred animal food over plant food. In our recent study of 229 hunter-gatherer societies, published in the *American Journal of Clinical Nutrition*, my research team showed that 73 percent of these cultures obtained between 56 and 65 percent of their daily subsistence from animal foods. In a follow-up study published in the *European Journal of Clinical Nutrition*, involving 13 additional hunter-gatherer groups whose diets were more closely analyzed, we found almost identical results. Our colleague, Mike Richards, PhD, of the University of Bradford in the United Kingdom, has taken a slightly different approach in determining the plant-to-animal balance in Stone Age diets. He has measured chemicals called stable isotopes in skeletons of hunter-gatherers that lived during the Paleolithic Era. His results dovetailed nicely with ours and confirmed that hunter-gatherers living 12,000 to 28,000 years ago were no different from contemporary hunter-gatherers—the majority of their daily calories also came from animal sources.

Based upon the best available evidence, you should try to eat a little more than half (50 to 55 percent) of your daily calories from lean meats, fish, and seafood. Avoid fatty meats, but fatty fish such as salmon, mackerel, and herring are perfectly acceptable because of their high concentrations of healthful omega-3 fatty acids and cholesterol-lowering monounsaturated fats. Table 9.1 lists some of the animal foods you should include in your diet as well as those you should avoid.

HOW ABOUT FATTY MEATS?

Some people who have adopted what they think are "Paleolithic diets" have embraced fatty meats such as bacon, T-bone steaks, and ribs as staples. Even some of the diet doctors with high-fat, low-carbohydrate weight-loss schemes have tried to jump on the Paleolithic bandwagon by suggesting that fatty meats would

TABLE 9.1

Fat and Protein Content of Meat and Seafood (percentage of total calories)

MEATS AND SEAFOOD TO EAT	% Protein	% Fat
Beef		
Veal steak	68	32
Sirloin steak	65	35
Lean flank steak	62	38
Poultry		
Skinless turkey breasts	94	5
Skinless chicken breasts	63	37
Pork		
Lean tenderloin	72	28
Lean chops	62	38
Organ Meats		
Beef sweetbreads	77	23
Beef heart	69	30
Chicken livers	65	32
Beef liver	63	28
Seafood		
Boiled shrimp	90	10
Orange roughy	90	10
Pollock fish	90	10
Broiled lobster	89	5
Red snapper	87	13
Dungeness crab	86	10
Broiled halibut	80	20
Steamed clams	73	12
Broiled tuna	68	32
Broiled salmon	62	38
Game Meats		
Buffalo roast	84	16
Roast venison	81	19

MEATS TO AVOID	% Protein	% Fat
Beef		
T-bone steak	36	64
Ground beef (15% fat)	35	63
Beef ribs	26	74
Poultry		
Chicken wings	38	59
Chicken thighs/leg	36	63
Pork		
Ribs	27	73
Shoulder roast	45	55
Lamb		
Shoulder roast	32	68
Chops	25	75
Processed Meats		
Ham lunch meat	39	54
Dry salami	23	75
Link pork sausage	22	77
Bacon	21	78
Liverwurst sausage	18	79
Bologna	15	81
Hot dog	14	83

have been normal fare for Stone Agers. Let's take a look at the real story.

Because animals had yet to be domesticated, Stone Age hunters could eat only wild animals whose body fat naturally waxes and wanes with the seasons. In contrast, virtually all of the meat in the typical US diet comes from grain-fattened animals, slaughtered at peak body-fat percentage regardless of the time of year. For instance, modern feedlot operations typically produce an obese (30 percent body fat or greater) 1,200-pound steer ready for slaughter in about 14 months. These animals are produced like clockwork, 12 months a year, no matter whether it is spring, summer, fall, or winter. That's quite the opposite of wild animals such as caribou, whose body fat changes with the seasons, as shown in Figure 9.1. Note that for 7 months out of the year, total body fat averages less than 5 percent. Only in the fall and early winter are significant body fat stores present, but these values are one-half to two-thirds less than the obese feedlot-produced steer!

Even more telling is how the types of fat change seasonally in the carcasses of wild animals. Remember, hunter-gatherers relished

FIGURE 9.1

Seasonal Change in Wild Caribou Body Fat %

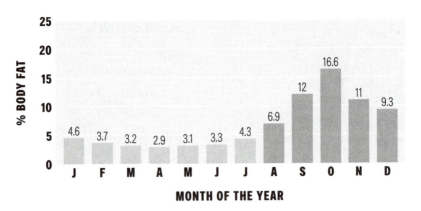

all edible body parts—they ate everything except bones, hooves, hide, and horns. By analyzing the total amount of fat and the kinds of fat in muscle, storage fat, and all of the edible organs, our research team was able to show how the animal's total body content of saturated fat varied with the seasons. Take a look at Figure 9.2 on page 168; you can see that for 7 months out of the year, the saturated fat from the edible carcass averages only 11.1 percent of its total available calories—meaning that hunter-gatherers simply did not have a high, year-round dietary source of saturated fat. To lower our blood cholesterol levels and reduce the risk of heart disease, the American Heart Association recommends that our dietary saturated fat intake be 10 percent of our total daily calories—remarkably close to what hunter-gatherers could have obtained from eating wild animals on a year-round basis! For this reason, we recommend that you always eat the leanest cuts of meat.

There is absolutely no doubt that hunter-gatherers favored the fattiest parts of animals. There is incredible fossil evidence from Africa, dating back to 2.5 million years ago, showing this scenario to be true. Stone-tool cut marks on the inner jawbone of antelope reveal that our ancient ancestors removed the tongue and almost certainly ate it. Other fossils show that Stone Age hunter-gatherers smashed open long bones and skulls of their prey and ate the contents. Not surprisingly, these organs are all relatively high in fat; but, more important, analyses from our laboratories showed the types of fat in the tongue, brain, and marrow are healthful, unlike the high concentrations of saturated fats found in fatty domestic meats. Brain is extremely high in polyunsaturated fats, including the health-promoting omega-3 fatty acids, whereas the dominant fats in tongue and marrow are the cholesterol-lowering monounsaturated fats.

Most of us would not savor the thought of eating brains,

FIGURE 9.2

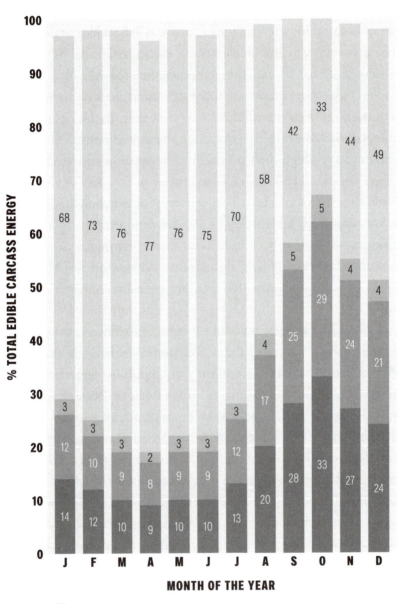

marrow, tongue, liver, or any other organ meat on a regular basis; therefore, a few 21st-century modifications of the original Paleolithic diet are necessary to get the fatty acid balance "right." First, we suggest you limit your choice of meats to very lean cuts, but don't worry about fatty fish—they're good for you, just like the organ meats our ancestors preferred. Second, we recommend that you add healthful vegetable oils to your diet. By following these simple steps, together with the other nuts and bolts of this plan, the fatty acid balance in your diet will approximate what our Stone Age ancestors got.

From our analyses of 229 hunter-gatherer diets and the nutrient content of wild plants and animals, our research team has demonstrated that the most representative fat intake would have varied from 28 to 57 percent of total calories. To reduce risk of heart disease, the American Heart Association recommends limiting total fat to 30 percent or less of daily calories. On the surface, it would appear that, except for the extreme lower range, there would be too much fat in the typical hunter-gatherer diet—at least according to what we (the American public) have heard for decades: Get the fat out of your diet! The Food Pyramid cautions us to cut out as much fat as possible and replace it with grains and carbohydrate. Not only is this message misguided, it is flat-out wrong. Scientists have known for more than 50 years that it is not the total amount of fat in the diet that promotes heart disease but, rather, the kind of fat. Plain and simple, it is a qualitative issue, not a quantitative one! Polyunsaturated fats are good for us, particularly when we correctly balance the omega-3 and omega-6 fatty acids. Monounsaturated fats are heart-healthy, and even some saturated fats such as stearic acid (found in animal fat) do not promote heart disease. Deadly fats are three specific saturated fats (palmitic acid, lauric acid, and myristic acid) and the trans fats found in margarine, shortening, and hydrogenated vegetable oils, as well as processed foods made with these products.

169

Now let's get back to the fat content of our ancestral hunter-gatherer diet. They frequently ate more fat than we do, but it was almost invariably healthy fats. Using computerized dietary analyses of the wild plant and animal foods, our research team has shown that the usual fat breakdown in hunter-gatherer diets was 55 to 65 percent monounsaturated fat, 20 to 25 percent polyunsaturated fat (with an omega-6-to-omega-3 ratio of 2:1), and 10 to 15 percent saturated fat (about half being the neutral stearic acid). This balance of fats is exactly what you will get when you follow our dietary recommendations.

FOODS NOT ON THE PALEOLITHIC MENU

Let's get down to the specifics of the diet. Table 9.2 on page 172 includes an inventory of modern foods that should be avoided. These recommendations might at first seem like a huge laundry list, with seemingly needless elimination of entire food groups. Most dyed-in-the-wool nutritionists wouldn't object to our advice to cut down or eliminate sugars and highly refined, processed foods. They would have no problem with our suggestions to reduce saturated and trans fats and salt, and they would be ecstatic about our recommendations to boost fresh fruit and vegetable consumption. But they would, guaranteed, react violently to the mere thought of eliminating "sacred" whole grains from your diet. If they heard we also advocate reducing or eliminating dairy products, they almost certainly would brand this diet unhealthful, if not outright dangerous. You may wonder why, just because hunter-gatherers did not regularly eat grains or dairy products, you should follow suit. After all, aren't whole grains healthful, and isn't milk good for everybody? How can you get calcium without dairy? And won't eating a lot of meat increase blood cholesterol levels?

In science, decisions should be made based upon what the data tell us and not upon human bias and prejudice. With these ground rules in mind, let's take a look at the reasons for and potential benefits of eliminating or severely restricting entire food groups with the Paleo Diet for Athletes. One of the major goals of any diet, for both athletes and nonathletes alike, is to supply you, the consumer, with a diet rich in nutrients (vitamins, minerals, and phytochemicals) that promote good health, which in turn promotes good performance. Table 9.3 on page 174 shows the nutrient density of seven food groups.

From top to bottom, here's the ranking of the most nutritious food groups: fresh vegetables, seafood, lean meats, fresh fruits, whole grains and milk (tied for second to last), and nuts and seeds. Why in the world would the USDA place grains at the Pyramid's base if the goal is an adequate intake of vitamins and minerals? This strategy makes no sense for the average American, much less athletes like you. Had we included refined grains in the list, they would have ended up dead last because the refining process strips this nutrient-poor food group even further of vitamins and minerals. Unfortunately, in the United States, 85 percent of the grains we eat are highly refined, and grains typically make up 24 percent of our daily calories.

Not only are grains and dairy foods poor sources of vitamins and minerals, they also retain nutritional characteristics that clearly are not in your best interest, whether you're an athlete or not. From Chapter 5, you now know all about the glycemic index and acid/base balance in foods, along with how they impact your performance. Virtually all refined grains and grain products yield high glycemic loads. Further, all grains, whether whole or refined, are net acid producing. Dairy products are one of the greatest sources of artery-clogging saturated fats in the American diet, and cheeses produce the highest acidic loads of any foods. If that's not bad enough, a recent study found that dairy products, despite having low glycemic indices, spike blood insulin levels similar to white

TABLE 9.2

Modern Foods to Avoid

DAIRY FOODS

Milk

Cheese

Butter

Cream

Yogurt

Ice cream

Ice milk

Frozen yogurt

Powdered milk

Nonfat creamer

Dairy spreads

All processed foods made with dairy products

CEREAL GRAINS

Wheat (bread, rolls, muffins, noodles, crackers, cookies, cake, doughnuts, pancakes, waffles, pasta, tortillas, pizza, pita bread, flat bread, and all processed foods made with wheat or wheat flour)

Rye (bread, crackers, and all processed foods made with rye)

Barley (soup, bread, and all processed foods made with barley)

Oats (instant oatmeal, rolled oats, and all processed foods made with oats)

Corn (corn on the cob, corn tortillas, cornstarch, corn syrup)

Rice (including brown, white, wild, and basmati; ramen and rice noodles; rice cakes; rice flour; and all processed foods made with rice)

Millet

Sorghum

CEREAL GRAINLIKE SEEDS

Amaranth

Quinoa

Buckwheat

LEGUMES

All beans except string beans (kidney, pinto, navy, white, lima, black, and broad beans)

bread. Do yourself a favor—get the grains and dairy out of your diet and replace them with more healthful fruits, veggies, lean meats, and seafood.

If you, like most Americans, have been swayed by those milk mustache ads, you probably are part of the mass hysteria, largely generated by the dairy industry, suggesting there is a nationwide calcium shortage that underlies osteoporosis. Not true! Calcium intake from dairy, or any other food, is only part of the story behind bone mineral health. More important is calcium balance, the dif-

Lentils

Peas, snowpeas

Peanuts (peanuts are legumes, not nuts)

Soybeans and all soybean products

Chickpeas and garbanzo beans

STARCHY TUBERS

Potatoes

YEAST-CONTAINING FOODS

Breads, doughnuts, rolls, muffins

All fermented foods (beer, wine, pickled foods, foods containing vinegar, and tofu)

FATTY, PROCESSED, AND CANNED MEATS AND FISH

Sausages, bacon

Fatty hamburger

Fatty cuts of meat (T-bone steaks, beef ribs, and lamb roasts and chops)

Processed meats (lunch meats, deli meats, preserved or smoked meats such as ham and turkey, and smoked or dried and salted fish)

Canned or pickled meats and fish (tuna, sardines, herrings, smoked oysters and clams, and canned salmon and mackerel, chicken, beef)

ALCOHOLIC BEVERAGES

All alcoholic beverages (permitted in moderation; see Chapter 11)

SWEETS

All candy

Honey

Dried fruit (permitted in moderation; see Chapter 11)

Note that these foods are not forever banned from your diet, but to be regularly avoided; see Chapter 11.

ference between how much calcium goes into your body from diet and how much leaves in urine. You will be out of balance if more calcium leaves than what comes in, no matter how much milk you drink. What we really need to pay attention to is the other side of the equation—the calcium leaving our bodies. Dietary acid/base balance is the single most important factor influencing calcium loss in the urine. Net acid-producing diets overloaded with grains, cheeses, and salty processed foods increase urinary calcium losses, whereas the Paleo Diet for Athletes is rich in alkaline-yielding fruit

TABLE 9.3

Nutrient Density for Various Food Groups (100 kilocalorie samples)

	WHOLE GRAINS	WHOLE MILK	FRUITS
Vitamin B$_{12}$ (µg)	0.00[4]	0.58[5]	0.00[4]
Vitamin B$_3$ (mg)	1.12[4]	0.14[1]	0.89[3]
Phosphorus (mg)	90[3]	152[5]	33[1]
Vitamin B$_2$ (mg)	0.05[3]	0.26[6]	0.09[4]
Vitamin B$_1$ (mg)	0.12[5]	0.06[2]	0.11[4]
Folate (µg)	10.3[3]	8.1[2]	25.0[6]
Vitamin C (mg)	1.53[3]	74.2[5]	221.3[7]
Iron (mg)	0.90[4]	0.08[1]	0.69[2]
Vitamin B$_6$ (mg)	0.09[3]	0.07[1]	0.20[5]
Vitamin A (RE)	2[3]	50[5]	94[6]
Magnesium (mg)	32.6[4]	21.9[2]	24.6[3]
Calcium (mg)	7.6[2]	194.3[7]	43.0[4]
Zinc (mg)	0.67[4]	0.62[3]	0.25[1]
Sum Rank Score	**44**	**44**	**48**

Superscripts represent relative ranking per nutrient (7 = highest; 1 = lowest).

Nutrient values represent average of food types within each food group: 8 whole grains, 20 fruits, 18 vegetables, 20 types of seafood, 4 lean meats, 10 seeds and nuts. Food types within food groups were based upon the most commonly consumed foods in the US diet for the 13 vitamins and minerals most frequently lacking or deficient in the US diet.

and vegetables that bring us back into calcium balance and promote bone mineral health.

DIETARY STAPLES: LEAN MEATS

With the Paleo Diet for Athletes, you'll be eating lean meat and seafood, and lots of it, at almost every meal. Should you be worried about your blood cholesterol levels rising? Absolutely not, and here's why. In the 1950s, when scientists began to realize that saturated fats promote heart disease, a nationwide campaign was initiated to reduce dietary fats, and meat became a primary target. As

VEGETABLES	SEAFOOD	LEAN MEATS	NUTS/SEEDS
0.00[4]	7.42[7]	0.63[6]	0.00[4]
2.73[5]	3.19[6]	4.73[7]	0.35[2]
157[6]	219[7]	151[4]	80[2]
0.33[7]	0.09[4]	0.14[5]	0.04[2]
0.26[7]	0.08[3]	0.18[6]	0.12[5]
208.3[7]	10.8[4]	3.8[1]	11.0[5]
93.6[6]	1.9[4]	0.1[1]	0.4[2]
2.59[7]	2.07[6]	1.10[5]	0.86[3]
0.42[7]	0.19[4]	0.32[6]	0.08[2]
687[7]	32[4]	1[2]	2[3]
54.5[7]	36.1[6]	18.0[1]	35.8[5]
116.8[6]	43.1[5]	6.1[1]	17.5[3]
1.04[5]	7.6[7]	1.9[6]	0.6[2]
81	**65**	**50**	**38**

this strategy gained momentum in the late '60s and early '70s, meat, and red meat in particular, became vilified. In the eyes of overzealous vegetarians, nutritionists, and physicians, meat consumption was the scapegoat underlying the epidemic of heart disease and cancer in the United States. But the problem was oversimplified—they threw out the baby with the bathwater. It was not meat, per se, that was the problem; rather, it was the fatty meats such as hamburger, T-bone steaks, bologna, and hot dogs that had become the norm in the US diet.

This fact was strikingly demonstrated by my colleague, Andy

Sinclair, PhD, from the Royal Melbourne Institute of Technology, with a clever dietary intervention in which people were fed a diet either of lean beef trimmed of visible fat or with the trimmed fat added back in. When lean beef was consumed, LDL (bad) cholesterol in the blood declined, but (not surprisingly) it increased when the fat was added back in. These results have been duplicated numerous times in independent labs. In fact, experiments by Bernard Wolfe, MD, at the University of Western Ontario have decisively shown that when low-fat animal protein replaces dietary saturated fat, it is more effective in lowering blood cholesterol and improving blood chemistry than are low-fat carbohydrates. In nutritional interventions such as Dr. Wolfe's, the key to scientific credibility is replication—replication, replication, replication! It is absolutely essential that other scientists get similar results from comparable experiments. To the surprise of some party-line nutritionists, a series of four recent (2003) papers from independent researchers around the world confirmed Dr. Wolfe's earlier work.

Is there a limit to a good thing? You now know that lean animal protein lowers your blood LDL (bad) cholesterol levels, increases HDL (good), and provides muscle-building branched-chain amino acids. How much protein should—or can—you eat?

There is a limit to the amount of protein you can physiologically tolerate. Nineteenth- and 20th-century explorers, frontiersmen, and trappers who were forced to eat nothing but the fat-drained flesh of wild game in late winter or early spring developed nausea, diarrhea, and lethargy and eventually died. Studies conducted in the laboratory of Daniel Rudman, MD, at Emory University have examined the causal mechanisms underlying the protein ceiling and found that toxicity occurs when the liver can't eliminate nitrogen from the ingested protein fast enough. Nitrogen is normally excreted as urea in the urine and feces, but with protein toxicity, ammonia and excessive amino acids from protein degradation build up in the bloodstream and produce adverse symptoms. For most people, the maximum dietary protein limit is between 200 and 300 grams per day, or about 30 to 40 percent of the normal daily caloric intake. On the Paleo Diet for Athletes, you will never have to worry about protein toxicity, as you will eat unlimited amounts of carbohydrates in the form of fruits and vegetables. Further, in the postexercise window, as fully explained in Chapters 2, 3, and 4, you will be encouraged to consume high glycemic, alkaline-yielding carbohydrates to fully replenish your glycogen stores.

From our analyses of hunter-gatherer diets and the nutrient content of wild plants and animals, our research team has shown that the protein intake in the average hunter-gatherer diet would have ranged from 19 to 35 percent of daily calories. Since the protein intake in the normal US diet is about 15 percent of daily energy, we recommend that for peak performance during Stage V of recovery (the period following short-term recovery, lasting until your next preexercise feeding), you boost your protein intake to between 25 and 30 percent of daily calories. At values higher than 30 percent of energy, some people may begin to experience symptoms indicative of the physiologic protein ceiling.

MACRONUTRIENT BALANCE

We've already mentioned that the fat content in Paleolithic diets (28 to 57 percent total calories) was quite a bit higher than values (30 percent or less) recommended by the American Heart Association. We suggest consuming between 30 and 40 percent of your Stage V energy as fat. But remember, you will be eating the bulk of your fats as healthful monounsaturated and polyunsaturated fats (particularly the omega-3s). How about carbohydrates? In hunter-gatherer diets, carbohydrate normally ranged from 22 to 40 percent of total daily energy. Because of your special need as an athlete to restore muscle glycogen on a daily basis, you should boost these values a bit higher. We suggest that Stage V carbohydrate intake should typically range from 35 to 45 percent of calories. As you personalize the Paleo Diet for Athletes to your specific training schedule and body needs, you will be able to fine-tune your daily intake of carbohydrate, fat, and protein.

NUTRITIONAL ADEQUACY

Regardless of your final ratio of protein to fat to carbohydrate, you will be eating an enormously enriched and nutrient-dense diet, compared with what you were probably eating before. We've partially addressed this concept in Chapter 1, where we compared the Paleo Diet for Athletes with the recommended USDA Food Pyramid diet, and also in Table 9.3 on page 174. An even better way to appreciate how much more nutritious your diet will become when you adopt the Paleo Diet for Athletes is by looking at what the average American eats. Figure 9.3 shows the breakdown by food group in the typical US diet. Notice that grains are the highest contributor to total calories (23.9 percent), followed by refined sugars (18.6 percent) and refined vegetable oils (17.8 percent). When you add in dairy products (10.6 percent of total energy) to grains, refined sugars, and refined oils, the total is 70.9 percent of daily calo-

FIGURE 9.3

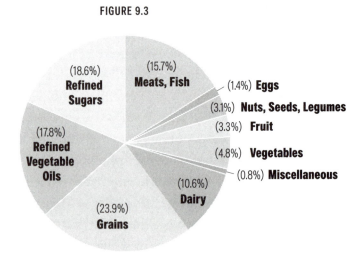

ries. None of these foods would have been on the menu for our Paleolithic ancestors, as fully discussed in Chapter 8.

Refined sugars are devoid of any vitamins or minerals, and except for vitamins E and K, refined vegetable oils are in the same boat. Think of it: More than a third of your daily calories come from foods that lack virtually any vitamins and minerals. When you add in the nutrient lightweights we call cereals and dairy products (check out Table 9.3 on page 174), you can see just how bad the modern diet really is. The staple foods (grains, dairy, refined sugars, and oils) introduced during the agricultural and industrial revolutions have displaced more healthful and nutrient-dense lean meats, seafood, and fresh fruits and vegetables. Once you begin to get these delicious foods back into your diet, not only will your vitamin, mineral, and phytochemical intake improve, but so will your performance.

Chapter 10

THE PALEOLITHIC ATHLETE: THE ORIGINAL CROSS-TRAINER

Ten thousand years sounds like a long, long time ago. But if you think about it in terms of how long the human genus (*Homo*) has existed (2.5 million years), 10,000 years is a mere blink of the eye on an evolutionary time scale. Somewhere in the Middle East about 10,000 years ago, a tiny band of people threw in the towel and abandoned their hunter-gatherer lifestyle. These early renegades became the very first farmers. They forsook a mode of life that had sustained each and every individual within the human genus for the previous 100,000 generations. In contrast, only a paltry 500 human generations have come and gone since the first seeds of agriculture were sown. What started off as a renegade way of making a living became a revolution that would guarantee the complete and absolute eradication of every remaining hunter-gatherer on the planet. At the dawn of the 21st century, we are at the bitter end. Except for perhaps a half dozen uncontacted tribes in South America and a few others on the Andaman Islands in the Bay of Bengal, pure hunter-gatherers have vanished from the face of the earth.

So what difference does that make? Why should 21st-century

endurance athletes care one iota about whether or not there are any hunter-gatherers left? Because once these people are gone, we will no longer be able to examine their lifestyle for invaluable clues to the exercise and dietary patterns that are built into our genes. When I was a track athlete in the late 1960s and early '70s, runners rarely or never lifted weights, and no runners worth their Adidas or Puma flats would even think about swimming. Fast-forward 30 years. What progressive coach now doesn't know the value of cross-training? Those benefits might have been figured out much earlier, had we only taken notice of clues from our hunter-gatherer ancestors.

Very few modern people have ever experienced what it is like to "run with the hunt." One of the notable exceptions is Kim Hill, PhD, an anthropologist at the University of New Mexico who has spent the last 30 years living with and studying the Ache hunter-gatherers of Paraguay and the Hiwi foragers of southwestern Venezuela. His description of these amazing hunts represents a rare glimpse into the activity patterns that would have been required of us all, were it not for the Agricultural Revolution.

I have only spent a long time hunting with two groups, the Ache and the Hiwi. They were very different. The Ache hunted every day of the year if it didn't rain. Recent GPS data I collected with them suggests that about 10 km per day is probably closer to their average distance covered during search. They might cover another 1–2 km per day in very rapid pursuit. Sometimes pursuits can be extremely strenuous and last more than an hour. Ache hunters often take an easy day after any particularly difficult day, and rainfall forces them to take a day or two a week with only an hour or two of exercise. Basically they do moderate days most of the time, and sometimes really hard days usually followed by a very easy day. The difficulty of the terrain is really what killed me (ducking under low branches and vines about once every 20 seconds all day long, and climbing over fallen trees, moving through tangled thorns, etc.). I was often drenched in sweat within an hour of leaving camp, and usually didn't return for 7–9 hours with not more than 30 minutes rest during the day. The Ache seemed to have an easier time because they "walk better" in the forest than me (meaning the vines and branches don't bother them as much). The really hard days when they literally ran me into the ground were long distance pursuits of peccary herds when the Ache hunters move at a fast trot through thick forest for about 2 hours before they catch up with the herd. None of our other grad students could ever keep up with these hunts, and I only kept up because I was in very good shape back in the 1980s when I did this.

The Hiwi on the other hand only hunted about 2–3 days a week and often told me they wouldn't go out on a particular day because they were "tired." They would stay home and work on tools, etc. Their travel was not as strenuous as among the Ache (they often canoed to the hunt site), and their pursuits were usually shorter. But the Hiwi sometimes did amazing long distance walks that would have really hurt the Ache. They would walk to visit another village maybe 80–100 km away and then stay for only an hour or two before returning. This often included walking all night long as well as during the day. When I hunted with Machiguenga, Yora, Yanomamo Indians in the 1980s, my focal man days were much much easier than with the Ache. And virtually all these groups take an easy day after a particularly difficult one.

By the way, the Ache do converse and even sing during some of their search, but long distance peccary pursuits are too difficult for any talking. Basically men talk to each other until the speed gets up around 3km/hour which is a very tough pace in thick jungle. Normal search is more like about 1.5 km/hour, a pretty leisurely pace. Monkey hunts can also be very strenuous because they consist of bursts of sprints every 20–30 seconds (as the mon-

keys are flushed and flee to new cover), over a period of an hour or two without a rest. This feels a lot like doing a very long session of wind sprints.

Both my graduate student Rob Walker and Richard Bribiescas of Harvard were very impressed by Ache performance on the step test. Many of the guys in their mid 30s to mid 50s showed great aerobic conditioning compared to Americans of that age. (VO_2 max/kg body weight is very good.) While hunter-gatherers are generally in good physical condition if they haven't yet been exposed to modern diseases and diets that come soon after permanent outside contact, I would not want to exaggerate their abilities. They are what you would expect if you took a genetic cross section of humans and put them in lifetime physical training at moderate to hard levels. Most hunting is search time not pursuit, thus a good deal of aerobic long distance travel is often involved (over rough terrain and carrying loads if the hunt is successful). I used to train for marathons as a grad student and could run at a 6:00 per mile pace for 10 miles, but the Ache would run me into the ground following peccary tracks through dense bush for a couple of hours. I did the 100 yd in 10.2 in high school (I was a fast pass catcher on my football team), and some Ache men can sprint as fast as me.

But hunter-gatherers do not generally compare to world class athletes, who are probably genetically very gifted and then undergo even more rigorous and specialized training than any forager. So the bottom line is foragers are often in good shape and they look it. They sprint, jog, climb, carry, jump, etc., all day long but are not specialists and do not compare to Olympic athletes in modern societies.

Dr. Hill's wonderful imagery and insight tell us part of the story, but not everything. In this day and age of gender equality, women are just as likely as men, if not more so, to be found at the gym, lifting weights, or out on the trails, running or riding a bike.

In stark contrast, hunter-gatherer women almost never participated in hunting large game animals. Nearly without exception, ethnographic accounts of hunter-gatherers agree on this point. Does this mean that women did no hard aerobic work? Absolutely not! Women routinely gathered food every 2 or 3 days. The fruits of their labors included not only plant foods but also small animals such as tortoises, small reptiles, shellfish, insects, bird eggs, and small mammals. They spent many hours walking to sources of food, water, and wood. Sometimes they would help carry butchered game back to camp. Their foraging often involved strenuous digging, climbing, and then hauling heavy loads back to camp, often while carrying infants and young children. Other common activities, some physically taxing, included tool making, shelter construction, childcare, butchering, food preparation, and visiting. Dances were a major recreation for hunter-gatherers and could take place several nights a week and often last for hours. Table 10.1 shows the caloric costs of typical hunter-gatherer activities and their modern counterparts.

The overall activity pattern of women, like men's, was cyclic, with days of intense physical exertion (both aerobic and resistive) alternating with days of rest and light activity. What hunter-gatherers did in their day-to-day lives appears to be good medicine for modern-day athletes. When Bill Bowerman, a well-known track coach at the University of Oregon, advocated the easy/hard concept back in the '60s, it was thought to be both brilliant and revolutionary. Using his system of easy/hard, athletes recovered more easily from hard workouts and reduced their risk of injury. Ironically, Coach Bowerman's "revolutionary" training strategy was as old as humanity itself. Similarly, during the same decade, weight training combined with swimming was a stunning innovation at Doc Counsilman's world-famous swim program at Indiana University. Now it is the rare world-class endurance coach who doesn't advocate cross-training to improve performance, increase strength, and help pre-

TABLE 10.1

Calories Burned per Hour in Hunter-Gatherer and Modern Activities

HUNTER-GATHERER		MODERN HUMAN	
Activity	Calories Burned	Activity	Calories Burned
Carrying logs	893	Carrying logs	670
Running (cross-country)	782	Running (cross-country)	587
Carrying meat (20 kg) back to camp	706	Climbing hills (20 kg load)	529
Carrying young child	672	Climbing hills (10 kg load)	504
Hunting, stalking prey (carrying bows and spears)	619	Climbing hills (5 kg load)	464
Digging (in a field)	605	Digging (in the garden)	454
Dancing (ceremonial)	494	Dancing (aerobic)	371
Stacking firewood	422	Stacking firewood	317
Butchering large animal	408	Chopping slowly with ax	306
Walking (normal pace in fields and hills)	394	Walking (normal pace in fields and hills)	295
Gathering plant foods	346	Weeding garden	259
Archery	312	Archery	234
Scraping a hide	302	Scraping paint	227
Shelter construction	250	Carpentry	187
Flint knapping	216	Shoe repair	162

Calorie burn (kilocalories per hour) is based on a 176-pound man or 132-pound woman.

vent injury. Once again the rationale behind the success of cross-training can be found in the hunter-gatherer genes in all of us.

WHY WE ARE DESIGNED TO EXERCISE

It may seem obvious, but sometimes the obvious is rarely considered. Do you know why the Aches and, for that matter, all hunter-gatherers exercise? Before we go down this road, let's clarify the word exercise. No adult hunter-gatherers in their right minds would have ever set off on a run or repeatedly lifted a heavy stone simply to expend energy and "get exercise." Virtually all their movement resulted from the day's mandatory activities: food and water procurement, shelter building, journeys, tool making, wood gathering, escape from dangers, child rearing, and social activities. Hunter-gatherers had no choice but to do physical labor of all kinds, big and small, day in and day out, for their entire lives. There were no retirements, vacations, layoffs, career changes, or labor-saving devices. Except for the very young or the very old, everyone did labor of one form or another on a regular basis.

Let's get back to the obvious that you may never have considered. Hunter-gatherers "exercised" because they had to. They had no other choice—period! For all humans living before the Agricultural Revolution, energy input (food) and energy expenditure (exercise) were directly linked. If Stone Age people wanted to eat, they had to hunt, gather, forage, or fish. Now you can see what may have motivated the Ache hunters as they furiously chased that herd of peccaries hour after hour through the tropical forest in Paraguay. Whether you do a long, hard workout or none at all, food is always there for you at the end of the day. Wouldn't it be disappointing to do your long, hard workout and come home to an empty fridge? Would an empty belly motivate you even more on the next workout (hunt) if the intensity of the exercise was directly related to the amount of food in the refrigerator?

In the modern world, we have totally obliterated the ancient evolutionary link between energy expenditure and food intake. As you lazily stroll down the grocery aisle and throw one item after another into the cart, you don't give a single thought to "search time" or "pursuit" of your prey, as Dr. Hill graphically portrayed for us with his description of the Ache hunters. In a supermarket, the search and pursuit times are identical, whether you toss a smoked ham or a head of lettuce into your cart.

The consequences of severing this primeval evolutionary connection between energy expenditure and intake are not pretty. When we eat more energy than we expend, we gain weight. And when we gain weight, our health suffers. Unless you haven't read a newspaper or a magazine lately, you know that we are in the midst of an obesity epidemic in the United States. Two-thirds of all Americans are either overweight or obese, 40 million have type 2 diabetes, and cardiovascular disease is the leading cause of death in this country. There is little doubt in my mind that none of this would be possible without the uncoupling of energy intake and expenditure that was handed to us when we deserted our ancestral hunter-gatherer way of life.

COMPARING THE LIFESTYLES OF HUNTER-GATHERERS AND MODERN ATHLETES

After reading Dr. Hill's description of the Ache hunters (see page 181), you probably have a pretty good feel for how their daily workout compares with yours, whether you're a recreational athlete, an accomplished local and regional endurance athlete, or an elite athlete of national or international caliber. How would the average hunter-gatherer stack up when it comes to high-level endurance performance on race day?

First, let's take a look at the advantages on the hunter-gatherer's side. From the time of weaning until very old age, hunter-gatherer athletes would have done moderate to hard aerobic activity, month in and month out, for their entire lives. They would have regularly rotated hard days with easy ones, and strength activities would have commonly accompanied aerobic work. This pattern of movement would have diminished their chance of injury, so they could get up morning after morning to hunt and gather again and again.

In exercise physiology there is a well-known law stating that aerobic capacity (max VO_2) within an individual may increase based upon exercise frequency, intensity, and duration. Of these three factors, intensity is the most important feature in squeezing out the last bit of aerobic capacity from already trained subjects. The problem is that as intensity increases, the chance of injury and illness also increase. Hunter-gatherers were in it for the long haul. Their objectives were to obtain food day in and day out, year in and year out. Regular high-intensity exercise would have been a liability because injury and illness meant less food. On the other hand, today's endurance athletes don't have to worry about injuries or illness getting in the way of eating; food is always available, no matter what your condition. Accordingly, endurance athletes can take their chances with high-intensity training. As a matter of fact, high-intensity workouts (>85 percent max VO_2) are not an anomaly but rather a requisite to perform at the highest levels upon the world's stage.

As we previously outlined, it is virtually impossible to exercise at >85 percent max VO_2 for extended periods unless muscle glycogen stores are fully topped off. Without daily consumption of high glycemic load carbs, regular high-intensity workouts simply are not feasible. Since high glycemic load carbs were not on the hunter-gatherers' menus, they could not have eked out the last 2 to 5 percent of their genetic aerobic potential by doing high-intensity workouts, as can modern athletes. On the other hand, because they ate more fat and fewer daily meals than we do, their intramuscular triglyceride stores would have been much higher, thereby allowing them to do aerobic work at moderate intensity for extended periods—just what the doctor ordered if you need to go hunting daily and high glycemic carbs don't exist. For the modern-day endurance athlete who is solely interested in maximum performance, an alternative exists: Both can be done. You can maximize muscle glycogen and triglyceride stores by following the diet we have summarized in Chapters 2, 3, 4, and 9.

Because the protein content of their diet was higher than ours, the concentration of the anabolic branched-chain amino acids (leucine, isoleucine, and valine) would have been much higher. As pointed out previously, these dietary amino acids promote muscle resynthesis following exercise and may also delay the onset of fatigue. Unless you are eating lots of lean meats and fish, hunter-gatherers would have had the advantage here. The high protein content of our ancestral diet meant that another amino acid, glutamine, would also have been higher than what you get in a vegetarian diet of beans and brown rice, or simply the standard American junk-food diet. A classic symptom of overtraining in endurance athletes is low blood levels of glutamine.

The trick with glutamine is not just how much you are getting but how much you are losing. Losing excess glutamine is just like not getting enough. If you are eating a high-carb, low-fat diet—pretty much the standard endurance-athlete fare—it is almost certain that your body will be in a slight state of net metabolic acidosis. As we have previously shown, a net acid-producing diet causes your body to excrete more and more of the muscle's glutamine in an attempt to restore acid/base balance. The loss of muscle glutamine from an acid-yielding diet and from insufficient intake of glutamine-rich foods (lean meats, fish, and seafood) may adversely affect performance. Chalk up another advantage to hunter-gatherers.

One of the most important variables leading to athletic success is staying healthy and free of illness and colds. There is little doubt that proper nutrition is absolutely essential for optimizing your immune system. Because hunter-gatherers ate no processed foods, cereal grains, or refined sugars or oils, their intake of trace nutrients (vitamins, minerals, and phytochemicals) was way higher than what the average US citizen gets. Also, they consumed more healthful omega-3 fatty acids than most of us now do. These dietary advantages would have again allowed our hunter-gatherer ancestors to go out day after day to hunt and forage without interruption from illness. For our species, natural selection had no interest in winning a 10-K or marathon; the name of the evolutionary game was adequate calories, not maximum exercise performance.

So let's get down to the nitty-gritty. Was there ever a hunter-gatherer who could have taken home the Olympic gold in any endurance event in the last 30 years? The answer is no. The average hunter-gatherer was clearly more fit than the average American couch potato, as we pointed out in the Introduction. Most foragers, both men and women, could have run any recreational runner into the ground. At the local and regional levels, their best athletes would have been competitive. But there is no comparison between them and elite national and international athletes for two basic reasons.

First are the numbers. The primary determinant of aerobic capacity is maximum oxygen consumption, or max VO_2. If you want to be a world-class endurance athlete, you better choose your parents well, because max VO_2 is almost entirely determined by genetics. One of the highest max VO_2 values ever reliably recorded for an elite male athlete in the United States is about 84 milliliters per kilogram per minute (ml/kg/min). Contrast this value to about 40 ml/kg/min for the average American male. So what happens if the 40 ml/kg/min guy wants to become world class and sets off upon an incredibly intense training program for years and years? Does he have a chance of getting to 84 ml/kg/min? Not even close! Max VO_2 can increase by about 10 to 15 percent in the best of all worlds, but no more. In the United States, we now have more than 260 million residents. Compare this with the fewer than 1,000 Ache hunter-gatherers that Dr. Hill accompanied. If only one person out of 1,000 has a genetically determined max VO_2 of greater than 70 ml/kg/min, then in the US population, there will be 26,000 people who have the genetic potential to perform at extremely high aerobic capacities. Among the Ache hunter-gatherers, only one person in their entire population will have this genetic capacity.

Hunter-gatherers wouldn't stand a chance against Olympian endurance athletes, not only because of the numbers game, but because they were limited to low-octane fuel. Intramuscular triglyceride is a great energy source for moderate to hard exercise lasting for hours, but it can't hold a candle to glycogen when it comes to high level exertion at 85 percent or greater of the VO_2 required to make Olympic champions. Because hunter-gatherers ate less carbohydrate and more fat, along with fewer daily meals, their intramuscular triglyceride stores would have been higher than ours. But they also ate no high glycemic load carbs, so their muscle glycogen reserves would have always been lower than ours. They simply lacked the fuel injection of high glycemic load carbs to restore muscle glycogen concentrations following hard exercise. You now have this option. Not only can you increase muscle glycogen concentrations via careful dietary manipulation but, by following our nutritional plan, you can also increase intramuscular triglycerides.

You, as a 21st-century endurance athlete, are no longer reliant upon the current scientific status quo relating diet to performance—you have the added advantage of knowing how the wisdom of your ancestral dietary background can improve performance. By combining the best of their world with the best of ours, your performance will soar.

PART IV

PUTTING
IT INTO
PRACTICE

Chapter 11

THE TRAINING TABLE

You won't need to buy any exotic foods to properly follow the Paleo Diet for Athletes. No matter if you live in a big city or in the country, the diet's mainstays (lean meats, fish, and fresh fruits and vegetables) are almost always on hand at your local grocery store or supermarket. In Chapter 9 we laid out a comprehensive list of the foods you should limit or exclude from your diet. In this chapter, we'll show you all the delicious, health-giving choices you have the luxury to eat. We'll also give you some practical pointers on how to pull off a Stone Age diet in the 21st century.

YOUR PRIORITY: FRESH FOODS

When you're hungry in the United States, getting something to eat is as easy as the nearest vending machine, fast-food restaurant, or convenience store. But you know what? You have to look long and hard to find "real" food—food that is not adulterated with sugar, salt, refined grains, and unhealthy fats—at any of these places. The incredible overabundance and easy access to processed foods in this country make it easy to derail your plans to improve your diet—particularly when you're famished and need food now.

One of the keys to the Paleo Diet for Athletes is fresh foods. I repeat—fresh foods! They really are so much better for you than their canned, processed, frozen, and prepackaged counterparts that there is no comparison. Canned, sugar-laced peaches don't hold a candle to fresh peaches, either in taste or nutrition. A fatty hot dog with its added salt, sugar, and preservatives, whether it's ground from leftover pork or beef, bears little nutritional resemblance to fresh, lean pork loin or beef flank steak.

As an athlete, you know that small but perceptible extra efforts during training, day in and day out, season in and season out, will pay off over the long haul. Pushing that last interval to the max hurts, but by doing so regularly, you will become fitter and stronger and your performance will improve—maybe by only 1 to 2 percent, but, as we pointed out in Chapter 8, that seemingly minuscule difference can be huge when it comes to racing. This same principle holds true with the foods you eat. By methodically eating fresh, wholesome foods whenever and wherever you can, the overall trace nutrient (vitamins, minerals, and phytochemicals) density of your diet will ultimately improve. And, as we have previously pointed out, there is a mountain of scientific evidence to show that your immune system functions better when properly nourished. A healthy immune system can more effectively ward off illness and help you to recover more rapidly from injuries, thereby allowing you to train at higher levels. Do yourself a favor—get fresh fruits, veggies, lean meats, and seafood into your diet whenever you can.

If you're like most Americans, fresh fruits and veggies occupy a small drawer in your fridge, where they get wilted, soft, and brown, and they end up thrown out more often than eaten. This will change with your new diet, and here are some practical pointers to help you get more fresh produce into your meal plans.

1. Thoroughly wash your fresh veggies and put them in plastic bags before you put them in your refrigerator.

These simple steps will prevent wilting, increase storage life, and reduce contaminants.

2. Buy enough produce to last for no more than 5 to 7 days. It's better to get fresh supplies at least once a week.

3. If food preparation time is an issue, you can purchase a lot of produce that's packaged and ready to go with little or no prep. Examples include shredded lettuce and salad mixes; precut broccoli florets; baby spinach leaves; washed and peeled baby carrots; precut chunks of melon, pineapple, and other fruit; and shelled nuts. But remember, you'll pay a bit more for the convenience.

4. Make a very large mixed salad at the beginning of the week and put it in a large, sealed plastic container; dish out portions as needed throughout the week.

Organic Produce

How about organic produce—any advantages to it? Should you pay the higher price? Table 11.1 on page 198 is adapted from the results of a study that compiled numerous publications comparing the nutrient content of organic versus conventionally produced plant foods. Data from this study as well as other comprehensive reviews of the literature generally conclude that, except for a slightly higher vitamin C content and possibly protein in organically produced vegetables (but not fruit), no differences exist for any other vitamins or minerals. So, if you're contemplating buying organic produce for its greater nutritional value, it's simply not worth it.

However, do note that the levels of nitrate in organically produced fruits and veggies are consistently lower than in conventional produce. Both the World Health Organization and the Environmental Protection Agency (EPA) in the United States have set limits for daily nitrate intake (1.6 milligrams/nitrate/kilogram body weight). Generally, both conventional and organic fruits and vegetables fall below acceptable limits. Similarly, some studies have

TABLE 11.1

Comparison of Organic versus Conventionally Grown Plant Foods. Percentage of Studies in Which Organic Crops Have Increased, Remained the Same, or Decreased Compared to Conventionally Grown Crops.

NUTRIENT	% INCREASED	% REMAINED SAME	% DECREASED	NO. OF STUDIES
Vitamin C	58.3	33.3	8.3	36
Beta-carotene	38.5	38.5	23.0	13
Zinc	25.0	56.3	18.7	16
B vitamins	12.5	75.0	12.5	16
Calcium	44.7	42.5	12.8	47
Protein	100	0	0	3
Magnesium	37.7	53.3	8.0	45
Nitrate	12.5	25.0	62.5	40
Iron	42.9	40.0	17.1	35

demonstrated reduced amounts of pesticides in organic produce. Elevated environmental and dietary exposure to both nitrates and pesticides are associated with elevated risk for developing certain cancers. If either of these issues is of concern to you, then go with organic produce.

Acceptable Fresh Vegetables

Potatoes maintain high glycemic loads and should be eaten only during the postexercise window, as explained in Chapter 4. Otherwise, virtually all fresh vegetables are perfectly acceptable: asparagus, parsnip, radish, broccoli, lettuce, mushrooms, dandelion greens, mustard greens, watercress, purslane, onions, green onions, carrots, parsley, squash of all varieties, all peppers, artichokes, tomatoes, cauliflower, cabbage, Brussels sprouts, celery, cucumbers, tomatillos, collards, Swiss chard, endive, beet greens, beets, turnips, rutabaga, kohlrabi, kale, eggplant, pumpkin, sweet potatoes, turnip greens, spinach, seaweed, yams.

Acceptable Fresh Fruit

As with vegetables, any fresh fruit you can get your hands on is fair game. The only exceptions are dried fruits (such as raisins, dates, and figs), which, like potatoes, have high glycemic loads and should be limited to the postexercise window. Reach for these and other fruits anytime: apples, oranges, pears, peaches, plums, kiwifruit, pomegranates, grapes, watermelon, cantaloupe, honeydew melon, cassava melon, pineapple, guava, nectarines, apricots, strawberries, blackberries, blueberries, raspberries, avocado, carambola, cherimoya, cherries, grapefruit, lemon, lime, lychee, mango, papaya, passion fruit, persimmon, tangerine, starfruit, gooseberries, boysenberries, cranberries, rhubarb.

GETTING THE FATTY ACID BALANCE RIGHT

As you know by now, getting the fatty acid balance right is essential in replicating hunter-gatherer diets with modern foods. For our Stone Age ancestors, this problem was a no-brainer. Because their only food choices were wild plants and animals, the fatty acid balance always fell within healthful limits. By following our simple advice of eating lean meats along with healthful oils, you won't have to give a second thought to the correct balance, either.

Acceptable Domestic Animal Products

Always choose lean cuts of meat, such as the examples that follow, and trim all visible fat from the product before cooking: beef flank steak, top sirloin steak, London broil, chuck steak, extra-lean ground beef (drain excess fat); pork loin and pork chops; skinless breasts of chicken, turkey, and game hens.

Eggs are actually a high-fat food; a single egg averages 62 percent fat by energy. We recommend that you limit egg consumption to six per week and buy omega-3-enriched eggs whenever possible.

Organ meats, except for marrow and brains, of commercially

produced animals are quite lean. However, the liver and kidneys, which cleanse and detoxify the animal's body, frequently contain high concentrations of environmental contaminants. We recommend eating only calves' liver because virtually all calves slaughtered in the United States haven't found their way to the toxic feedlot environment; all are pasture fed. Brains contain high concentrations of omega-3 fatty acids and were relished by our hunter-gatherer ancestors. However, because of the small risk of developing prion disease (mad cow disease), we do not advise eating the brains of any animal, domestic or wild. Cholesterol-lowering monounsaturated fatty acids are the dominant (about 65 percent) fatty acids in marrow and tongue, both of which are quite healthful and tasty. Beef, lamb, and pork sweetbreads are also lean and contain healthful fatty acids.

Grass-Fed or Free-Ranging Meats

If you can find it, grass-fed (or free-ranging) meat will always be a better choice than domestic beef, pork, or poultry because it is richer in healthful omega-3 fatty acids, lower in fat (like wild game), and less likely to be tainted with hormones and pesticides. Figure 11.1 contrasts the total fat percentage among wild game, grass-fed beef, and feedlot-produced beef, while Table 11.2 compares the differences in fatty acid content.

One of the largest mail-order suppliers of grass-fed meats in the United States is Slanker's Grass Fed Meats: http://texasgrassfed beef.com/. You can often find organically produced beef and other meat items in health food stores. However, organic meat and grass-fed meat are not always one and the same. Frequently, organic beef or buffalo is fattened with "organically produced" grains, yielding the same poor ratio of omega-6 to omega-3 found in feedlot animals.

Commercially Available Game Meat and Other Exotic Meats

In the United States, the commercial sale of hunted, wild game is prohibited. So, unless you are a hunter, the only way to obtain

FIGURE 11.1

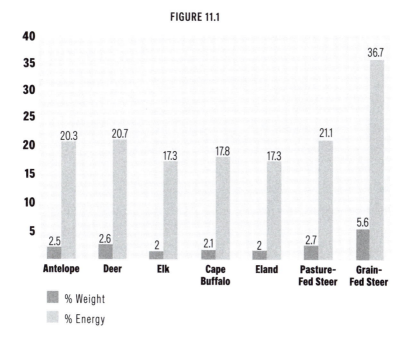

game meat is to purchase meat that has been produced on game farms or ranches—but even that, except for buffalo, is difficult to find. (One of the largest mail-order suppliers of game meat that can be found in the United States is Game Sales International: www.gamesalesintl.com.) Generally, this meat is superior to feedlot products, but it may not be as lean or as healthful as wild

TABLE 11.2

Comparison of Animals' Muscle Fatty Acid Concentrations
(mg fatty acids/100 g sample)

FATTY ACID	ELK	MULE DEER	ANTELOPE	PASTURE-FED STEER	GRAIN-FED STEER
SAT	610	989	895	910	1,909
MUFA	507	612	610	793	1,856
PUFA	625	746	754	262	341
Omega-3 PUFA	178	225	216	61	46
Omega-6 PUFA	448	524	536	138	243

SAT = total saturated fatty acids; MUFA = total monounsaturated fatty acids; PUFA = total polyunsaturated fatty acids game. It is not an uncommon practice to feed grain to elk and buffalo to fatten them before slaughter.

Other exotic meats you may want to try include kangaroo, venison, elk, alligator, reindeer, pheasant, quail, Muscovy duck, goose, wild boar, ostrich, rattlesnake, emu, turtle, African springbok antelope, New Zealand Cervena deer, squab, wild turkey, caribou, bear, buffalo, rabbit, and goat.

Fish

We no longer live in a healthy, pristine, unpolluted environment; pesticides, heavy metals, chemicals, and other toxic compounds frequently make their way into our food chain. No one knows precisely how low-level exposure to these toxins affects health over the course of a lifetime. It is prudent to try to reduce our exposure to toxic compounds whenever possible, but it is virtually impossible to eliminate exposure to environmental toxins because they now permeate even such places as the Antarctic. Fish can frequently contain high concentrations of mercury and pesticides. To minimize your risk of eating contaminated fish, avoid eating freshwater fish from lakes and rivers, particularly the Great Lakes and other industrialized areas. Also avoid large, long-lived fish such as swordfish, tuna, and shark because they tend to concentrate mercury in their flesh.

Desirable commercially available fish include salmon, halibut, herring, trout, catfish, bass, mackerel, cod, scrod, northern pike, sunfish, haddock, grouper, walleye, flatfish, red snapper, monkfish, rockfish, perch tilapia, striped bass, turbot, mullet, bluefish, drum, eel, and orange roughy.

Shellfish

About 15 to 20 years ago, people were told to avoid shellfish, which were believed to have too much cholesterol. It's true that shellfish are high in cholesterol—but the good news is that we don't have to avoid them. It turns out that dietary cholesterol has a very small influence upon blood cholesterol levels when the food's total saturated fat content is low. Table 11.3 shows that all shellfish are extremely low in both saturated and total fat, despite having relatively high cholesterol concentrations. We encourage you to eat as much shellfish as you like.

Healthful Oils, Nuts, and Seeds

Table 11.4 on page 204 provides you with all the information you need to pick out the most healthful oils. Oils you use for cooking need to be stable and more resistant to the oxidizing effects of heat, whereas those you use in your salads don't. Saturated fatty acids (SAT) are the most stable and heat resistant, followed by monounsaturated fatty acids (MUFA), then polyunsaturated fatty acids (PUFA). Because SAT elevate blood cholesterol levels, your choice of cooking oils should be high in MUFA and relatively low in both SAT and PUFA. Good oils for cooking include olive, avocado, and canola. All oils, regardless of their fatty acid makeup,

TABLE 11.3

Comparison of Cholesterol and Fat in Shellfish, Bacon, and Cheese (100 g portions)

FOOD	CHOLESTEROL (MG)	SATURATED FAT (G)	TOTAL FAT (% TOTAL ENERGY)
Shrimp	200	0.4	15
Crayfish	114	0.2	11
Lobster	95	0.2	9
Abalone	85	0.2	7
Whelk	65	0.03	3
Crab	59	1	10
Oysters	50	0.5	26
Clams	34	1	12
Scallops	33	0.1	8
Mussels	28	0.4	23
Bacon	107	14.3	77
Cheddar cheese	104	21.0	74

oxidize during cooking. Consequently, you should not fry at high or searing heats; instead, sauté at low to medium temperatures and cook for shorter periods.

The stability of oil is determined not only by its relative ratio of SAT to MUFA to PUFA but also by the type of PUFA. Omega-3 PUFA are more fragile than omega-6 PUFA because of the location and number of the double bonds in the fatty acid molecule. Consequently, flaxseed and walnut oils should not be used for cooking because of their high concentrations of total PUFA and

TABLE 11.4

Fatty Acid Composition of Salad and Cooking Oils

TYPE OF OIL	OMEGA-6:OMEGA-3 RATIO	% MUFA	% PUFA	% SAT
Flaxseed	0.24	20.2	66.0	9.4
Canola	2.00	58.9	29.6	7.1
Walnut	5.08	22.8	63.3	9.1
Soybean	7.5	23.3	57.9	14.4
Wheat germ	7.9	15.1	61.7	18.8
Avocado	13.0	67.9	13.5	11.6
Olive	13.1	72.5	8.4	13.5
Rice bran	20.9	39.3	35.0	19.7
Oat	21.9	35.1	40.9	19.6
Tomato seed	22.1	22.8	53.1	19.7
Corn	83.0	24.2	58.7	12.7
Sesame	137.2	39.7	41.7	14.2
Cottonseed	258	17.8	51.9	25.9
Sunflower	472.9	19.5	65.7	10.3
Grape seed	696	16.1	69.9	9.6
Poppy seed	extremely high (no omega-3s)	19.7	62.4	13.5
Hazelnut	extremely high (no omega-3s)	78	10.2	7.4
Peanut	extremely high (no omega-3s)	46.2	32	16.9
Coconut	extremely high (no omega-3s)	5.8	1.8	86.5
Palm	extremely high (no omega-3s)	11.4	1.6	81.5
Almond	extremely high (no omega-3s)	70	17.4	8.2
Apricot kernel	extremely high (no omega-3s)	60	29.3	6.3
Safflower	extremely high (no omega-3s)	14.4	74.6	6.2

MUFA = monounsaturated fatty acids; PUFA = polyunsaturated fatty acids; SAT = saturated fatty acids omega-3 PUFA. However, both oils are good choices for dressing salads. Flaxseed oil is the richest vegetable source of omega-3 fatty acids. Pour it over steamed veggies or incorporate it into a marinade added to meat and seafood after cooking. Both strategies are great ways to get more omega-3 fatty acids into your diet.

Because of their high MUFA and low SAT and PUFA, olive and avocado oils are good choices for cooking and add a wonderful flavor to any dish. However, both have too many omega-6s to omega-3s (13:1). You can lower the ratio by mixing either oil with canola oil prior to cooking. Strive to use a bit more flaxseed oil than olive oil on a daily basis, and you will get your fatty acid balance correct.

The only oils we recommend are flaxseed, canola, walnut, avocado, and olive. Although soybean and wheat germ oils appear on paper to have acceptable fatty acid balances, both are concentrated sources of antinutrients known as lectins. Wheat germ oil is the highest dietary source of the lectin wheat germ agglutinin (WGA), and soybean oil contains soybean agglutinin (SBA). In animal models, both of those lectins have been shown to adversely influence gastrointestinal and immune function. Similarly, peanuts are not nuts but legumes. Peanut oil, just like soybean oil, is a concentrated source of the lectin peanut agglutinin (PNA).

What's Wrong with Peanut Oil and Peanuts?

If you look at peanut oil fatty acid composition in Table 11.4, you'll see that it contains little saturated fat, and almost 80 percent is made up of cholesterol-lowering monounsaturated and polyunsaturated fats. Hence, on the surface, you might think that peanut oil would be helpful in preventing the artery-clogging process (atherosclerosis) that underlies coronary heart disease. Well, your idea is not a whole lot different than what nutritional scientists believed—that is, until they got around to actually testing peanut oil in laboratory animals. Starting in the 1960s and continuing into the 1980s, scientists found peanut oil to be unexpectedly atherogenic, causing arterial plaques to form in rabbits, rats, and primates—only a single study showed otherwise. In fact, peanut oil is so atherogenic that it continues to be routinely fed to rabbits to stimulate atherosclerosis to study the disease itself.

At first, it was not clear how a seemingly healthful oil could be so toxic in such a wide variety of animals. Then, in a series of experiments, David Kritchevsky, PhD, and colleagues at the Wistar Institute in Philadelphia showed that peanut oil lectin (PNA) was most likely responsible for the artery-clogging properties. Lectins are fairly large protein molecules, and most nutritional scientists had assumed that digestive enzymes in the gut would degrade it into its component amino acids, so the intact lectin molecule would not be able to get into the bloodstream to do its dirty work. But they were wrong. It turned out that lectins were highly resistant to the gut's protein-shearing enzymes. An experiment conducted by Dr. Wang and colleagues and published in the prestigious medical journal *Lancet* revealed that PNA gets into the bloodstream intact in as little as 1 to 4 hours after participants ate a handful of roasted, salted peanuts. Even though the concentrations of PNA in the blood were quite low, they were still at amounts known to cause atherosclerosis in experimental animals. Lectins are a lot like superglue—it doesn't take much. Because these proteins contain carbohydrates, they can bind to a wide variety of cells in the body, including the cells lining the arteries. And indeed, it was found that PNA did its damage to the arteries by binding to a specific sugar receptor. So, the practical point here is to stay away from both peanuts and peanut oil. There are better choices.

How about Canola Oil?

One of the enormous achievements of humankind is the creation of the Internet, with its incredible potential for the communication of information and ideas. Unfortunately, the downside of the Web is its lack of checks and balances. Anybody can say literally anything, with absolutely no regard to any semblance of the truth. In contrast, scientists communicate their ideas to their colleagues and to the world through peer-reviewed publications. Although this process can and does stifle creativity, it also prevents sheer nonsense from filtering to the surface. Unfortunately, the same cannot be said for some of the information you can download from the Internet. Such is the case for canola oil, which is totally and nonobjectively trashed by a number of Web sites. If you direct your Web browser to Pub Med (www.ncbi.nlm.nih.gov/entrez/query.fcgi) and investigate canola oil's true effects upon health and well-being, you get a much different story.

We recommend canola oil because it is high in monounsaturated fats (58.9 percent) and low in saturated fats (7.1 percent), and it has an omega-6:omega-3 ratio (2:0) that mimics the ratio found in preagricultural diets. These fatty acid characteristics have been shown in numerous clinical trials to reduce the risk of atherosclerosis and heart disease, currently the number one cause of death in the United States.

Canola oil comes from the seeds of the rape plant (*Brassica rapa* or *Brassica campestris*), which is a close relative of broccoli, cabbage, Brussels sprouts, and kale. Humans have eaten cabbage and its relatives since prior to historical times. In their original form, rape plants produced a seed oil that contained high levels (20 to 50 percent) of a monounsaturated fat called erucic acid, which was shown to cause a wide variety of deleterious health effects in laboratory animals. In the early 1970s, plant breeders from Canada developed a strain of rape that produced a seed with less than 2 percent erucic acid and christened this new variety canola. The erucic acid content of commercially available canola oil averages 0.6 percent. Numerous animal experiments show that the previous health effects identified with erucic acid do not occur at this low concentration; in fact, canola oil prevents potentially fatal heart arrhythmias in animal models. There is no credible scientific evidence showing that canola oil is harmful to humans.

Nuts and Seeds

Except for peanuts, we recommend all nuts and seeds as healthful components of the Paleo Diet for Athletes. Many people have food allergies, and nuts are one of the more common ones. Always listen to your body; if you know or suspect that nuts do not agree with you, then don't eat them. This advice holds for all foods, including shellfish, which also frequently cause allergies. In Table 11.5, you can see the fatty acid balance for commonly available nuts. Notice that except for walnuts and macadamia nuts, all other nuts maintain high ratios of omega-6 to omega-3. The ideal ratio in your diet should be about 2:1 or slightly lower. Because nuts are so calorically dense, they can very easily derail the best-laid dietary plans. If you use nuts as staples—rather than lean meats, seafood, healthful oils, and fresh fruits and veggies—chances are that you will not get sufficient omega-3 fatty acids in your diet. Enjoy nuts, but use them sparingly.

CHEATING

The Paleo Diet for Athletes is actually not a diet at all but, rather, a lifelong pattern of eating that will, besides improving athletic performance, normalize body weight and reduce the risk for heart disease, cancer, and osteoporosis. It also plays a significant role in treating diabetes, hypertension, high blood cholesterol, inflammatory gut conditions, and certain autoimmune diseases. The positive health effects are thoroughly explained in *The Paleo Diet*.

In order for most people to make lifelong dietary changes, a number of behavioral techniques seem to be helpful. When giving certain foods up, most people do better psychologically when they know that they do not have to completely and forever ditch some of their favorite foods. The Paleo Diet for Athletes allows for what we call the 95:5 rule, which means that what you do infrequently will have little negative impact on the favorable effects of what you do most of the time.

Most people consume about 20 meals per week, plus snacks.

TABLE 11.5

Fatty Acid Composition of Nuts and Seeds

NUT	OMEGA-6:OMEGA-3 RATIO	% MUFA	% PUFA	%SAT
Walnuts	4.2	23.6	69.7	6.7
Macadamia nuts	6.3	81.6	1.9	16.5
Pecans	20.9	59.5	31.5	9
Pine nuts	31.6	39.7	44.3	16
Cashews	47.6	61.6	17.6	20.8
Pistachios	51.9	55.5	31.8	12.7
Sesame seeds	58.2	39.5	45.9	14.6
Hazelnuts (filberts)	90	78.7	13.6	7.7
Pumpkin seeds	114.4	32.5	47.6	19.9
Brazil nuts	377.9	36.2	38.3	25.5
Sunflower seeds	472.9	20	69	11
Almonds	Extremely high (no omega-3s)	66.6	25.3	8.1
Coconut	Extremely high (no omega-3s)	4.4	1.3	94.3
Peanuts	Extremely high (no omega-3s)	52.1	33.3	14.6

MUFA = monounsaturated fatty acids; PUFA = polyunsaturated fatty acids; SAT = saturated fatty acids

It's perfectly acceptable and pleasurable if one or two of those meals include any food you want, as long as lean meats, seafood, fruits, vegetables, healthful oils, and nuts and seeds make up roughly 95 percent of the balance of your weekly calories. The Paleo Diet for Athletes allows moderate alcohol and coffee consumption or occasional chocolates, bagels, or whatever your favorite food may be. Cheating and digressions now and then are of great emotional benefit, but—so long as they make up 5 percent or less of the overall diet—will have little impact on athletic performance and health effects. This recommendation, of course, does not include the non-Paleo foods that may be eaten immediately before, during, and after some workouts, as described in Chapters 2, 3, and 4.

EATING OUT AND ON THE ROAD

Many restaurants cater to vegetarians and increasingly more are offering menus for low-carb dieters. But, to date, none offer Paleo meals. However, by ordering carefully, you can usually approximate the Paleo Diet for Athletes. The best strategy for breakfast is to order either an egg dish or some kind of lean meat along with a bowl of fresh fruit. Poached eggs are a good bet because they will not be prepared with the wrong kinds of fat, which invariably accompany omelets and fried eggs. Also, poached or hard-boiled eggs are less likely to contain oxidized cholesterol, a by-product of fried eggs that especially promotes atherosclerosis in laboratory animals.

Lunch and dinner are usually no problem; most restaurants offer some kind of fish, seafood, or lean-meat entrée for these meals. Remember, the key is to get a big piece of lean protein as your main dish. Strive for simplicity: Forsake fancy entrées made with complicated sauces for simpler versions. To even out the acid load, order a salad (hold the croutons) and request steamed veggies instead of the compulsory bread or potatoes. For the salad dressing, vinegar and oil—particularly olive oil—are fine in a pinch. See if you can get fresh fruit for dessert.

For road trips, pack a cooler with fruits, veggies, salads, and leftover meats and seafood. A good strategy at dinnertime is to cook about two or three times as much meat or seafood as you will eat, and keep the rest for breakfast and lunch the next few days. For example, barbecue a big chunk of London broil for dinner one evening, refrigerate the leftovers, and the next day slice the beef into a mixed salad and toss with flaxseed oil and lemon juice. Voilà—an instant Paleo picnic lunch! If you don't have a cooler, check out the deli or seafood section of a supermarket to get cooked meat or shrimp. Proceed to the produce section and grab some fresh fruit, avocados, and crisp veggies. Always keep a sharp knife and some utensils in your car, so you don't have to deal with cutting up meat with a plastic knife.

Chapter 12

PALEO RECIPES

The bottom line in creating Paleo Diet recipes with modern foods is to keep it simple. Our Stone Age ancestors ate virtually all of their foods fresh and minimally processed. If you do likewise, your health and performance will soar. Whenever possible, choose your foods in this order: (1) fresh, (2) frozen, (3) canned. When you prepare Stone Age recipes with contemporary foods, bear in mind that you want to make sure the ingredients are free of grains, dairy products, salt, refined sugars, legumes (including peanut), and yeast and yeast-containing foods such as baked goods, pickled foods, vinegar, and fermented foods and beverages. Be sure your food choices contain only permitted oils, and remember to select the leanest cuts of meats and trim away visible fat. Keep in mind the foundation of the Paleo Diet for Athletes: lean meats, seafood, and fresh fruits and veggies!

PALEO FOOD REPLACEMENTS

Our modern palettes have become jaded with the never-ending onslaught of salt, starch, sugar, and fat laced everywhere into processed foods. After a few weeks of Paleo dieting, you will notice a wonderful change emerging in your taste buds.

Subtle flavors that you never knew existed will materialize. You won't need to add sugar to your fresh strawberries—they will taste delightfully sweet all by themselves. Avocados will have a luscious, creamy flavor that needs no added salt or anything else. Once you have given up sweet, sticky doughnuts, a fresh nectarine will never have tasted so good. Spices you never knew existed will enliven your steaks and roasts, and you will be able to discern these subtle yet incredible flavors because you will no longer be drowning your taste buds in salt and refined sugars.

Vinegar: Vinegar contains acetic acid in a 5 percent solution and consequently contributes to the net metabolic acidosis that plagues the typical American diet. Additionally, unless the vinegar is distilled, it will contain small quantities of yeast—another non-Paleo food substance that should be avoided. We recommend you replace vinegar in your recipes with either lemon or lime juice.

Salt: One of the toughest modern dietary routines to kick is the salt habit. Salt is added to almost everything. In fact, most of us take in an appalling 10 grams per day! These salt substitutes will not only help you get the salt out but will enliven your recipes: lemon crystals, lemon pepper devoid of salt, powdered garlic, powdered onion, ground red pepper, chili powder, black pepper, cumin, turmeric, celery seeds, coriander seeds, and any commercially available salt-free spice mixtures.

Sugars: There is absolutely no doubt that our Stone Age ancestors had a sweet tooth. Field studies of hunter-gatherers show that they would endure enormous numbers of bee stings to get hold of honey. During certain times of the year, they would gorge themselves with a pound or more of honey a day. However, they couldn't eat it day in and day out, all year long, because it simply wasn't available. Similarly, other naturally occurring sweets such as dates, figs, or maple sugar would have been available seasonally for only a few short weeks during the entire year. We should follow the hunter-gatherer example and get refined sugars out of our diets. That doesn't mean you have to ban sweets entirely—you can eat all of the fresh fruit that you like, and you can add certain spices such as vanilla, ginger, mint leaves, cinnamon, and nutmeg to recipes. Also, it is entirely permissible to add fruit purees sweetened with lemon or lime juice to your recipes.

Fat: Replace the "bad" fats (lard, butter, margarine, and shortening) with these oils: olive, flaxseed, walnut, canola, and avocado. Remember that flaxseed and walnut oils are delicate and susceptible to breakdown by heat and therefore should be used after, not during, cooking.

Alcohol: Perhaps the most important component of any dietary plan is getting people to stick with it. The best way to make you instantly give up on the Paleo Diet for Athletes—or any diet, for that matter—is to make "Thou Shalt Nots." You will notice from Chapter 9 that there are no—repeat, no—absolute requirements in the Paleo Diet for Athletes. We have deliberately incorporated this strategy into our nutritional plan to help you with compliance. If you enjoy an occasional glass of wine with your dinner—have it! Realize that you have a certain number of open meals during the week (as fully outlined in Chapter 11), which allow you to enjoy any food you like. However, bear in mind, the further you deviate from the basic plan, the less likely you are to achieve your health and performance goals. Obviously, alcohol was not part of any hunter-gatherer diet, and we do not recommend regular consumption of alcohol for athletes, either. However, it's perfectly acceptable to use certain alcoholic beverages such as wine to add flavor to marinades and sauces. Much of the alcohol is vaporized during cooking.

RECIPES

Meat Dishes
Pork

BARCELONA PORK LOIN

⅓ cup chili powder
1 teaspoon dried leaf thyme
1 teaspoon Mexican oregano
⅛ teaspoon cloves
⅛ teaspoon allspice
1–2 tablespoons chicken stock
2 pounds boneless pork loin
½ cup water

Preheat the oven to 350°F. In a small bowl, mix together the chili powder, thyme, oregano, cloves, allspice, and stock to form a paste. Thoroughly rub the paste over all sides of the pork loin. Put the pork loin in a small lidded roasting pan. Add the water to the pan. Cover the pan and place in the oven for 2 hours, until tender. Remove the pork from the oven and let stand, covered, for 30 minutes before slicing.

Serves 4.

BARBECUED LEMON-PEPPER PORK STEAKS

1 onion, minced
2 teaspoons thyme
¼ teaspoon ground black pepper
¼ teaspoon ground red pepper
2 cloves garlic, minced

½ cup olive oil

6 pork steaks, each 1" thick

⅓ cup fresh lemon juice

1½ teaspoons grated lemon peel

Warm up your grill. Combine the onion, thyme, and ground peppers in a small bowl. Add the garlic and oil, and thoroughly blend the ingredients with a whisk. Mop the steaks with a paper towel, and then smother with the lemon juice. Brush both sides of the steaks with some of the sauce. Briefly flame the steaks over high heat and sprinkle with the lemon peel. Put the steaks on a cool side of the grill and baste liberally with the remaining sauce. Cook about 10 minutes per side under a closed grill.

Serves 6.

OVEN-BAKED PECAN PORK CHOPS

1 egg, beaten

2 tablespoons olive oil

1 tablespoon dry sherry or water
    Ground ginger and garlic powder

4 lean pork chops

¼ cup finely chopped pecans

Preheat the oven to 350°F. In a shallow bowl, beat together the egg, oil, and sherry. Add ginger and garlic powder to taste. Dip the chops in the mixture, and then coat evenly with the pecans. Arrange the pork chops in a single layer in a glass baking dish coated with additional oil. Bake for 30 minutes, turn, and bake until tender, about 20 minutes longer.

Serves 4.

MEXICO CITY 1968 PORK LOIN APPETIZER

½ pound pork tenderloin
3 tablespoons olive oil
1 small carrot, sliced
1 small onion, sliced
4 bay leaves
2 teaspoons minced garlic
2 large tomatoes, peeled and chopped
1 teaspoon black peppercorns
2 stems fresh rosemary
2 tablespoons lime juice

In a large skillet, brown the pork loin in the oil, and then brown the carrot and onion. Place in a 4- to 6-quart pot lightly coated with olive oil, and add the bay leaves, garlic, tomatoes, peppercorns, and rosemary. Add water to cover, and simmer for 1½ hours, adding the lime juice during the last few minutes. Remove the pork loin and thinly slice it. Place in a dish and cover with the vegetables and sauce. Discard the bay leaves before serving.

Serves 6.

Chicken and Poultry

ANKARA CHICKEN

4 whole skinless chicken breasts
1 large carrot, cut into 1" pieces
1 large rib celery, cut into 1" pieces
½ onion, sliced
2 bay leaves
6 peppercorns

  ½ teaspoon cumin
  ½ pound shelled walnuts
  3 cloves garlic
     Freshly ground black pepper
  2 tablespoons olive oil
  1 teaspoon paprika

Place the chicken breasts, carrot, celery, onion, bay leaves, and peppercorns in a large Dutch oven. Add cold water to cover the chicken by 1½". Heat to a boil, and skim off all froth and solids that rise to the top. Reduce heat to low. Simmer gently until the chicken is tender, 20 to 30 minutes. Remove the chicken and allow to cool, then debone it. Set aside the cooking liquid, discarding the bay leaves. In a blender or food processor, combine the cumin, walnuts, garlic, and ground pepper. Blend well, and then pour in 1 cup of the cooking liquid. Continue blending until smooth. Cut the chicken breasts in half crosswise, and shred the meat. Mix with the sauce and add ground pepper as needed. Arrange the meat on a platter. Blend the oil and paprika together, and drizzle over the chicken.

Serves 6.

LEBANESE WALNUT CHICKEN

     1 tablespoon olive oil
     ½ teaspoon powdered cinnamon
     ½ teaspoon ground nutmeg
  2 or 3 cloves
     ⅓ pound seedless grapes
    1½ cups dry white wine
     1 tablespoon lemon juice
     2 tablespoons chicken stock
     1 tablespoon finely chopped onion

2 tablespoons walnut meal
Freshly ground black pepper
½ teaspoon dried thyme
¼ teaspoon chili powder
2¼ pounds skinless chicken breasts
2 large tomatoes, sliced
1 tablespoon chopped walnuts

Preheat the oven to 375°F. Pour the oil in a skillet over medium heat. Add the cinnamon, nutmeg, and cloves. Sear for a few seconds, then take out the cloves. Add the whole grapes and cook for 2 minutes. Add the wine, lemon juice, and stock, and cook to reduce the mixture by half (roughly 8 minutes). When the sauce has reduced to a syrupy consistency, remove from the heat and let cool. Mix the onion, walnut meal, pepper, thyme, and chili powder together in a bowl, and pat onto each chicken breast. Place the chicken breasts in a flat glass baking dish lightly coated with olive oil, and bake for 35 to 40 minutes, or until done. Place on a bed of sliced tomatoes, pour the sauce over them, and sprinkle with the chopped walnuts.

Serves 2.

CHICKEN À LA MADRID

4 large skinless chicken breasts
2 red bell peppers, chopped
1 green bell pepper, chopped
6 plum tomatoes, peeled
2 onions, finely chopped
½ teaspoon crushed Anaheim chilies
1 small sprig fresh rosemary
3 cloves garlic, crushed
1 pint reconstituted lime juice

1 pint boiling water
½ teaspoon cayenne pepper
Freshly ground black pepper

Place all the ingredients into a large saucepan. Bring to a boil, then reduce the heat and simmer for 40 minutes, until the chicken is tender.

Serves 4.

ZESTY GRILLED TURKEY BREAST

5 cloves garlic, minced
¼ cup lime juice
¼ cup lemon juice
¼ cup flaxseed oil
1 teaspoon paprika
1 teaspoon cumin
1 teaspoon turmeric
½ teaspoon white pepper
1½ pounds turkey breast slices, pounded ¼" thick
1 tablespoon olive oil (for basting)

Mix all sauce ingredients together in a blender. Grill or broil the turkey breasts while brushing with the oil to keep them moist. Grill on each side for about 5 minutes. Top each slice with about 2 to 3 tablespoons of the sauce.

Serves 4.

ROASTED CORNISH GAME HENS

3 Cornish hens (1½ pounds each)
½ cup unsweetened applesauce
2 teaspoons lemon juice

¼ teaspoon rubbed sage

¼ teaspoon freshly ground black pepper

¼ teaspoon paprika

¼ teaspoon garlic powder

Preheat the oven to 350°F. Remove the skins from the hens and cut the hens in half lengthwise. Place in a shallow glass roasting pan lightly coated with olive oil. Combine the applesauce and remaining ingredients. Brush half over the hens, and set aside the remaining mixture. Bake for 30 minutes. Baste the hens with the reserved applesauce mixture, and bake for 15 to 30 minutes longer, or until done.

Serves 6.

Beef

SIRLOIN TIPS AND TOMATO SAUCE

1½ pounds tomatoes, peeled

2 tablespoons lemon juice

1 onion, thinly sliced

2 tablespoons olive oil

1½ pounds sirloin tips, cubed

1 teaspoon garlic powder

½ teaspoon cinnamon

Freshly ground black pepper

Puree the tomatoes in a blender along with the lemon juice. In a large skillet, brown the onion in the oil. Add the sirloin and cook until brown, stirring frequently. Add the pureed tomato sauce and spices, and simmer for 1 hour.

Serves 4 to 6.

BRAISED BEEF WITH WALNUTS, PRUNES, AND PEACHES

    3 pounds lean beef
    2 cloves garlic, minced
    3 tablespoons chopped fresh parsley
    3 tablespoons olive oil
    1 medium onion, chopped
    3 stems fresh thyme
    7 ounces white wine
    1 large tomato, chopped
    3 ounces walnuts, chopped
   10 dried prunes, chopped (nonsulfured; available at health
       food stores)
   10 dried peaches, chopped (nonsulfured; available at health
       food stores)

Cover the beef with the garlic and parsley. Heat the oil in a large casserole dish and brown the beef. Mix in the onion, thyme, and wine, and cook over medium heat for 10 minutes, stirring frequently. Add the tomato and walnuts. Cover and cook over medium-low heat for 90 minutes. Stir in the prunes and peaches, and cook for 15 minutes longer, covered, until the beef is tender and the sauce is thickened.

Serves 6.

ISOLA POT ROAST

  3–4 pounds lean pot roast
    2 tablespoons olive oil
       Freshly ground black pepper
    1 pound tomatoes, peeled
    1 cup dry red wine
    1 medium onion, chopped

1 cup chopped celery

1 tablespoon minced parsley

2 teaspoons oregano

1 clove garlic, minced

Preheat the oven to 300°F. In a Dutch oven, brown the roast in the oil. Add pepper to taste. Puree the tomatoes in a blender and pour over the meat. Stir in the remaining ingredients. Cover and bake for 3 to 4 hours, checking occasionally. If pan liquid seems low, add a small amount of water while roasting.

Serves 6 to 8.

BEEF KEBABS

1 pound top sirloin steak

1 small onion, finely chopped

½ cup Pinot Noir red wine

8 cubes (1" × 1") fresh pineapple

8 cherry tomatoes

1 can (8 ounces) salt-free water chestnuts, drained

Cut the steak into ¼"-thick strips. Combine the onion and wine in a bowl with the beef strips. Marinate for 4 hours. Alternately thread beef strips, pineapple cubes, cherry tomatoes, and water chestnuts onto metal skewers. Place kebabs on grill over medium coals. Grill 4 minutes, turning once.

Serves 4.

GRILLED LONDON BROIL

1½ pounds London broil steaks, each 1½" thick

5 large cloves garlic, minced

1 teaspoon powdered onion

¼ cup dry red wine

¼ cup lime juice

Place all the ingredients in a shallow dish and marinate in the refrigerator for at least 4 and up to 24 hours. Remove the steaks from the marinade and grill for 12 to 16 minutes for medium-rare, turning once. Place on a cutting board and, holding a sharp knife at a 45-degree angle, cut the steak across the grain into thin slices.

Serves 2 to 4.

Organ Meats

APRICOT-RAISIN TONGUE

1 beef tongue

1 tablespoon garlic powder

3 bay leaves

1 tablespoon marjoram

1 pound dried apricots (nonsulfured; available at health food stores)

1 pound tomatoes, peeled

½ cup lime juice

½ cup lemon juice

¼ teaspoon basil

¼ teaspoon ground red pepper

1 tablespoon mustard powder

½ cup raisins

Put the tongue in a large pot, cover completely with water, and bring to a rapid boil. Replace the water and bring to a second boil. Replace the water again and bring to a slow, easy boil. Add the garlic powder, bay leaves, and marjoram, and cook until done, about 2 hours. Discard the water and bay leaves. Skin the tongue and let it cool. Cut into thin slices. Preheat the oven to 350°F. Place the apricots in a saucepan. Puree the tomatoes in a blender. Add the tomato sauce and the remaining ingredients to the apricots, and bring to a boil. Continue to simmer until the mixture thickens. Layer the sliced tongue in a flat casserole dish and pour the sauce over it. Bake for about 20 minutes.

Serves 4.

BASQUE BEEF HEART

½ pound beef heart
½ white onion, chopped
4 peppercorns
2 whole cloves
2 teaspoons garlic powder
1 tablespoon flaxseed oil
1 tablespoon lemon juice
1 cup thinly sliced celery
1 cup chopped red onion
1 cup diced tomatoes
½ teaspoon rosemary
½ teaspoon thyme

Put the beef heart in a large pot filled with cold water and add the white onion, peppercorns, cloves, and garlic powder. Bring to a rolling boil, then reduce the heat, cover, and cook until the beef heart is fork-tender. Cool, then cut off the surface covering of the heart and slice it into cubes. Mix together the remaining ingredients and ladle over the beef cubes prior to serving.

Serves 2.

BEEF LIVER IN LIME SAUCE

  1 pound beef liver, sliced ⅜" thick
  1 clove garlic, slivered
  ½ teaspoon cumin
     Freshly ground black pepper
  2 tablespoons salt-free tomato sauce
  2 tablespoons olive oil
  2 tablespoons lime juice
1½ tablespoons pecan nut flour
  2 tablespoons water

Broil the liver on both sides until lightly browned but not fully cooked. Cut into 1" squares. Place the liver, garlic, cumin, and pepper to taste in a shallow skillet over low heat. Add the tomato sauce and oil and cover with water. Bring to a boil and simmer. In a bowl, mix the lime juice, nut flour, and water until the mixture is the texture of soft custard. Pour into the center of a pan and stir until smooth. Fold into the cooking liver and simmer 5 minutes longer. Serve hot over steamed fresh vegetables.

Serves 4 to 6.

HUNGARIAN CHICKEN LIVERS WITH MUSHROOMS

  1 onion, finely chopped
  1 green pepper, finely chopped
  7 tablespoons olive oil
  ½ pound mushrooms, sliced
1½ pounds chicken livers, cut into bite-size piece
  1 tablespoon paprika
  1 tablespoon nut flour
  ½ cup chicken stock
     Freshly ground black pepper

4 tablespoons dry red wine

3 tablespoons finely chopped parsley

In a large skillet, cook the onion and green pepper in 5 tablespoons of the oil for 3 to 5 minutes or until soft, stirring frequently. Add the mushrooms and cook for 3 to 5 minutes longer. Put in a bowl and add the remaining 2 tablespoons of oil. Add the chicken livers to the skillet and cook for 5 minutes. Return the vegetables to the skillet. Add the paprika and nut flour and stir until the liver and vegetables are evenly coated. Add the stock and simmer until the livers are cooked to the desired state. Season with pepper and reduce the heat. Pour in the wine and reheat, but do not boil. Serve the chicken livers garnished with parsley.

Serves 6.

ROCKY MOUNTAIN OYSTERS

2 pounds beef testicles

2 bay leaves

1 tablespoon basil

Freshly ground black pepper

1 cup nut flour

Garlic powder

Turmeric

1 cup red wine

Ground red pepper

Olive oil

With a sharp knife, cut and remove the sturdy membrane that covers each testicle. Place in a large pot filled with water and add the bay leaves and basil. Bring to a slow boil and simmer until done. Let cool and slice each testicle into ¼"-thick ovals. Sprinkle with black pepper to taste. Mix the nut flour, garlic powder, and turmeric to taste in a bowl. In a separate bowl, season the wine with red pepper to taste. Roll each slice in the dry mixture, then dip into the seasoned wine. Sauté in olive oil until slightly browned or tender. Drain on paper towels.

Serves 4 to 6.

Game Meats

ROOKE'S ROAST VENISON

2 yellow onions, sliced
3 carrots, sliced diagonally
1 rib celery, finely chopped
¼ cup olive oil
3 cups red wine
½ cup lemon juice
¼ cup Grand Marnier
1 quart water
1 branch fresh thyme
1 bay leaf
2 tablespoons black peppercorns
5 pounds venison roast
2 cups beef stock
3 tablespoons flaxseed oil
  Freshly ground black pepper

In a medium-size pot, cook the onions, carrots, and celery in the olive oil about 5 minutes, until soft, stirring frequently. Add the wine, lemon juice, Grand Marnier, water, thyme, bay leaf, and peppercorns. Bring to a boil and simmer for 20 minutes. Cool, then pour over the venison and refrigerate for 1 to 2 days, stirring occasionally. Remove the venison from the marinade 2 hours prior to cooking. Preheat the oven to 450°F. Place the venison in a roasting pan and roast for 10 minutes, then reduce the heat to 350°F and roast for 1½ to 2 hours longer, until done. In the meantime, bring the marinade to a boil over medium heat and reduce to 2 cups, about 45 minutes. Add the stock and simmer to reduce the marinade until it starts to thicken, about 12 minutes. Turn off the heat, cool the marinade to lukewarm, pour in the flaxseed oil, and season to taste with ground pepper. Discard the bay leaf. Cool the venison, slice into serving portions, and cover with the sauce.

Serves 5 or more.

MOOSE RUMP ROAST

5 to 6 pounds moose rump roast
      Olive oil
   1 teaspoon garlic powder
      Freshly ground black pepper
   1 large onion, sliced
   2 tablespoons lemon juice
   2 tablespoons lime juice
   ½ cup red Zinfandel wine
   1 cup water
      Cumin

Preheat the oven to 325°F. Rub the roast completely with oil. Sprinkle on the garlic powder and pepper to taste. Put the onion into the bottom of a roasting pan. Pour 1 tablespoon each of the lemon and lime juices over the onions. Place the roast on the onion slices. Pour the rest of the juices over the meat. Add the wine and water. Cover the pan tightly with foil and bake for 3½ to 4 hours, adding more water as necessary to keep moist. Add cumin and more pepper to taste.

Serves 8 to 10.

BUFFALO STEAKS WITH MUSHROOM SAUCE

1½ pounds buffalo steak
3 tablespoons freshly chopped thyme
¼ teaspoon garlic powder
Freshly ground black pepper
2 teaspoons + 4 tablespoons olive oil
2 shallots, chopped
½ pound fresh mushrooms, sliced
1½ cups red wine
1 cup beef stock
1 tablespoon chopped parsley
1 tablespoon chives
1 tablespoon flaxseed oil

Cut the steak into 4 pieces and cover with the thyme, garlic powder, and pepper. Cook on both sides in 2 teaspoons of the olive oil for 2 to 3 minutes, or until the centers are still pink, stirring frequently. Remove to a platter and keep warm. Cook the shallots and mushrooms in the remaining 4 tablespoons olive oil, turning frequently. Add the wine and cook to reduce until only about one-fourth is left. Add the stock and reduce until about one-half is left. Season with more pepper to taste and cool. Add the parsley, chives, and flaxseed oil. Pour over the steaks before serving.

Serves 2 to 3.

TARRAGON RABBIT

4 rabbit legs (boned)
1 tablespoon olive oil
1 cup dry sherry
1 tablespoon tomato puree
1 teaspoon garlic powder

1 teaspoon onion powder
2 tablespoons dried tarragon
  Freshly ground black pepper

In a large pan, cook the rabbit slowly in the oil, stirring frequently, but do not brown. Add the sherry, tomato puree, and garlic and onion powders. Stir in 1 tablespoon of the tarragon and season to taste with pepper. Cover and simmer gently for 30 to 40 minutes. Just before serving, turn off the heat and stir in the remaining tablespoon of tarragon.

Serves 4.

BARBECUED OSTRICH MEDALLIONS

8 ounces Cabernet Sauvignon wine
1 red onion, finely chopped
1 Jerusalem artichoke, finely chopped
1 green onion, finely chopped
1 rib celery, finely chopped
2 tablespoons fresh or frozen (thawed) mashed blueberries
2 stems fresh thyme
2 stems fresh basil
  Juice and chopped rind of 1 lemon
  Juice and chopped rind of 1 lime
1 pound ostrich medallions

Combine all the ingredients except the ostrich into a marinade in a large bowl. Add the ostrich and refrigerate for 12 hours. Remove the medallions and save the marinade. Grill the meat until it is cooked to taste. Reduce the marinade until it turns into a thick sauce. Pour over the ostrich.

Serves 4.

Seafood
Shellfish

PELOPONNESIAN SHRIMP

  1 teaspoon garlic, finely chopped
  2 tablespoons olive oil
  2 cups tomatoes, diced
  ½ cup dry white wine
  ¼ cup fresh basil, chopped
  1 teaspoon dried oregano
      Freshly ground black pepper
1½ pounds shrimp, peeled and deveined
  ⅛ teaspoon ground red pepper

Briefly cook the garlic in 1 tablespoon of the oil, stirring frequently. Add the tomatoes and cook for about a minute. Add the wine, basil, oregano, and black pepper to taste. Cook over moderate heat for 8 to 10 minutes. Heat the remaining 1 tablespoon of oil in a large skillet and add the shrimp. Cook rapidly, 1 to 2 minutes, or until the shrimp turn pink. Dust with the red pepper. Pour the tomato sauce over the shrimp.

Serves 4.

CANCUN ZESTY MUSSELS

5 pounds mussels
2 tablespoons olive oil
1 cup water
2 cups white wine
½ teaspoon cumin
½ teaspoon garlic powder

¼ teaspoon ground red pepper

3 to 4 large red onions, cut in rings

Freshly ground black pepper

1 bunch parsley

Lemon slices

Rinse and clean the mussels. In a 1-gallon pot, combine the oil, water, wine, cumin, garlic powder, red pepper, onions, and black pepper to taste. Bring to a boil. Add the drained mussels and return to a boil for 15 to 20 minutes. When all of the mussel shells have opened, they are done. Garnish with parsley and serve with lemon slices.

Serves 2 to 4.

TILLAMOOK STEAMED CLAMS

6 ounces clams (if open, tap on shell; if it does not close, discard)

Chopped parsley

Olive oil (for serving)

Under cold running water, scrub the sand from the clams with a stiff brush. Place the clams on a rack in a steamer. Fill with enough water to just cover the bottom of the rack. Bring to a boil, reduce the heat, cover the steamer, and steam the clams until they just open, 5 to 10 minutes. Drain and sprinkle with parsley. Serve in soup bowls with oil on the side. To eat the clams, pull them from their shells by their necks and dip in olive oil.

Serves 1.

OMEGA-3 STUFFED CRAB

   1 pound shredded crabmeat (6 crabs)
      Freshly ground black pepper
      Paprika
      Turmeric
      Flaxseed Oil Mayonnaise (see page 236)
   1 clove garlic
      Olive oil
      Cucumber slices

Combine the crabmeat with the pepper, paprika, and turmeric to taste. Add sufficient mayonnaise to moisten. Rub six crab shells with the garlic and oil. Pile the crab mixture in the shells. Cover with foil and place in a large baking dish. Bake at 400°F for 20 to 25 minutes, or until done. Garnish with cucumber slices.

Serves 6.

LEMON DILL SHRIMP

   3 cloves garlic, minced
  ⅓ cup olive oil
   1 pound large shrimp, shelled and deveined
   2 tablespoons lemon juice
  ⅓ cup fresh dill, minced

In a large skillet, cook the garlic in the oil until soft, stirring frequently. Stir in the shrimp and cook until just pink. Add the lemon juice and dill and blend well.

Serves 4.

Fish

CORDAIN'S FENNEL SALMON

   3 tablespoons extra-virgin olive oil
   1 small bulb fresh fennel, cored and slivered
   1½ pounds salmon fillets
   1 teaspoon dried dill weed
   1 teaspoon dried basil

Preheat the oven to 400°F. Coat the bottom and sides of a glass baking dish with 2 tablespoons of the oil. Spread the fennel over the bottom of the dish. Carefully place the salmon on top of the fennel and drizzle the remaining 1 tablespoon of oil over it. Sprinkle with the dill and basil. Cover with foil and bake for 20 to 25 minutes. Serve with steamed broccoli and sliced raw cucumbers.

Serves 4 to 6.

SAUTERNE SQUID

   1 pound squid, each about 2" long
     Pecan nut flour
   1 teaspoon garlic powder
   ½ cup olive oil
   ¼ cup Sauterne wine
   1 tablespoon lemon juice
   2 tomatoes, cut into wedges
     Parsley sprigs

Wash the squid completely, remove the ink sack and soft backbone from each head, and strip off the black membrane covering the squid. Coat the squid with the nut flour and sprinkle with the garlic powder. Heat the oil in a heavy skillet and cook the squid until brown, stirring frequently. Turn off the heat. Pour the wine over the squid and add the lemon juice. Let stand for 5 to 10 minutes, then drain. Garnish with tomato wedges and parsley sprigs.

Serves 4.

ORANGE POACHED FISH

4 medium fillets of any whitefish
¼ cup dry white wine
6 black peppercorns
1 bay leaf
1 small onion, sliced
1 medium orange, quartered
   Dried dill weed

In a large skillet, place the fish in a single layer. Add the wine, peppercorns, bay leaf, onion, and enough water to just cover the fish. Poach over medium heat until tender, then remove the fish from the pan and drain on paper towels. Squeeze the juice from the orange over the fish, and dust with dill before serving.

Serves 4.

LITTLE VALLEY STUFFED TROUT

½ teaspoon dried dill weed
2 tablespoons finely chopped fresh parsley
2 tablespoons finely chopped yellow onion
¼ cup slivered almonds
1 pound trout (brook trout if you can get one; rainbow trout will do)
   Lemon juice
   Freshly ground black pepper

Preheat the oven to 400°F. In a small bowl, mix the dill, parsley, onion, and almonds. Fill the cavity of the trout with this mixture. Place the fish on foil and liberally squeeze lemon juice over the fish. Add pepper to taste. Seal the foil and bake for about 25 minutes, until the fish flakes easily with a fork.

Serves 2 to 4.

REESE RIVER BARBECUED CATFISH WITH PEACH SALSA

4 catfish fillets
½ teaspoon freshly ground black pepper
½ teaspoon garlic powder
1 teaspoon ground red pepper
Peach Salsa (see page 240)

Oil and preheat the grill. Sprinkle the catfish fillets with pepper, garlic powder, and red pepper. Place the grill about 4" from the heat source. Cook for about 5 minutes on each side, or until the fish flakes easily with a fork. Serve with Peach Salsa spooned over the fillets.

Serves 2 to 4.

Condiments

FLAXSEED OIL MAYONNAISE

1 egg
1 tablespoon lemon juice
¼ teaspoon mustard powder
1 cup flaxseed oil

In a blender, combine the egg, lemon juice, and mustard and blend for 3 to 5 seconds. Continue blending and slowly add the oil. Blend until thick. Put into a tightly sealed plastic container and refrigerate. The mayonnaise should keep for 5 to 7 days.

Makes 1½ cups.

ALL NATURAL CATSUP

4 cups vine-ripened fresh tomatoes, diced
1 small sweet onion, diced
¼ teaspoon crushed garlic
½ sweet red bell pepper, diced
1 whole bay leaf
½ Granny Smith apple, peeled, cored, and diced
½ teaspoon allspice
½ teaspoon ground mace
½ cinnamon stick
1 tablespoon black peppercorns
½ teaspoon celery seed
½ cup lemon juice
⅛ teaspoon cayenne pepper

Into a 4-quart saucepan, place the tomatoes, onion, garlic, pepper, bay leaf, and apple. In a small cloth spice bag, put the allspice, mace, cinnamon stick, peppercorns, and celery seed, and place into the tomato mixture. Bring to a boil, and cook until reduced by half, stirring frequently. Remove spice bag and bay leaf. Puree in a food processor until well blended. Return to the saucepan and add lemon juice and cayenne pepper. Continue cooking until catsup reaches a thick, spreadable consistency. Stir frequently, and watch for sticking and scorching as it thickens. Refrigerate or freeze in a well-sealed container.

Makes about 2 cups.

TARTAR SAUCE

    1 cup Flaxseed Oil Mayonnaise (see page 236)
    ¼ cup finely chopped onion
    1 tablespoon lemon juice
    ½ teaspoon dried dill weed

Mix all the ingredients together. Chill before serving.

Makes 1 cup.

COLORADO RANCH DRESSING

    1 cup Flaxseed Oil Mayonnaise (see page 236)
    1 cup coconut milk
    1 teaspoon dried dill weed
    ½ teaspoon garlic powder
    ½ teaspoon dried basil
       Freshly ground black pepper

Mix all the ingredients together. Refrigerate at least 1 hour before serving.

Makes 1¾ cups.

RUSSIAN FLAXSEED SALAD DRESSING

    1 cup fresh tomatoes
    ½ cup flaxseed oil
    ½ cup lemon juice
    1 tablespoon honey
    1 teaspoon paprika
    1 teaspoon onion powder
    ½ teaspoon garlic powder

Put all the ingredients into a blender and blend until smooth. Refrigerate.

Makes 1½ cups.

TOMATO FLAXSEED DRESSING

⅓ cup tomato puree

½ cup flaxseed oil

⅓ cup lime juice

½ teaspoon garlic powder

½ teaspoon onion powder

1 tablespoon honey

Put all the ingredients into a blender and blend until smooth. Refrigerate.

Makes 1¼ cups.

GARDEN-FRESH SALSA

2 cloves garlic

1 large yellow onion, quartered

1 green bell pepper, quartered and seeded

2 jalapeño peppers, stemmed, seeded, and chopped

6 tomatoes, peeled, seeded, and chopped

1 cup fresh cilantro

Freshly ground black pepper

Mince the garlic in a food processor. Add the onion, bell pepper, and jalapeño peppers, and pulse until barely chopped. Add the tomatoes and cilantro, and process until combined but slightly chunky. Add pepper to taste. Refrigerate before using.

Makes 6 to 8 cups.

PEACH SALSA

1 cup peeled and finely chopped fresh peaches
¼ cup chopped red onions
¼ cup chopped Anaheim chile peppers
½ tablespoon lime juice
½ tablespoon lemon juice
½ teaspoon honey
   Cayenne pepper

Combine all the ingredients in a medium bowl. Cover and chill up to 6 hours.

Makes 1½ cups.

SACRAMENTO GUACAMOLE

3 ripe avocados
1 teaspoon fresh lemon juice
1 teaspoon coarsely ground black pepper
1 teaspoon garlic powder
1 jalapeño pepper, stemmed, seeded, and finely diced

Mash the avocados with a fork or potato masher until smooth. Stir in the remaining ingredients until well mixed. Refrigerate if not eaten immediately.

Makes 3 cups.

CORONADO BARBECUE SAUCE

2 teaspoons olive oil
¼ cup minced onion
1 tablespoon minced seeded jalapeño pepper
¼ cup All Natural Catsup (see page 237)

1 tablespoon honey
¼ teaspoon mustard powder
  Dash of ground red pepper
2 cups diced tomatoes
  Freshly ground black pepper

Heat the oil in a stainless steel saucepan. Add the onion and jalapeño pepper and cook over moderate heat, stirring, until soft, about 3 minutes. Add the ketchup, honey, mustard, and red pepper and bring to a simmer. Add the tomatoes and simmer over low heat, stirring until thickened, about 10 minutes. Puree the sauce in a blender or food processor until smooth. Pass through a strainer and season with black pepper to taste. Serve at room temperature.

Makes 2 cups.

Vegetable Dishes

STIR-FRIED GARLIC ASPARAGUS

1 clove garlic, minced
2 tablespoons olive oil
1 pound fresh asparagus spears
1 tablespoon lemon juice

Cook the garlic in the oil until soft, stirring frequently. Add the asparagus spears. Cook until tender, 3 to 5 minutes. Pour the lemon juice over the asparagus.

Serves 4.

SPICY LEMON BROCCOLI

4 cups small broccoli florets
1 tablespoon olive oil
2 teaspoons freshly grated lemon peel
   Crushed red pepper

Place a vegetable steamer in a medium saucepan and fill with water to the bottom of the steamer. Place the broccoli in the steamer and bring to a boil. Cover and cook for 2 to 3 minutes. Remove the broccoli. Heat the oil in a skillet over medium heat. Add the lemon peel and crushed red pepper to taste. Cook, stirring frequently, until the peel begins to brown, about 1 minute. Add the broccoli and stir until hot, about 1 minute.

Serves 4.

CRUNCHY GARLIC BROCCOLI

1 tablespoon olive oil
4 cups broccoli florets
2 cloves garlic, run through a press

Heat the oil in a large skillet. Add the broccoli, cover, and cook for 3 minutes, stirring occasionally. Turn the heat to low and cook for 2 minutes, or until just tender. Add the garlic, and cook for 1 minute.

Serves 4.

MARINATED BROCCOLI STALKS

2 pounds fresh broccoli
1 tablespoon lemon juice
1 tablespoon olive oil

¼ teaspoon dried dill weed

1 clove garlic, minced

Red cabbage leaves

Detach broccoli florets from the stalks, leaving only the secondary stalks attached to the main stalk. (Reserve florets for another use.) Cut off and discard the tough bottom end of the main stalk. Cut the remaining stalks diagonally into ½" slices. (You should have about 2 cups.) Whisk together the lemon juice, oil, dill, and garlic in a medium bowl. Add the sliced stalks and stir to coat evenly. Cover and refrigerate for 3 hours. Serve on cabbage leaves.

Serves 4.

BAKED WALNUT-STUFFED CARROTS

4 large carrots, washed and pared

1 medium onion, chopped

¼ cup chopped walnuts

½ green bell pepper, chopped

3 tablespoons olive oil

Freshly ground black pepper

Boil the carrots for 30 minutes, then cut in half lengthwise. Preheat the oven to 350°F. Hollow out the centers and puree the extracted portions. Combine the onion, walnuts, and bell pepper with 1 tablespoon of the oil. Add ground pepper to taste. Mix in the pureed carrots, and stuff the eight carrot halves with the mixture. Bake in a dish coated with the remaining 2 tablespoons of oil. Bake for about 30 minutes.

Serves 8.

STEAMED BABY CARROTS WITH BASIL

20 small carrots, washed and trimmed
 1 tablespoon lemon juice
    Dried basil

Put a vegetable steamer in the bottom of a medium saucepan, and fill with water to the bottom of the steamer. Bring to a boil, place the carrots in the steamer, cover, and reduce the heat. Steam until tender, 5 to 10 minutes. Pour the lemon juice over the carrots and sprinkle with basil to taste.

Serves 4.

LEMON-VINAIGRETTE CARROTS

 1 pound carrots, peeled
 ½ cup flaxseed oil
 ⅓ cup lemon juice
 1 teaspoon minced garlic
 1 teaspoon onion powder
 ¼ teaspoon freshly ground black pepper

Cut the carrots into very thin diagonal slices. Place in a large skillet, cover with water, and boil until tender, 3 to 5 minutes. Whisk together the remaining ingredients in a small bowl. Drain the carrots and toss with the lemon vinaigrette.

Serves 4.

TOMATO-PECAN ZUCCHINI

 2 zucchini, cut in half lengthwise
 1 small red onion, finely chopped
 4 tablespoons unsalted tomato sauce

½ teaspoon dried parsley

1 clove garlic, chopped

2 tablespoons pecans, chopped

Preheat the oven to 450°F. Hollow out the zucchini halves. In a saucepan, heat the pulp with the onion, tomato sauce, parsley, garlic, and pecans for 5 minutes. Stuff the zucchini shells with the mixture. Place in a baking dish with a little water on the bottom. Bake for 30 minutes, until the zucchini is soft.

Serves 2.

SAUTÉED CAULIFLOWER AND ZUCCHINI

1 head cauliflower

½ cup olive oil

1 teaspoon lime juice

1½ teaspoons cumin

¼ teaspoon freshly ground black pepper

1 teaspoon dried basil

1 teaspoon dried oregano

1 tablespoon chopped yellow onion

3 zucchini, cut into ½" slices

Detach the florets from the cauliflower and place in a large skillet with boiling water. Cook until just tender, about 5 minutes. Pour out the water and remove the florets. Pour the oil into the skillet and stir in the lime juice, cumin, pepper, basil, oregano, and onion. Add the zucchini and cauliflower. Cover and cook over low heat for 10 to 15 minutes, or until the zucchini is tender.

Serves 6.

LIVORNO EGGPLANT

2 eggplants, peeled and cubed

2 cloves garlic, minced

1 yellow onion, diced

2 tablespoons olive oil

1 teaspoon dried basil

1 teaspoon dried oregano

½ teaspoon cumin

3 medium tomatoes, diced

Preheat the oven to 375°F. Add the eggplant to boiling water and boil for 1 minute. Remove and drain the eggplant. Place the eggplant in a bowl and set aside. Cook the garlic and onion in the olive oil about 5 minutes or until soft, stirring frequently. Add the onion, garlic, basil, oregano, and cumin to the eggplant; blend well. Put the mixture into a well-oiled glass baking dish. Layer with the diced tomatoes and bake uncovered for 25 to 30 minutes.

Serves 4.

Salads

COLORADO COLESLAW

2 tablespoons lemon juice

2 Granny Smith apples, thinly sliced

3 cups shredded cabbage

1 rib celery, chopped

1 carrot, grated

1 medium yellow onion, thinly sliced

¼ teaspoon garlic powder

½ cup Flaxseed Oil Mayonnaise (see page 236)

In a large bowl, pour the lemon juice over the apple slices and add the cabbage, celery, carrot, and onion. Mix together the garlic powder and mayonnaise, and combine with the cabbage mixture.

Serves 4.

BASIL TOMATOES

4 medium tomatoes, sliced
¼ cup flaxseed oil
1½ tablespoons lemon juice
½ teaspoon onion powder
½ teaspoon dried basil
⅛ teaspoon cayenne pepper
1 clove garlic, minced

Place the tomatoes in a shallow dish. Combine the remaining ingredients and pour the dressing over the tomatoes. Cover and refrigerate before serving.

Serves 4.

OMEGA-3 SPINACH SALAD

1 pound fresh spinach
2 tablespoons lime juice
¼ cup flaxseed oil
1 tablespoon honey
Freshly ground black pepper
1 avocado, diced
8 ounces pork loin (precooked, cooled, and diced)
2 omega-3 eggs, hard-boiled and chopped

Wash the spinach and dry with paper towels. Mix together the lime juice, oil, honey, and pepper to taste in a large bowl. Fold the avocado cubes into the dressing. Toss the spinach, pork loin, and chopped eggs with the avocado and dressing.

Serves 4.

GREEK CUCUMBER-TOMATO SALAD

1 large cucumber, cut into ½" slices, then quartered
2 medium tomatoes, cut into eighths
¼ red onion, very thinly sliced
½ green bell pepper, very thinly sliced
¼ cup lemon juice
2 tablespoons extra-virgin olive oil
   Freshly ground black pepper

Mix the cucumber, tomatoes, onion, and bell pepper in a bowl. Toss with the lemon juice and oil. Add black pepper to taste.

Serves 2.

AVOCADO-CUCUMBER SALAD

1 medium unwaxed cucumber, peeled and very thinly sliced
1 yellow bell pepper, sliced
1 tablespoon fresh lime juice
1 jalapeño pepper, seeded and finely diced
1 teaspoon minced onion
   Lettuce
1 avocado, sliced
   Fresh parsley

In a bowl, combine the cucumber slices with the bell pepper, lime juice, jalapeño pepper, and onion. Arrange lettuce leaves on six serving plates. Pile the cucumber mixture in the center of each plate. Add avocado slices and garnish with parsley.

Serves 6.

BOMBAY CHICKEN SALAD

2 whole skinless chicken breasts, visible fat removed
1 tablespoon curry
4 tablespoons Flaxseed Oil Mayonnaise (see page 236)
1 tablespoon garam masala spice mixture
4 fresh pineapple slices, diced
1 tablespoon raisins
½ teaspoon freshly grated ginger
1 cucumber, peeled and finely chopped
2 ribs celery, finely chopped

Place the chicken breasts and curry in a pot filled with water. Simmer slowly until completely cooked; drain and cool. Cut the chicken into ½" cubes or smaller. In a medium serving dish, combine the mayonnaise with the remaining ingredients. Add the chicken and mix well.

Serves 4.

GUACAMOLE SALAD

4 avocados
2½ tablespoons lime juice
1 clove garlic, minced
1 Anaheim chile pepper with seeds, finely chopped
1 teaspoon onion powder
Butter lettuce leaves
1 tomato, diced

Mash the avocados into a chunky paste and add the lime juice, garlic, chili pepper, and onion powder. Stir well and spoon onto the lettuce leaves. Cover with diced tomato.

Serves 2.

OMEGA-3 CRAB SALAD

 2 cups cooked crabmeat, cooled and flaked
 1 cup diced celery
 ¼ cup chopped red bell pepper
 1 teaspoon onion powder
 ¼ teaspoon freshly ground black pepper
 1 tablespoon fresh lemon juice
 3 tablespoons Flaxseed Oil Mayonnaise (see page 236)
  Mixed salad greens
 6 avocado wedges

Mix the crabmeat with the celery, bell pepper, onion powder, black pepper, lemon juice, and mayonnaise. Serve over mixed greens with avocado.

Serves 2.

SALSA SHRIMP SALAD

 2 cups boiled shrimp
 ½ cup diced celery
 1 teaspoon finely chopped onion
 3 omega-3 eggs, hard-boiled and chopped
 ⅓ cup Flaxseed Oil Mayonnaise (see page 236)
 ¼ cup Garden-Fresh Salsa (see page 239)
 3 tablespoons lemon juice
  Butter lettuce leaves

Combine the shrimp, celery, onion, and eggs. Mix together the mayonnaise, salsa, and lemon juice. Toss together all the ingredients and spoon onto lettuce leaves. Chill before serving.

Serves 4.

LEAN BEEF SALAD

½ cup All Natural Catsup (see page 237)

⅓ cup flaxseed oil

¼ cup lemon juice

½ teaspoon ground ginger

3 cups cooked lean beef, cut into strips

2 tomatoes, cut into wedges

1 green bell pepper, cut into strips

1 cup fresh mushrooms, sliced

1 cup sliced celery

½ cup green or sweet onion, thinly sliced

4 cups salad greens (romaine lettuce, Chinese cabbage, spinach)

Mix the ketchup, oil, lemon juice, and ginger together to make a marinade. Combine the beef, tomatoes, bell pepper, mushrooms, celery, and onion and cover with the marinade. Chill for 2 hours. Put the salad greens into a serving bowl. Drain the marinade from the beef and vegetable mixture; reserve the marinade. Spoon the beef and vegetables onto the greens and toss. Serve with the extra marinade for dressing.

Serves 4.

Soups

ACAPULCO AVOCADO SOUP

2 avocados, diced

1 tablespoon chopped green onions

1 jalapeño pepper, seeded and finely chopped

1 tablespoon extra-virgin olive oil

2 cups chicken stock

Freshly ground black pepper
Ground cumin
1 sprig cilantro
1 tomato, diced

Place the avocados in a blender or food processor and puree until smooth. Cook the onions and jalapeño pepper in the oil until tender, stirring frequently. In a large bowl, combine the avocado with the stock and the onions and jalapeño pepper, mixing until smooth. Add black pepper and cumin to taste. Chill for 60 minutes prior to serving. Garnish with cilantro and diced tomato.

Serves 4.

BROCCOLI SOUP

1 large onion, chopped
3 cloves garlic, chopped
1 tablespoon olive oil
1½ pounds broccoli florets
3 cups chicken stock
¼ teaspoon ground nutmeg
Freshly ground black pepper

In a large saucepan, cook the onion and garlic in the oil until tender, stirring frequently. Add the broccoli and stock and bring to a boil. Reduce the heat and simmer 10 to 15 minutes, until the broccoli is tender. Put the mixture in a blender and puree until smooth, return it to the saucepan, and heat slowly. Season with the nutmeg and pepper to taste.

Serves 4 to 6.

KARACHI CARROT SOUP

   1 butternut squash, cut in half, seeds removed
   1 onion, diced
   3 cloves garlic, minced
   2 tablespoons olive oil
   4 cups water
   1 pound carrots, peeled and diced
1½" fresh ginger, peeled and thinly sliced
      Pinch of ground cinnamon
      Freshly ground black pepper
   1 sprig parsley

Preheat the oven to 375°F. Place the squash, cut side down, onto a greased baking sheet. Bake for 35 to 40 minutes, or until softened. Cool, then spoon the flesh out of the skin. Cook the onion and garlic in a large saucepan with the oil until soft but not browned, stirring frequently. Pour in the water and add the squash flesh, carrots, and ginger. Bring to a boil and cook for at least 20 minutes, or until the carrots and ginger are tender. Put the mixture in a blender and puree. Return the soup to the saucepan and reheat. Add the cinnamon, season to taste with pepper, and garnish with parsley.

Serves 4.

FRESH TOMATO-BASIL SOUP

   2 large yellow onions, diced
  ¼ cup extra-virgin olive oil
   2 pounds fresh tomatoes, peeled
   1 tablespoon finely grated orange peel
   1 tablespoon lemon juice
      Freshly ground black pepper
      Fresh basil leaves

In a large saucepan, cook the onions in the oil until translucent, stirring frequently. Put the tomatoes in a blender and puree. Add the orange peel, lemon juice, and pureed tomatoes to the saucepan, and cook over medium-low heat, stirring occasionally, for 15 to 20 minutes. Season to taste with pepper and garnish with basil.

Serves 4 to 6.

LEAN CHICKEN-VEGGIE SOUP

2 large skinless chicken breasts
½ teaspoon thyme
½ teaspoon marjoram
1 bunch celery, chopped
1 medium head cabbage, chopped
1 large green bell pepper, chopped
1 zucchini, chopped
6 onions, chopped
8 tomatoes, chopped
1 tablespoon onion powder
2 cloves garlic, minced
8 whole peppercorns
1 bay leaf

In a large pot filled with water, simmer the chicken breasts with the thyme and marjoram for 15 to 20 minutes, or until the chicken is fully cooked. Remove the chicken and debone. Chop the chicken into ½" or smaller cubes, discard the bones, and put the chicken back into the pot. Add the remaining ingredients. Bring to a boil, then reduce the heat and simmer for 1½ to 2 hours, until the vegetables are tender and the flavors are well blended. Discard the bay leaf before serving.

Serves 12.

Fruits and Desserts

GRANNY'S APPLESAUCE

8 Granny Smith apples, peeled, cored, and cut into eighths
½ cup water
2 tablespoons lemon juice
1 tablespoon grated lemon peel

Combine the apples and water in a large saucepan and cook over low heat until the apples are tender. Add the lemon juice and cook until the apples are easily mashed with a fork. Remove from the heat and add the lemon peel. Mash with the tines of a fork or a potato masher, leaving a bit of coarse texture. Serve warm.

Serves 4.

BAKED CINNAMON-APPLE RINGS

4 Rome baking apples
½ teaspoon powdered cloves
½ teaspoon cinnamon
1 tablespoon honey
½ cup water

Preheat the oven to 400°F. Core the apples and slice into ½" rings. Place into a shallow baking dish lightly greased or coated with cooking spray. Mix the remaining ingredients and pour over the apples. Bake for 15 minutes, or until tender.

Serves 4.

BAKED BANANAS

4 bananas
¼ cup olive oil
   Juice and grated rind of 2 lemons
1 tablespoon vanilla
1 teaspoon cinnamon

Preheat the oven to 350°F. Cut the bananas in half lengthwise and place cut side down in a baking dish greased with the oil. Drizzle the bananas with the lemon juice and vanilla and sprinkle with the grated lemon rind and cinnamon. Bake for 15 to 20 minutes.

Serves 4.

CANTALOUPE-PINEAPPLE AMBROSIA

2 cantaloupes
1 pineapple
1 large Granny Smith apple
1 cup raisins
1 cup fresh shredded coconut
1 cup chopped walnuts
   Juice of 1 orange

Remove the skins, seeds, and cores from the cantaloupes, pineapple, and apple and cut the fruit into small chunks. In a large salad bowl, mix the fruit with the raisins, coconut, and walnuts and sprinkle with the orange juice.

Serves 4.

WALNUT-CRUSTED STRAWBERRIES

Fresh strawberries, sliced lengthwise
Honey
Lemon juice
Finely diced walnuts

Wash the strawberries, remove the stems, and cut in thin lengthwise sections. Mix together equal parts honey and lemon juice. Dip the strawberries into the mixture. Arrange on a serving tray and sprinkle with the walnuts.

Servings vary with quantity.

Stage IV Recovery Recipes

The following recipes are intended only for Stage IV recovery and are based on potatoes, sweet potatoes, and yams. Many of these include small amounts of salt as recovery therapy.

Electrolytes are the salts sodium, chloride, potassium, calcium, and magnesium, which occur naturally either within the body's cells or in the extracellular fluids surrounding them. Dissolved in the body fluids as ions, they conduct electric currents and are therefore critical for muscle contraction and relaxation and also for maintaining fluid levels. The body loses a small portion of these salts during exercise, primarily through sweat. The loss is typically not critical in events shorter than 4 hours or in cool-weather events, when the sweat rate is low. But after longer events and exercise in extreme heat, replacement is of greater significance, especially for sodium and possibly for potassium.

There is no doubt that you are losing sodium during extensive exercise. The white blotches on your skin and clothes are visible signs of this. The problem with this is that the excessive loss of sodium during exercise can result in hyponatremia—levels of sodium so low that your health and well-being are at risk. The key to preventing hyponatremia is balancing fluid and sodium intakes during long exercise sessions.

In the postexercise recovery period, replacing lost electrolytes will help speed recovery. Most of the electrolytes are found in abundance in natural foods, which makes their replacement fairly easy. Drinking any juices or eating fruits will easily replace nearly all of the electrolytes lost—except sodium, which is also the one most likely to need replenishment. This must be added to postexercise recovery drink and food by adding a bit of table salt. Once beyond Stages III and IV, salt should be restricted in your diet.

MARINATED MUSHROOMS

  1 pound button mushrooms
  ¼ cup olive oil
     Juice of 1 lemon
  2 tablespoons Johannisberg Riesling or other quality Riesling wine
  3 cloves garlic, mashed
  ½ teaspoon mustard powder
  ¼ teaspoon paprika
     Pinch of red pepper flakes
  1 tablespoon chopped fresh oregano
  1 tablespoon chopped fresh basil
  1 tablespoon chopped fresh parsley
     Salt
     Freshly ground black pepper

In a large glass bowl, toss the mushrooms with all the other ingredients except salt and pepper and marinate for at least 20 minutes. Cook the mushrooms in a dry skillet over high heat for 3 to

5 minutes, until just tender, stirring frequently. Season with salt and pepper to taste. Serve over baked Idaho potatoes, sweet potatoes, or yams. Can be made ahead and refrigerated for quick use.

Serves 4.

HERBED NEW POTATOES

8 small new red potatoes
2 tablespoons olive oil
½ tablespoon chopped fresh parsley
½ tablespoon chopped fresh basil
　Salt
　Freshly ground pepper

Boil the potatoes until tender, about 12 minutes. Drain and place on a plate or in a bowl. Drizzle with the oil and toss with the herbs and salt and pepper to taste. Make ahead and microwave for quick use.

Serves 2.

HERB-PEPPER-ALMOND POTATO TOPPERS

4 tablespoons olive oil
2 cups whole almonds
4 teaspoons herb pepper seasoning (or make your own mixture of parsley, lemon pepper, black pepper, and garlic powder)

Preheat the oven to 325°F. Spread the oil on a jelly roll pan or flat baking sheet. Stir the nuts and seasonings together and place on the baking sheet. Bake for 20 minutes, stirring occasionally. Remove with a slotted spoon and drain on a paper towel. Sprinkle on potatoes or salad.

Serves 8.

MEXICAN PECAN POTATO TOPPERS

4 tablespoons olive oil

4 cups pecan halves

1 tablespoon chili powder

2 teaspoons ground cumin

Dash of salt

Preheat the oven to 325°F. Spread the oil on a jelly roll pan or flat baking sheet. Stir the nuts and seasonings together and place on the baking sheet. Bake for 20 minutes stirring occasionally. Remove with a slotted spoon and drain on a paper towel. Sprinkle on potatoes or salad.

Serves 16.

HORSERADISH-GARLIC SAUCE

2 egg yolks

1 tablespoon white wine

¼ teaspoon salt

1 teaspoon honey

½ teaspoon freshly ground black pepper

⅔ cup olive oil

3 tablespoons prepared horseradish, or to taste

3 cloves garlic, smashed

Place the egg yolks, wine, salt, honey, and pepper in a food processor or blender and mix lightly. With the machine running, add the oil in a thin stream to thoroughly mix. Add half the horseradish and half the garlic, taste, and adjust the seasonings to your liking. Chill and serve as a topping for potatoes, vegetables, or meat. Keeps for 1 week in the refrigerator.

Makes 1 cup.

BRAISED ONION SAUCE

1½ pounds sweet onions (about 6 medium), sliced
½ cup olive oil
1 tablespoon honey
¼ cup Madeira wine
Freshly ground nutmeg

Cook the onions in the oil until they're soft and transparent, stirring frequently. Drizzle in the honey, reduce the heat, and simmer slowly for 1 hour. Stir in the wine and cook briefly. Serve as is or puree for a smooth sauce. Sprinkle with nutmeg before serving. Great on potatoes or as a side vegetable.

Makes 4 cups.

FRESH TOMATO SAUCE

1 medium onion, sliced
4 tablespoons olive oil
2½ pounds tomatoes, peeled, seeded, and chopped (or equivalent amount of canned unsalted tomatoes)
½ teaspoon salt
1 tablespoon fresh basil (or 1 teaspoon dried)

Cook the onion in the oil until soft and transparent, stirring frequently. Add the tomatoes and seasonings. Simmer gently for 10 minutes. Pour over potatoes or yams.

Variation: Sauté ½ pound thinly sliced mushrooms with the onion.

Makes 4 cups.

ALMOND-AVOCADO SPREAD

1 large ripe avocado, seeded, peeled, and mashed
1 tablespoon lime juice
¼ teaspoon chili powder
  Pinch of salt
¼ cup toasted chopped almonds
2 tablespoons diced green chile pepper (Anaheim or other mild variety)

Mix together the avocado, lime juice, chili powder, and salt. Stir in the almonds and pepper. Cover with plastic wrap and refrigerate for 4 hours. Put on baked potatoes, sweet potatoes, or yams.

Makes 1½ cups.

TOMATO-GINGER SAUCE

1½ cups chopped onion
4 thin slices fresh ginger, cut diagonally about 2" long
1 tablespoon olive oil
¼ teaspoon salt (optional)
½ teaspoon ground cumin
½ teaspoon turmeric
⅓ teaspoon allspice
½ teaspoon ground fennel
1 tablespoon minced garlic
½ cup water
1½ pounds crushed tomatoes (if canned, use unsalted tomatoes)

Cook the onion and ginger in the oil, stirring frequently. Add the spices and garlic, and simmer for 5 minutes. Stir in the water and tomatoes. Cook over medium heat for 10 minutes. Spoon over baked potatoes, sweet potatoes, or yams.

Makes 4 cups.

SPICED ORANGE SAUCE

    3 tablespoons olive oil
    3 cups chopped onions
    3 tablespoons allspice
   ¼ teaspoon salt
  1½ teaspoons minced garlic
       Juice of 3 oranges
    1 cup pitted, chopped plums, prunes, or other dried fruit

Heat the oil in a large, heavy saucepan. Add the onions, allspice, and salt, and cook over medium heat, stirring frequently, for 5 minutes. Stir in the garlic and orange juice. Simmer for 5 minutes longer. Add the fruit and simmer for another 5 minutes. Serve hot over potatoes or yams.

Makes 4 cups.

Bibliography

INTRODUCTION

Bar-Yosef, O. "The Natufian culture in the Levant, threshold to the origins of agriculture." *Evolutionary Anthropology,* 1998; 6:159–77.

Blurton Jones, N. G., Smith, L. C., O'Connell, J. F., Hawkes, K., and Kamuzora, C. L. "Demography of the Hadza, an increasing and high density population of Savanna foragers." *American Journal of Physiological Anthropology,* 1992; 89:159–81.

Burke, E. R., and Berning, J. R. *Training Nutrition.* Carmel, Indiana: Cooper Publishing Group, 1996. Cabeza de Vaca, N. *Cabeza de Vaca's Adventures in the Unknown Interior of America.* New York: Collier Books, 1961.

Caesar, Julius Gaius. *Commentaries on the Gallic War, Book VI.* (The second passage of the Rhine, with some notes on the Druids and the remarkable animals found in the Hercynian forest, paragraph 28, 53 B.C.) Translated by W. A. McDevitte and W. S. Bohn. New York: Harper & Brothers, 1869.

Cook, J. *A Voyage Towards the South Pole and Round the World.* London: W. Strahan & T. Cadell, 1777.

DeVries, A. *Primitive Man and His Food.* Chicago: Chandler Book Company, 1952.

Eaton, S. B., Cordain, L., and Lindeberg, S. "Evolutionary health promotion: a consideration of common counterarguments." *Preventive Medicine,* 2002; 34:119–23.

Eaton, S. B., Konner, M., and Shostak, M. "Stone agers in the fast lane: chronic degenerative diseases in evolutionary perspective." *American Journal of Medicine,* 1988 Apr; 84(4):739–49.

Eaton, S. B., Shostak, M., and Konner, M. *The Paleolithic Prescription.* New York: Harper Row, 1988.

Galloway, J. H. "Sugar." In Kiple, K. F., Ornelas, K. C., editors. *The Cambridge World History of Food, Volume 1,* pp. 437–49. Cambridge: Cambridge University Press, 2000.

Gerrior, S., and Bente, L. *Nutrient Content of the U.S. Food Supply, 1,909–99: A Summary Report.* U.S. Department of Agriculture, Center for Nutrition Policy and Promotion. Home Economics Report No. 55, 2002.

Hill, K., and Hurtado, A. M. *Ache Life History.* New York: Aldine de Gruyter, 1996.

Honeman, W. *American Bicyclist,* 1945.

Jaffee, A. J. "Length of life: short and not so merry." In *The First Immigrants from Asia: A Population History of the North American Indians.* A. J. Jaffee, ed., pp. 55–66. New York: Plenum Press, 1992.

James, S. R. "Hominid use of fire in the lower and middle Pleistocene." *Current Anthropology,* 1989; 30:1–26.

Laudonniere, R. G. *Histoire Notable de la Florida.* Gainesville: University of Florida Press, 1975.

Lee, R. B. "The Kung Bushmen of Botswana." In *Hunters and Gatherers Today*, M. G. Bicchieri, ed., pp. 327–35. New York: Holt, Rinehart and Winston, 1972.

Neel, J. V. "Health and disease in unacculturated American Indian population." *Ciba Foundation Symposium*, 1977; 49:155–77.

Oliver, W. J., Cohen, E. L., and Neel, J. V. "Blood pressure, sodium intake, and sodium related hormones in the Yanomamo Indians, a 'no-salt' culture." *Circulation*, 1975 Jul; 52(1):146–51.

Savage-Landor, A. H. *Across Unknown South America*. London: Hodder and Stoughton, 1913.

Stefansson, V. "Eskimo longevity in northern Alaska." *Science*, 1958; 127:16–19.

United States Department of Agriculture, Agricultural Research Service. 1997. "Data tables: Results from USDA's 1994–96 Continuing Survey of Food Intakes by Individuals and 1994–96 Diet and Health Knowledge Survey" [Online]. ARS Food Surveys Research Group. Available (under "Releases"): http://www.barc.usda.gov/bhnrc/foodsurvey/ home.htm.

United States Department of Agriculture, Economic Research Service, 2002. "Food consumption (per capita) data system, sugars/sweeteners." Washington, DC, http://www.ers.usda.gov/ Data/foodconsumption/datasystem.asp.

Wright, K. "The origins and development of ground stone assemblages in Late Pleistocene Southwest Asia." *Paleorient*, 1991; 17:19–45.

CHAPTER 1

Anthony, J. C., Lang, C. H., Crozier, S. J., Anthony, T. G., MacLean, D. A., Kimball, S. R., and Jefferson, L. S. "Contribution of insulin to the translational control of protein synthesis in skeletal muscle by leucine." *American Journal of Physiology Endocrinology Metabolism*, 2002; 282: E1092–101.

Atkins, R. C. *New Diet Revolution*. New York: Avon Books, 1998.

Ballmer, P. E., and Imoberdorf, R. "Influence of acidosis on protein metabolism." *Nutrition*, 1995; 11:462–8. http://www.arrs.net/CY_O10K2.htm, http://www.usatf.org/events/2003/ USAOutdoorTFChampionships/results/F27.asp.

Calder, P. C., and Kew, S. "The immune system: a target for functional foods?" *British Journal of Nutrition*, 2002; 88 Suppl 2:S165–77.

Cordain, L. "The nutritional characteristics of a contemporary diet based upon Paleolithic food groups." *Journal of American Neutraceutical Association*, 2002; 5:15–24.

Cordain, L., Watkins, B. A., Florant, G. L., Kehler, M., Rogers, L., and Li, Y. "Fatty acid analysis of wild ruminant tissues: Evolutionary implications for reducing diet-related chronic disease." *European Journal of Clinical Nutrition*, 2002; 56:181–91.

Eades, M. R., Eades, M. D. *Protein Power*. New York: Bantam Books, 1996.

Farnsworth, E., Luscombe, N. D., Noakes, M., Wittert, G., Argyiou, E., and Clifton, P. M. "Effect of a high-protein, energy-restricted diet on body composition, glycemic control, and lipid concentrations in overweight and obese hyperinsulinemic men and women." *American Journal of Clinical Nutrition*, 2003; 78:31–39.

Ferencik, M., and Ebringer, L. "Modulatory effects of selenium and zinc on the immune system." *Folia Microbiology (Praha)*, 2003; 48:417–26.

Foster, G. D., Wyatt, H. R., Hill, J. O., McGuckin, B. G., Brill, C., Mohammed, B. S., Szapary, P. O., Rader, D. J., Edman, J. S., and Klein, S. "A randomized trial of a low-carbohydrate diet for obesity." *New England Journal of Medicine*, 2003; 348:2,082–90.

Frassetto, L., Morris, R. C., and Sebastian, A. "Potassium bicarbonate reduces urinary nitrogen excretion in postmenopausal women." *Journal of Clinical Endocrinology Metabolism*, 1997; 82:254–59.

Frassetto, L., Morris, R. C. Jr., Sellmeyer, D. E., Todd, K., and Sebastian, A. "Diet, evolution and aging—the pathophysiologic effects of the post-agricultural inversion of the potassium-to-sodium and base-to-chloride ratios in the human diet." *European Journal of Nutrition*, 2001; 40:200–13.

Hawley, J. A., Schabort, E. J., Noakes, T. D., and Dennis, S. C. "Carbohydrate-loading and exercise performance. An update." *Sports Medicine*, 1997; 24:73–81.

Helge, J. W. "Adaptation to a fat-rich diet: effects on endurance performance in humans." *Sports Medicine*, 2000; 30:347–57.

Kris-Etherton, P. M., Taylor, D. S., Yu-Poth, S., Huth, P., Moriarty, K., Fishell, V., Hargrove, R. L., Zhao, G., and Etherton, T. D. 2000. "Polyunsaturated fatty acids in the food chain in the United States." *American Journal of Clinical Nutrition*, 71(1 Suppl):179S-88S.

Layman, D. K. "Role of leucine in protein metabolism during exercise and recovery." *Canadian Journal of Applied Physiology*, 2002; 27:646–62.

Lemon, P. W., Berardi, J. M., and Noreen, E. E. "The role of protein and amino acid supplements in the athlete's diet: does type or timing of ingestion matter?" *Current Sports Medicine Reports*, 2002; 1:214–21.

Levenhagen, D. K., Gresham, J. D., Carlson, M. G., Maron, D. J., Borel, M. J., and Flakoll, P. J. "Postexercise nutrient intake timing in humans is critical to recovery of leg glucose and protein homeostasis." *American Journal of Physiology—Endocrinology and Metabolism*, 2001; 280:E982–93.

Ludwig, D. S. "The glycemic index: physiological mechanisms relating to obesity, diabetes, and cardiovascular disease." *Journal of the American Medical Association*, 2002; 287:2414–23.

May, R. C., Bailey, J. L., Mitch, W. E., Masud, T., and England, B. K. "Glucocorticoids and acidosis stimulate protein and amino acid catabolism in vivo." *Kidney International*, 1996; 49:679–83.

Remer, T. "Influence of nutrition on acid-base balance—metabolic aspects." *European Journal of Nutrition*, 2001; 40:214–20.

Remer, T., and Manz, F. "Potential renal acid load of foods and its influence on urine pH." *Journal of the American Dietetic Association*, 1995; 95:791–97.

Samaha, F. F., Iqbal, N., Seshadri, P., Chicano, K. L., Daily, D. A., McGrory, J., Williams, T., Williams, M., Gracely, E. J., and Stern, L. "A low-carbohydrate as compared with a low-fat diet in severe obesity." *New England Journal of Medicine*, 2003; 348:2074–81.

Sears, B. *The Zone*. New York: Harper Trade, 1995.

Sebastian, A., Frassetto, L. A., Sellmeyer, D. E., Merriam, R. L., and Morris, R. C. Jr. "Estimation of the net acid load of the diet of ancestral preagricultural *Homo sapiens* and their hominid ancestors." *American Journal of Clinical Nutrition*, 2002; 76:1,308–16.

Sebastian, A., Harris, S. T., Ottaway, J. H., Todd, K. M., and Morris, R. C. Jr. "Improved mineral balance and skeletal metabolism in postmenopausal women treated with potassium bicarbonate." *New England Journal of Medicine*, 1994; 330:1,776–81.

Shaw, A., Fulton, L., Davis, C., and Hogbin, M. "Using the Food Guide Pyramid: A Resource for Nutrition Educators." US Department of Agriculture. Food, Nutrition, and Consumer Services, Center for Nutrition Policy and Promotion. Washington, DC. http://www.nal.usda.gov/fnic/Fpyr/guide.pdf.

Steward, H. L., Bethea, M. C., Andrews, S. S., and Balart, L. A. *Sugar Busters: Cut Sugar to Trim Fat.* New York: Ballantine Books, 1998.

Taubes, G. "What If It's All Been a Big Fat Lie?" *New York Times Magazine,* July 7, 2002.

Trinchieri, A., Zanetti, G., Curro, A., and Lizzano, R. "Effect of potential renal acid load of foods on calcium metabolism of renal calcium stone formers." *European Urology,* 2001; 39 Suppl 2:33–6.

CHAPTER 2

Berneis, K., Ninnis, R., Haussinger, D., and Keller, U. "Effects of hyper- and hypo-osmolality on whole body protein and glucose kinetics in humans." *American Journal of Physiology,* 1999; 276: E188–95.

Berning, J. R., Leeuders, M. M., Ratliff, K., et al. "The effects of a high-carbohydrate preexercise meal in the consumption of confectionaries of different glycemic indices." *Medical Science Sports Exercise,* 1993; 25(5):S125.

Jentjens, R. L., Cale, C., Gutch, C., and Jeukendrup, A. E. "Effects of preexercise ingestion of differing amounts of carbohydrate on subsequent metabolism and cycling performance." *European Journal of Applied Physiology,* 2003; 88(4–5):444–52.

Lemon, P. W., and Noreen, E. E. Unpublished paper, 2003.

McArdle, W. D., Katch, F. I., and Katch, V. L. *Exercise Physiology,* Baltimore: Williams & Wilkins, 1996.

Thomas, D. E., Brotherhood, J. R., and Brand, J. C. "Carbohydrate feeding before exercise: Effect of glycemic index." *International Journal of Sports Medicine,* 1991; 12:180–86.

Wilmore, J. H., and Costill, D. L. *Physiology of Sport and Exercise,* Champaign, IL: Human Kinetics, 1994.

Wolfe, R. R. "Effects of amino acid intake on anabolic processes." *Canadian Journal of Applied Physiology,* 2001; 26 Suppl:S220–27.

CHAPTER 3

Almond, C. S., Fortescue, E. B., Shin, A. Y., Mannix, R., and Greenes, D. S. "Risk Factors for Hyponatremia among Runners in the Boston Marathon." *Academy of Emergency Medicine,* 2003; 10(5):534–35.

Ball, T. C., Headley, S., and Vanderburgh, P. "Carbohydrate-electrolyte replacement improves sprint capacity following 50 minutes of high-intensity cycling." *Medical Science Sports Exercise,* 1994; 26:S196.

Barr, S. I., Costill, D. L., and Fink, W. J. "Fluid replacement during prolonged exercise: effects of water, saline, or no fluid." *Medical Science Sports Exercise,* 1991; 23(7):811–17.

Below, O., and Coyle, E. F. "Fluid and carbohydrate ingestion individually benefit exercise lasting one hour." *Medical Science Sports Exercise,* 1995; 27:200–10.

Blomstrand, E., Celsing, F., and Newsholme, E. A. "Changes in plasma concentrations of aromatic and branched-chain amino acids during sustained exercise in man and their possible role in fatigue." *Acta Physiology Scandinavia,* 1988; 133(1):115–21.

Blomstrand, E., Hassmen, P., Ek, S., Ekblom, B., and Newsholme, E. A. "Influence of ingesting a solution of branched-chain amino acids on perceived exertion during exercise." *Acta Physiology Scandinavia,* 1997; 159(1):41–49.

Blomstrand, E., Hassmen, P., Ekblom, B., and Newsholme, E. A. "Administration of branched-chain amino acids during sustained exercise—effects on performance and on plasma concentration of some amino acids." *European Journal of Applied Physiology and Occupational Physiology,* 1991; 63(2):83–88.

Blomstrand, E., and Newsholme, E. A. "Effect of branched-chain amino acid supplementation on the exercise-induced change in aromatic amino acid concentration in human muscle." *Acta Physiology Scandinavia,* 1992; 146(3):293–98.

Brouns, F., Saris, W., and Schneider, H. "Rationale for upper limits of electrolyte replacement during exercise." *International Journal of Sports Nutrition,* 1992; 2:229–38.

Brouns, F., Saris, W. H., Stroecken, J., et al. "Eating, drinking, and cycling. A controlled Tour de France simulation study, Part II. Effect of diet manipulation." *International Journal of Sports Medicine,* 1989; (10S):S41–S48.

Cade, J. R., Reese, R. M., Privette, R. M., et al. "Dietary intervention and training in swimmers." *European Journal of Applied Physiology,* 1991; 63(3–4):210–15.

Costill, D. L. "Sweating: its composition and effects on body fluids." *Annals of New York Academy of Science,* 1977; 301:160–74.

Fritzsche, R. G., Switzer, T. W., Hodgkinson, B. J., et al. "Water and carbohydrate ingestion during prolonged exercise increase maximal neuromuscular power." *Journal of Applied Physiology,* 2000; 88(2):730–37.

Gladden, L. B. "Lactate metabolism: A new paradigm for the third millennium." *Journal of Physiology,* 2004; 558:5–30.

Hawley, J. A., Sanders, B., Dennis, S. C., and Noakes, T. D. "Effect of ingesting varying concentrations of sodium on fluid balance during exercise." *Medical Science Sports Exercise,* 1996; 28(5): S350.

Hiller, W. D. "Dehydration and hyponatremia during triathlons." *Medical Science Sports Exercise,* 1989; 21(5 Suppl):S219–21.

Hiller, W. D., O'Toole, M. L., Fortess, E. E., Laird, R. H., Imbert, P. C., and Sisk, T. D. "Medical and physiological considerations in triathlons." *American Journal of Sports Medicine,* 1987; 15(2):164–67.

Ivy, J. L., Res, P. T., Sprague, R. C., et al. "Effect of a carbohydrate-protein supplement on endurance performance during exercise of varying intensity." *International Journal of Sports Nutrition Exercise Metabolism,* 2003; 13(3):388–401.

Kang, J., Utter, A., Nieman, D., et al. "Effect of carbohydrate substrate availability on ratings of perceived exertion during prolonged running." *Medical Science Sports Exercise,* 1997; 29(5):S111.

Malhotra, M. S., Sridharan, K., Venkataswamy, Y., Rai, R. M., Pichan, G., Radhakrishnan, U., and Grover, S. K. "Effect of restricted potassium intake on its excretion and on physiological responses during heat stress." *European Journal of Applied Physiology Occupational Physiology,* 1981; 47(2):169–79.

Mao, I. F., Chen, M. L., and Ko, Y. C. "Electrolyte loss in sweat and iodine deficiency in a hot environment." *Archives of Environmental Health,* 2001; 56(3):271–77.

McConnell, G., Kloot, K., and Hargreaves, M. "Effect of timing of carbohydrate ingestion on endurance exercise performance." *Medical Science Sports Exercise,* 1996; 28(10):1300–4.

McConnell, G., Snow, R. J., Proietto, J., and Hargreaves, M. "Muscle metabolism during prolonged exercise in humans: Influence of carbohydrate availability." *Journal of Applied Physiology,* 1999; 87(3):1083–86.

Millard-Stafford, M., Rosskopf, L. B., Snow, T. K., and Hinson, B. T. "Preexercise carbohydrate-electrolyte ingestion improves one-hour running performance in the heat." *Medical Science Sports Exercise,* 1994; 26:S196.

Miller, S. L., Maresh, C. M., Armstrong, L. E., Ebbeling, C. B., Lennon, S., and Rodriguez, N. R. "Metabolic response to provision of mixed protein-carbohydrate supplementation during endurance exercise." *International Journal of Sport Nutrition and Exercise Metabolism,* 2002; 12(4):384–97.

Newsholme, E. A., and Blomstrand, E. "The plasma level of some amino acids and physical and mental fatigue." *Experientia,* 1996; 52(5):413–15.

Newsholme, E. A., Blomstrand, E., and Ekblom, B. "Physical and mental fatigue: metabolic mechanisms and importance of plasma amino acids." *British Medical Bulletin,* 1992; 48(3): 477–95.

Nielsen, B., Hales, J. R., Strange, S., Christensen, N. J., Warberg, J., and Saltin, B. "Human circulatory and thermoregulatory adaptations with heat acclimation and exercise in a hot, dry environment." *Journal of Physiology,* 1993; 460:467–85.

Niles, E., Lachowetz, T., Garfi, J., et al. "Carbohydrate-protein drink improves time to exhaustion after recovery from endurance exercise." *Journal of Exercise Physiology online,* 2001; 4(1):45–52. (www.css.edu/users/tboone2/asep/Niles1Col.PDF)

Noakes, T. "Hyponatremia in distance runners: Fluid and sodium balance during exercise." *Current Sports Medicine Report,* 2002; 1(4):197–207.

Noakes, T. "IMMDA-AIMS advisory statement on guidelines for fluid replacement during marathon running." *New Studies in Athletics: IAAF Technical Quarterly,* 2003; 17(1):7–11.

Olsson, K. E., and Saltin, B. "Variation in total body water with muscle glycogen changes in man." *Acta Physiology Scandinavia,* 1970; 80(1):11–18.

O'Toole, M. L., Douglas, P. S., Laird, R. H., and Hiller, D. B. "Fluid and electrolyte status in athletes receiving medical care at an ultradistance triathlon." *Clinical Journal of Sport Medicine,* 1995; 5(2):116–22.

Rayssiguier, Y., Guezennec, C. Y., and Durlach, J. "New experimental and clinical data on the relationship between magnesium and sport." *Magnesium Research,* 1990; 3(2):93–102.

Robergs, R. A., Ghiasvand, F., and Parker, D. "Biochemistry of exercise-induced metabolic acidosis." *American Journal of Physiology Regulatory Integration Comparative Physiology,* 2004; 287: R502–R516.

Schena, F., Guerrini, F., Tregnaghi, P., and Kayser, B. "Branched-chain amino acid supplementation during trekking at high altitude. The effects on loss of body mass, body composition, and muscle power." *European Journal of Applied Physiology Occupational Physiology,* 1992; 65(5):394–98.

Shirreffs, S. M., and Maughan, R. J. "Whole body sweat collection in humans: an improved method with preliminary data on electrolyte content." *Journal of Applied Physiology,* 1997; 82(1): 336–41.

Speedy, D. B., Faris, J. G., Hamlin, M., Gallagher, P. G., and Campbell, R. G. "Hyponatremia and weight changes in an ultradistance triathlon." *Clinical Journal of Sport Medicine,* 1997; 7(3): 180–84.

Speedy, D. B., Noakes, T. D., and Schneider, C. "Exercise-associated hyponatremia: a review." *Emergency Medicine,* 2001; 13(1):17–27.

Speedy, D. B., Rogers, I. R., Noakes, T. D., et al. "Diagnosis and prevention of hyponatremia at an ultradistance triathlon." *Clinical Journal of Sport Medicine,* 2000; 10(1):52–58.

vanNieuwenhoven, M. A., Brummer, R.-J. M., and Brouns, F. "Gastrointestinal function during exercise: Comparison of water, sports drink, and sports drink with caffeine." *Journal of Applied Physiology,* 2000; 89(3):1079–85.

Vrijens, D. M. J., and Rehrer, N. J. "Sodium-free ingestion decreases plasma sodium during exercise in the heat." *Journal of Applied Physiology,* 1999; 86(6):1847–52.

Wagenmakers, A. J., Jeukendrup, A. E., and Saris, W. H. "Carbohydrate feedings improve 1 hour time trial cycling performance." *Medical Science Sports Exercise,* 1996; 28(5): S221.

Yamamoto, T., and Newsholme, E. A. "Diminished central fatigue by inhibition of the L-system transporter for the uptake of tryptophan." *Brain Research Bulletin,* 2000; 52(1):35–38.

Yaspelkis, B. B. III, Patterson, J. G., Anderla, P. A., et al. "Carbohydrate supplementation spares muscle glycogen during variable-intensity exercise." *Journal of Applied Physiology,* 1993; 75(4): 1477–85.

CHAPTER 4

Anthony, J. G., Anthony, T. G., Kimball, S. R., and Jefferson, L. S. "Signaling pathways involved in translational control of protein synthesis in skeletal muscle by leucine." *Journal of Nutrition,* 2001; 131:856S-860S.

Armstrong, L. E., Hubbard, R. W., Jones, B. H., and Daniels, J. "Preparing Alberto Salazar for the heat of the 1984 Olympic marathon." *Physiology and Sports Medicine,* 1986; 14(3):73–81.

Bassit, R. A., Sawada, L. A., Bacurau, R. F. P., Navarro, F., Martins, E., Santos, R. V. T., Caperuto, R. C., Rogeri, P., and Costa Rosa, L. F. P. B. "Branched-chain amino acid supplementation and the immune response of long-distance athletes." *Nutrition,* 2002; 18:376–79.

Brouns, F., Kovacs, E. M., and Senden, J. M. "The effect of different rehydration drinks on post-exercise electrolyte excretion in trained athletes." *International Journal of Sports Medicine,* 1998; 19(1):56–60.

Brouns, F., Saris, W., and Schneider, H. "Rationale for upper limits of electrolyte replacement during exercise." *International Journal of Sport Nutrition,* 1992; 2:229–38.

Burke, L. M. "Nutritional needs for exercise in heat." *Comparative Biochemical Physiology and Molecular Integrated Physiology,* 2001; 128(4):735–48.

Burke, L. M. "Nutrition for postexercise recovery." *Australian Journal of Science Medicine Sport,* 1997; 29(1):3–10.

Burke, L. M., Collier, G. R., and Hargreaves, M. "Muscle glycogen storage after prolonged exercise: effect of the glycemic index of carbohydrate feedings." *Journal of Applied Physiology,* 1993; 75(2):1019–23.

Burke, L. M., and Read, R. S. "Dietary supplements in sport." *Sports Medicine,* 1993; 15(1): 43–65.

Friedman, E., and Lemon, P. W. "Effect of chronic endurance exercise on retention of dietary protein." *International Journal of Sports Medicine,* 1989; 10(2):118–23.

Ivy, J. L. "Dietary strategies to promote glycogen synthesis after exercise." *Canadian Journal of Applied Physiology,* 2001; 26 Suppl: S236–45.

Ivy, J. L, Goforth, H.W. Jr., Damon, B.M., McCauley, T.R., Parsons, E.C., and Price, T.B. "Early postexercise muscle glycogen recovery is enhanced with a carbohydrate-protein supplement." *Journal of Applied Physiology,* 2002; 93(4):1337–44.

Ivy, J. L., Katz, A. L., and Cutler, C. L. "Muscle glycogen synthesis after exercise: Effect of time of carbohydrate ingestion." *Journal of Applied Physiology,* 1988; 64(4):1480–85.

Layman, D. K. "Role of leucine in protein metabolism during exercise and recovery." *Canadian Journal of Applied Physiology,* 2002; 27(6):646–63.

Lemon, P. W. "Effects of exercise on dietary protein requirements." *International Journal of Sport Nutrition,* 1998; 8(4):426–47.

Lemon, P. W., Dolny, D. G., and Yarasheski, K. E. "Moderate physical activity can increase dietary protein needs." *Canadian Journal of Applied Physiology,* 1997; 22(5):494–503.

Levenhagen, D. K., Carr, C., Carlson, M. G., et al. "Postexercise protein intake enhances whole-body and leg protein accretion in humans." *Medical Science Sports Exercise,* 2002; 34(5):828–37.

Levenhagen, D. K., Gresham, J. D., Carlson, M. G., et al. "Postexercise nutrient intake timing in humans is critical to recovery of leg glucose and protein homeostasis." *American Journal of Physiology Endocrinology Metabolism,* 2001; 280(6):E982–93.

Maughan, R. J., and Noakes, T. D. "Fluid replacement and exercise stress. A brief review of studies on fluid replacement and some guidelines for the athlete." *Sports Medicine,* 1991; 12(1):16–31.

Maughan, R. J., and Shirreffs, S. M. "Recovery from prolonged exercise: restoration of water and electrolyte balance." *Journal of Sports Science,* 1997; 15(3):297–303.

Mayer, K., Meyer, S., Reinholz-Muhly, M., Maus, U., Merfels, M., Lohmeyer, J., Grimminger, F., and Seeger, W. "Short-time infusion of fish oil–based lipid emulsions, approved for parenteral nutrition, reduces monocyte proinflammatory cytokine generation and adhesive interaction with endothelium in humans." *Journal of Immunology,* 2003; 171(9):4837–43.

Meredith, C. N., Zackin, M. J., Frontera, W. R., and Evans, W. J. "Dietary protein requirements and body protein metabolism in endurance-trained men." *Journal of Applied Physiology,* 1989; 66(6):2850–56.

Pendergast, D. R., Leddy, J. J., and Venkatraman, J. T. "A perspective on fat intake in athletes." *Journal of American College of Nutrition,* 2000; 19(3):345–50.

Remer, T., and Manz, F. "Potential renal acid load of foods and its influence on urine pH." *Journal of the American Dietetic Association,* 1995; 95:791–97.

Roy, B., Luttmer, K., Bosman, M. J., and Tarnopolsky, M. A. "The influence of postexercise macronutrient intake on energy balance and protein metabolism in active females participating in endurance training." *International Journal of Sport Nutrition and Exercise Metabolism,* 2002; 12:172–88.

Sherman, W. M. "Recovery from endurance exercise." *Medical Science Sports Exercise,* 1992; 24(9S):S336–S339.

Shirreffs, S. M., Taylor, A. J., Leiper, J. B., and Maughan, R. J. "Postexercise rehydration in man: effects of volume consumed and drink sodium content." *Medical Science Sports Exercise,* 1996; 28(10):1260–71.

Tarnopolsky, M. A., Bosman, M., Macdonald, J. R., Vandeputte, D., Martin, J., and Roy, B. D. "Postexercise protein-carbohydrate and carbohydrate supplements increase muscle glycogen in men and women." *Journal of Applied Physiology,* 1997; 83(6):1877–83.

Tarnopolsky, M. A., MacDougall, J. D., and Atkinson, S. A. "Influence of protein intake and training status on nitrogen balance and lean body mass." *Journal of Applied Physiology,* 1988; 64(1):187–93.

van Loon, L. J., Kruijshoop, M., Verhagen, H., Saris, W. H., and Wagenmakers, A. J. "Ingestion of protein hydrolysate and amino acid-carbohydrate mixtures increases postexercise plasma insulin responses in men." *Journal of Nutrition,* 2000 Oct; 130(10):2508–13.

Zawadzki, K. M., Yaspelkis, B. B. III, and Ivy, J. L. "Carbohydrate-protein complex increases the rate of muscle glycogen storage after exercise." *Journal of Applied Physiology,* 1992; 72(5): 1854–59.

Zhang, N., Terao, T., and Nakano, S. "Effect of time of carbohydrate ingestion on muscle glycogen resynthesis after exhaustive exercise in rats." *Tokai Journal of Experimental Clinical Medicine,* 1994; 19(3–6):125–29.

CHAPTER 5

Bohn, T., Davidsson, L., Walczyk, T., and Hurrell, R F. "Phytic acid added to white-wheat bread inhibits fractional apparent magnesium absorption in humans." *American Journal of Clinical Nutrition,* 2004 Mar; 79(3):418–23.

Chajes, V., and Bougnoux, P. "Omega-6/omega-3 polyunsaturated fatty acid ratio and cancer." *World Review of Nutrition and Diet,* 2003; 92:133–51.

Cordain, L. "Cereal grains: humanity's double-edged sword." *World Review of Nutrition and Diet,* 1999; 84:19–73.

Cordain, L. "The nutritional characteristics of a contemporary diet based upon Paleolithic food groups." *Journal of the American Nutraceutical Association,* 2002; 5:15–24.

Cordain, L., Brand Miller, J., Eaton, S. B, Mann, N., Holt, S. H. A., and Speth, J. D. "Plant to animal subsistence ratios and macronutrient energy estimations in world wide hunter-gatherer diets." *American Journal of Clinical Nutrition,* 2000; 71:682–92.

Cordain, L., Eaton, S. B., Brand Miller, J., Mann, N., and Hill, K. "The paradoxical nature of hunter-gatherer diets: meat-based, yet non-atherogenic." *European Journal of Clinical Nutrition,* 2002; 56 (suppl 1):S42–S52.

Foster-Powell, K., Holt, S. H. A., and Brand-Miller, J. C. "International table of glycemic index and glycemic load values: 2002." *American Journal of Clinical Nutrition,* 2002; 76:5–56.

Frassetto, L., Morris, R. C. Jr, and Sebastian, A. "Potassium bicarbonate reduces urinary nitrogen excretion in postmenopausal women." *Journal of Clinical Endocrinology Metabolism,* 1997 Jan; 82(1):254–59.

Gotshall, R. W., Mickleborough, T. D., and Cordain, L. "Dietary salt restriction improves pulmonary function in exercise-induced asthma." *Medical Science Sports Exercise,* 2000 Nov; 32(11):1815–19.

Harrington, M., and Cashman, K. D. "High salt intake appears to increase bone resorption in postmenopausal women but high potassium intake ameliorates this adverse effect." *Nutrition Review,* 2003 May; 61(5 Pt 1):179–83.

Holt, S. H., Miller, J. C., and Petocz, P. "An insulin index of foods: the insulin demand generated by 1000–kJ portions of common foods." *American Journal of Clinical Nutrition,* 1997 Nov; 66(5):1264–76.

Honein, M. A., Paulozzi, L. J., Mathews, T. J., Erickson, J. D., and Wong, L. Y. "Impact of folic acid fortification of the US food supply on the occurrence of neural tube defects." *Journal of the American Medical Association,* 2001 Jun 20; 285(23):2981–86.

Jenkins, D. J., Wolever, T. M., Taylor, R. H., Barker, H., Fielden, H., Baldwin, J. M., Bowling, A. C., Newman, H. C., Jenkins, A. L., and Goff, D. V. "Glycemic index of foods: a physiological basis for carbohydrate exchange." *American Journal of Clinical Nutrition,* 1981 Mar; 34(3):362–66.

Johnson, N. A., Stannard, S. R., and Thompson, M. W. "Muscle triglyceride and glycogen in endurance exercise: implications for performance." *Sports Medicine,* 2004; 34(3):151–64.

Lemon, P. W. "Effects of exercise on dietary protein requirements." *International Journal of Sport Nutrition,* 1998 Dec; 8(4):426–47.

Ludwig, D. S. "The glycemic index: physiological mechanisms relating to obesity, diabetes, and cardiovascular disease." *Journal of the American Medical Association,* 2002 May 8; 287(18):2414–23.

Machado Andrade Pde, M., and Tavares do Carmo, M. G. "Dietary long-chain omega-3 fatty acids and anti-inflammatory action: potential application in the field of physical exercise." *Nutrition,* 2004 Feb; 20(2):243.

Mickleborough, T., and Gotshall, R. "Dietary components with demonstrated effectiveness in decreasing the severity of exercise-induced asthma." *Sports Medicine,* 2003; 33(9):671–81.

Mickleborough, T. D., Gotshall, R. W., Cordain, L., and Lindley, M. "Dietary salt alters pulmonary function during exercise in exercise-induced asthmatics." *Journal of Sports Science,* 2001 Nov; 19(11):865–73.

Mickleborough, T. D., Gotshall, R. W., Kluka, E. M., Miller, C. W., and Cordain, L. "Dietary chloride as a possible determinant of the severity of exercise-induced asthma." *European Journal of Applied Physiology,* 2001 Sep; 85(5):450–56.

Mickleborough, T. D., Murray, R. L., Ionescu, A. A., and Lindley, M. R. "Fish oil supplementation reduces severity of exercise-induced bronchoconstriction in elite athletes." *American Journal of Respiratory Critical Care Medicine,* 2003 Nov 15; 168(10):1181–89.

O'Shaughnessy, K. M., and Karet, F. E. "Salt handling and hypertension." *Journal of Clinical Investigation,* 2004 Apr; 113(8):1075–81.

Ostman, E. M., Liljeberg Elmstahl, H. G., and Bjorck, I. M. "Inconsistency between glycemic and insulinemic responses to regular and fermented milk products." *American Journal of Clinical Nutrition,* 2001 Jul; 74(1):96–100.

Parry-Billings, M., Budgett, R., Koutedakis, Y., Blomstrand, E., Brooks, S., Williams, C., Calder, P. C., Pilling, S., Baigrie, R., and Newsholme, E. A. "Plasma amino acid concentrations in the overtraining syndrome: possible effects on the immune system." *Medical Science Sports Exercise,* 1992 Dec; 24(12):1353–58.

Pedersen, J. I. "More on trans fatty acids." *British Journal of Nutrition,* 2001 Mar; 85(3):249–50.

Salmeron, J., Ascherio, A., Rimm, E. B., Colditz, G. A., Spiegelman, D., Jenkins, D. J., Stampfer, M. J., Wing, A. L., and Willett, W. C. "Dietary fiber, glycemic load, and risk of NIDDM in men." *Diabetes Care.* 1997 Apr; 20(4):545–50.

Salmeron, J., Manson, J. E., Stampfer, M. J., Colditz, G. A., Wing, A. L., and Willett, W. C. "Dietary fiber, glycemic load, and risk of non-insulin-dependent diabetes mellitus in women." *Journal of the American Medical Association,* 1997 Feb 12; 277(6):472–77.

Schmitt, B., Fluck, M., Decombaz, J., Kreis, R., Boesch, C., Wittwer, M., Graber, F., Vogt, M., Howald, H., and Hoppeler, H. "Transcriptional adaptations of lipid metabolism in tibialis anterior muscle of endurance-trained athletes." *Physiology Genomics,* 2003 Oct 17; 15(2):148–57.

Sebastian, A., Frassetto, L. A., Sellmeyer, D. E., Merriam, R. L., and Morris, R. C. Jr. "Estimation of the net acid load of the diet of ancestral preagricultural *Homo sapiens* and their hominid ancestors." *American Journal of Clinical Nutrition,* 2002 Dec; 76(6):1308–16.

Simopoulos, A. P. "Omega-3 fatty acids in inflammation and autoimmune diseases." *Journal of American College Nutrition,* 2002 Dec; 21(6):495–505.

Simopoulos, A. P. "The importance of the ratio of omega-6/omega-3 essential fatty acids." *Biomedical Pharmacotherapy,* 2002 Oct; 56(8):365–79.

Stannard, S. R., and Johnson, N. A. "Insulin resistance and elevated triglyceride in muscle: more important for survival than 'thrifty' genes." *Journal of Physiology,* 2004; 554(Pt 3):595–607.

van der Merwe, N. J., Thackeray, J. F., Lee-Thorp, J. A., and Luyt, J. "The carbon isotope ecology and diet of Australopithecus africanus at Sterkfontein, South Africa." *Journal of Human Evolution,* 2003 May; 44(5):581–97.

Vermunt, S. H., Beaufrere, B., Riemersma, R. A., Sebedio, J. L., Chardigny, J. M., Mensink, R. P., and TransLinE Investigators. "Dietary trans alpha-linolenic acid from deodorised rapeseed oil and plasma lipids and lipoproteins in healthy men: the TransLinE Study." *British Journal of Nutrition,* 2001 Mar; 85(3):387–92.

Vogt, M., Puntschart, A., Howald, H., Mueller, B., Mannhart, C., Gfeller-Tuescher, L., Mullis, P., and Hoppeler, H. "Effects of dietary fat on muscle substrates, metabolism, and performance in athletes." *Medical Science Sports Exercise,* 2003 Jun; 35(6):952–60.

von Schacky, C. "Omega-3 fatty acids and cardiovascular disease." *Current Opinion Clinical Nutrition Metabolism Care,* 2004 Mar; 7(2):131–36.

Williams, M. H. "Facts and fallacies of purported ergogenic amino acid supplements." *Clinical Sports Medicine,* 1999 Jul; 18(3):633–49.

Williams, M. H. *Nutrition for Health, Fitness and Sport.* New York: McGraw Hill, 2002.

CHAPTER 6

Alessio, H. M. "Exercise-induced oxidative stress." *Medical Science Sports Exercise,* 1993 Feb; 25(2):218–24.

Alessio, H. M., Goldfarb, A. H., and Cao, G. "Exercise-induced oxidative stress before and after vitamin C supplementation." *International Journal of Sport Nutrition,* 1997 Mar; 7(1):1–9.

Armstrong, L. E. "Caffeine, body fluid-electrolyte balance, and exercise performance." *International Journal of Sport Nutrition and Exercise Metabolism,* 2002 Jun; 12(2):189–206.

Bell, D. G., and McLellan, T. M. "Exercise endurance 1, 3, and 6 hours after caffeine ingestion in caffeine users and nonusers." *Journal of Applied Physiology,* 2002 Oct; 93(4):1227–34.

Bhathena, S. J. "Relationship between fatty acids and the endocrine system." *Biofactors,* 2000; 13(1–4):35–39.

Brilla, L. R., and Landerholm, T. E. "Effect of fish oil supplementation and exercise on serum lipids and aerobic fitness." *Journal of Sports Medicine and Physical Fitness,* 1990 Jun; 30(2):173–80.

Castell, L. M., Poortmans, J. R., and Newsholme, E. A. "Does glutamine have a role in reducing infections in athletes?" *European Journal of Applied Physiological Occupational Physiology,* 1996; 73(5):488–90.

Cox, G. R., Desbrow, B., Montgomery, P. G., Anderson, M. E., Bruce, C. R., Macrides, T. A., Martin, D. T., Moquin, A., Roberts, A., Hawley, J. A., and Burke, L. M. "Effect of different protocols of caffeine intake on metabolism and endurance performance." *Journal of Applied Physiology,* 2002 Sep; 93(3):990–99.

Dragan, I., Dinu, V., Mohora, M., Cristea, E., Ploesteanu, E., and Stroescu, V. "Studies regarding the antioxidant effects of selenium on top swimmers." *Revue Roumaine de Physiologie,* 1990 Jan-Mar; 27(1):15–20.

Fielding, R. A., and Meydani, M. "Exercise, free radical generation, and aging." *Aging* (Milano), 1997 Feb-Apr; 9(1–2):12–18.

Graham, T. E., and Spriet, L. L. "Metabolic, catecholamine, and exercise performance responses to various doses of caffeine." *Journal of Applied Physiology,* 1995 Mar; 78(3):867–74.

Hemila, H. "Vitamin C and common cold incidence: a review of studies with subjects under heavy physical stress." *International Journal of Sports Medicine,* 1996 Jul; 17(5):379–83.

Holick, M. F. "Vitamin D: A millennium perspective." *Journal of Cell Biochemistry,* 2003; 88:296–307.

Horswill, C. A. "Effects of bicarbonate, citrate, and phosphate loading on performance." *International Journal of Sport Nutrition,* 1995 Jun; 5 Suppl:S111–19.

Itoh, H., Ohkuwa, T., Yamazaki, Y., Shimoda, T., Wakayama, A., Tamura, S., Yamamoto, T., Sato, Y., and Miyamura, M. "Vitamin E supplementation attenuates leakage of enzymes following 6 successive days of running training." *International Journal of Sports Medicine,* 2000 Jul; 21(5):369–74.

Jeukendrup, A. E., and Martin, J. "Improving cycling performance: how should we spend our time and money?" *Sports Medicine,* 2001; 31(7):559–69.

Ji, L. L. "Exercise at old age: does it increase or alleviate oxidative stress?" *Annual of the New York Academy of Science,* 2001 Apr; 928:236–47.

Kanter, M. "Free radicals, exercise and antioxidant supplementation." *Proceedings of the Nutrition Society,* 1998 Feb; 57(1):9–13.

Kelly, G. S. "Nutritional and botanical interventions to assist with the adaptation to stress." *Alternative Medical Review,* 1999 Aug; 4(4):249–65.

Lovlin, R., Cottle, W., Pyke, I., Kavanagh, M., and Belcastro, A. N. "Are indices of free radical damage related to exercise intensity?" *European Journal of Applied Physiology Occupational Physiology,* 1987; 56(3):313–16.

Matson, L. G., and Tran, Z. V. "Effects of sodium bicarbonate ingestion on anaerobic performance: a meta-analytic review." *International Journal of Sport Nutrition,* 1993 Mar; 3(1):2–28.

Meydani, M. "Vitamin E requirement in relation to dietary fish oil and oxidative stress in elderly." *EXS,* 1992; 62:411–18.

Meydani, M., Evans, W. J., Handelman, G., Biddle, L., Fielding, R. A., Meydani, S. N., Burrill, J., Fiatarone, M. A., Blumberg, J. B., and Cannon, J. G. "Protective effect of vitamin E on exercise-induced oxidative damage in young and older adults." *American Journal of Physiology,* 1993 May; 264(5 Pt 2):R992–98.

Monteleone, P., Maj, M., Beinat, L., Natale, M., and Kemali, D. "Blunting by chronic phosphatidylserine administration of the stress-induced activation of the hypothalamo-pituitary-adrenal axis in healthy men." *European Journal of Clinical Pharmacology,* 1992; 42(4):385–88.

Newsholme, E. A. "Biochemical mechanisms to explain immunosuppression in well-trained and overtrained athletes." *International Journal of Sports Medicine,* 1994 Oct; 15 Suppl 3:S142–47.

Niess, A. M., Hartmann, A., Grunert-Fuchs, M., Poch, B., and Speit, G. "DNA damage after exhaustive treadmill running in trained and untrained men." *International Journal of Sports Medicine,* 1996 Aug; 17(6):397–403.

Novak, F., Heyland, D. K., Avenell, A., Drover, J. W., and Su, X. "Glutamine supplementation in serious illness: a systematic review of the evidence." *Critical Care Medicine,* 2002 Sep; 30(9):2022–29.

Olinescu, R., Talaban, D., Nita, S., and Mihaescu, G. "Comparative study of the presence of oxidative stress in sportsmen in competition and aged people, as well as the preventive effect of selenium administration." *Romanian Journal of Internal Medicine,* 1995 Jan-Jun; 33(1–2):47–54.

Paluska, S. A. "Caffeine and exercise." *Current Sports Medicine Report,* 2003 Aug; 2(4):213–19.

Parry-Billings, M., Blomstrand, E., McAndrew, N., and Newsholme, E. A. "A communicational link between skeletal muscle, brain, and cells of the immune system." *International Journal of Sports Medicine,* 1990 May; 11 Suppl 2:S122–28.

Parry-Billings, M., Budgett, R., Koutedakis, Y., Blomstrand, E., Brooks, S., Williams, C., Calder, P. C., Pilling, S., Baigrie, R., and Newsholme, E. A. "Plasma amino acid concentrations in the overtraining syndrome: possible effects on the immune system." *Medical Science Sports Exercise,* 1992 Dec; 24(12):1353–58.

Schwenk, T. L., and Costley, C. D. "When food becomes a drug: nonanabolic nutritional supplement use in athletes." *American Journal of Sports Medicine,* 2002 Nov-Dec; 30(6):907–16.

Tarnopolsky, M. A., Atkinson, S. A., MacDougall, J. D., Sale, D. G., and Sutton, J. R. "Physiological responses to caffeine during endurance running in habitual caffeine users." *Medical Science Sports Exercise,* 1989 Aug; 21(4):418–24.

Van Soeren, M. H., Sathasivam, P., Spriet, L. L., and Graham, T. E. "Caffeine metabolism and epinephrine responses during exercise in users and nonusers." *Journal of Applied Physiology,* 1993 Aug; 75(2):805–12.

Wemple, R. D., Lamb, D. R., and McKeever, K. H. "Caffeine vs caffeine-free sports drinks: effects on urine production at rest and during prolonged exercise." *International Journal of Sports Medicine,* 1997 Jan; 18(1):40–46.

CHAPTER 7

Bailey, S. P., Davis, J. M., and Ahlborn, E. N. "Neuroendocrine and substrate responses to altered brain 5–HT activity during prolonged exercise to fatigue." *Journal of Applied Physiology,* 1993 Jun; 74(6):3006–12.

Balaban, E. P., Cox, J. V., Snell, P., Vaughan, R. H., and Frenkel, E. P. "The frequency of anemia and iron deficiency in the runner." *Medical Science Sports Exercise,* 1989 Dec; 21(6):643–48.

Bendich, A., and Chandra, R. K. *Micronutrients and Immune Functions.* New York: New York Academy of Sciences, 1990.

Cade, J. R., Reese, R. H., Privette, R. M., Hommen, N. M., Rogers, J. L., and Fregly, M. J. "Dietary intervention and training in swimmers." *European Journal of Applied Physiology Occupational Physiology,* 1991; 63:210–15.

Chandra, R. K. "Nutrition and immunity: lessons from the past and new insights into the future." *American Journal of Clinical Nutrition,* 1990; 53:1087–1101.

Clement, D. B., Lloyd-Smith, D. R., Macintyre, J. G., Matheson, G. O., Brock, R., and Dupont, M. "Iron status in Winter Olympic sports." *Journal of Sports Science,* 1987 Winter; 5(3):261–71.

Costill, D. L., Coyle, E., Dalsky, G., Evans, W., Fink, W., and Hoopes, D. "Effects of elevated plasma FFA and insulin on muscle glycogen usage during exercise." *Journal of Applied Physiology,* 1977 Oct; 43(4):695–99.

Costill, D. L., Flynn, M. G., Kirwan, J. A., Houmard, J. B., Mitchell, J. B., Thomas, R., and Park, S. H. "Effects of repeated days of intensified training on muscle glycogen and swimming performance." *Medical Science Sports Exercise,* 1988; 20:249–54.

Cunningham-Rundles, S. *Nutrient Modulation of the Immune Response.* New York: Marcel Dekker, 1993.

Davis, J. M., and Bailey, S. P. "Possible mechanisms of central nervous system fatigue during exercise." *Medical Science Sports Exercise,* 1997 Jan; 29(1):45–57.

Deuster, P. A., Kyle, S. B., Moser, P. B., Vigersky, R. A., Singh, A., and Schoomaker, E. B. "Nutritional intakes and status of highly trained amenorrheic and eumenorrheic women runners." *Fertility and Sterility,* 1986 Oct; 46(4):636–43.

Deuster, P. A., Kyle, S. B., Moser, P. B., Vigersky, R. A., Singh, A., and Schoomaker, E. B. "Nutritional survey of highly trained women runners." *American Journal of Clinical Nutrition,* 1986 Dec; 44(6):954–62.

Dressendorfer, R. H., and Sockolov, R. "Hypozincemia in runners." *Physiology Sports Medicine,* 1980; 8:97–100.

Dyck, D. J., Putman, C. T., Heigenhauser, G. J., Hultman, E., and Spriet, L. L. "Regulation of fat-carbohydrate interaction in skeletal muscle during intense aerobic cycling." *American Journal of Physiology,* 1993 Dec; 265(6 Pt 1):E852–59.

Flakoll, P. J., Judy, T., Flinn, K., Carr, C., and Flinn, S. "Postexercise protein supplementation improves health and muscle soreness during basic military training in marine recruits." *Journal of Applied Physiology,* 2004 Mar; 96(3):951–56. Epub 2003 Dec 02.

Fry, R. W., Morton, A. R., and Keast, D. "Overtraining in athletes. An update." *Sports Medicine,* 1991 Jul; 12(1):32–65.

Gershwin, M. E., Beach, R. S., and Hurley, L. S. *Nutrition and Immunity.* Orlando: Academic Press, 1985.

Hawley, J. A., and Hopkins, W. G. "Aerobic glycolytic and aerobic lipolytic power systems. A new paradigm with implications for endurance and ultraendurance events." *Sports Medicine,* 1995 Apr; 19(4):240–50.

Ivy, J. L., Goforth, H. W. Jr., Damon, B. M., McCauley, T. R., Parsons, E. C., and Price, T. B. J. "Early postexercise muscle glycogen recovery is enhanced with a carbohydrate-protein supplement." *Applied Physiology,* 2002 Oct; 93(4):1337–44.

Ivy, J. L., Res, P. T., Sprague, R. C., and Widzer, M. O. "Effect of a carbohydrate-protein supplement on endurance performance during exercise of varying intensity." *International Journal of Sport Nutrition and Exercise Metabolism,* 2003 Sep; 13(3):382–95.

Kirwan, J. P., Costill, D. L., Mitchell, J. B., Houmard, J. B., Flynn, M. G., Fink, W. J., and Beltz, J. D. "Carbohydrate balance in competitive runners during successive days of intense training." *Journal of Applied Physiology,* 1988; 65:2601–06.

Lambert, E. V., et al. "Enhanced endurance in trained cyclists during moderate-intensity exercise following two weeks adaptation to a high-fat diet." *European Journal of Applied Physiology,* 1994; 69:287–93.

Lambert, E. V., and Goedecke, J. H. "The role of dietary macronutrients in optimizing endurance performance." *Current Sports Medicine Report,* 2003 Aug; 2(4):194–201.

Lapachet, R. A., et al. "Body fat and exercise endurance in trained rats adapted to a high-fat and/or high-carbohydrate diet." *Journal of Applied Physiology,* 1996; 80(4):1173–79.

Muoio, D. M., Leddy, J. J., Horvath, P. J., Awad, A. B., and Pendergast, D. R. "Effect of dietary fat on metabolic adjustments to maximal VO_2 and endurance in runners." *Medical Science Sports Exercise,* 1994 Jan; 26(1):81–88.

Noakes, T., et al. "Effects of a low-carbohydrate, high-fat diet prior to carbohydrate loading on endurance cycling performance." *Clinical Science,* 1994; 87:S32–S33.

Nose, H., Mack, G. W., Shi, X. R., and Nadel, E. R. "Role of osmolality and plasma volume during rehydration in humans." *Journal of Applied Physiology,* 1988 Jul; 65(1):325–31.

Phinney, S. D., Bistrian, B. R., Evans, W. J., Gervino, E., and Blackburn, G. L. "The human metabolic response to chronic ketosis without caloric restriction: preservation of submaximal exercise capability with reduced carbohydrate oxidation." *Metabolism,* 1983 Aug; 32(8):769–76.

Shephard, R. J., and Shek, P. N. "Immunological hazards from nutritional imbalance in athletes." *Exercise Immunology Review,* 1998; 4:22–48.

Sherman, W. M., Doyle, J. A., Lamb, D. R., and Strauss, R. H. "Dietary carbohydrate, muscle glycogen, and exercise performance during 7 days of training." *American Journal of Clinical Nutrition,* 1993; 57:27–31.

Sherman, W. M., and Wimer, G. S. "Insufficient dietary carbohydrate during training: does it impair athletic performance?" *International Journal of Sport Nutrition,* 1991; 1:28–44.

Shirreffs, S. M., and Maughan, R. J. "Rehydration and recovery of fluid balance after exercise." *Exercise Sport Science Review,* 2000 Jan; 28(1):27–32.

Snyder, A. C., Kuipers, H., Cheng, B., Servais, R., and Fransen, E. "Overtraining following intensified training with normal muscle glycogen." *Medical Science Sports Exercise,* 1995; 27:1063–70.

Steinacker, J. M., Lormes, W., Lehmann, M., and Altenburg, D. "Training of rowers before world championships." *Medical Science Sports Exercise,* 1998 Jul; 30(7):1158–63.

van Erp-Baart, A. M., Saris, W. M., Binkhorst, R. A., Vos, J. A., and Elvers, J. W. "Nationwide survey on nutritional habits in elite athletes. Part II. Mineral and vitamin intake." *International Journal of Sports Medicine,* 1989 May; 10 Suppl 1:S11–16.

Vogt, M., Puntschart, A., Howald, H., Mueller, B., Mannhart, C. H., Gfeller-Tuescher, L., Mullis, P., and Hoppeler, H. "Effects of dietary fat on muscle substrates, metabolism, and performance in athletes." *Medical Science Sports Exercise,* 2003; 35(6):952–60.

Weiss, H. E. "Anamnestic, clinical and laboratory data of 1300 athletes in a basic medical check with respect to the incidence and prophylaxis of infectious diseases." *International Journal of Sports Medicine,* 1994; 6:360.

Wilson, W. M., and Maughan, R. J. "Evidence for a possible role of 5-hydroxytryptamine in the genesis of fatigue in man: administration of paroxetine, a 5-HT re-uptake inhibitor, reduces the capacity to perform prolonged exercise." *Experimental Physiology,* 1992 Nov; 77(6):921–24.

Wong, S. H., Williams, C., Simpson, M., and Ogaki, T. "Influence of fluid intake pattern on short-term recovery from prolonged, submaximal running and subsequent exercise capacity." *Journal of Sports Science,* 1998 Feb; 16(2):143–52.

Zawadzki, K. M., Yaspelkis, B. B. III, and Ivy, J. L. "Carbohydrate-protein complex increases the rate of muscle glycogen storage after exercise." *Journal of Applied Physiology,* 1992 May; 72(5):1854–59.

CHAPTER 8

Aiello, L. C., and Wheeler, P. "The expensive tissue hypothesis." *Current Anthropology,* 1995; 36:199–222.

Atkins, R. C., Ornish, D., and Wadden, T. "Low-carb, low-fat diet gurus face off." Interview by Joan Stephenson. *Journal of the American Medical Association,* 2003 Apr 9; 289(14):1767–68, 1773.

Blumenschine, R. J., and Cavallo, J. A. "Scavenging and human evolution." *Scientific American,* 1992; 267:90–96.

Brown, F., Harris, J., Leakey, R., and Walker, A. "Early *Homo erectus* skeleton from west Lake Turkana, Kenya." *Nature,* 1985 Aug 29–Sep 4; 316(6031):788–92.

Bunn, H. T., and Kroll, E. M. "Systematic butchery by plio/pleistocene hominids at Olduvai gorge, Tanzania." *Current Anthropology,* 1986; 27:431–52.

Burdge, G. C., Jones, A. E., and Wootton, S. A. "Eicosapentaenoic and docosapentaenoic acids are the principal products of alpha-linolenic acid metabolism in young men." *British Journal of Nutrition,* 2002 Oct; 88(4):355–63.

Burdge, G. C., and Wootton, S. A. "Conversion of alpha-linolenic acid to eicosapentaenoic, docosapentaenoic and docosahexaenoic acids in young women." *British Journal of Nutrition,* 2002 Oct; 88(4):411–20.

Chesney, R. W., Helms, R. A., Christensen, M., Budreau, A. M., Han, X. and Sturman, J. A. "The role of taurine in infant nutrition." *Advanced Experimental Medical Biology,* 1998; 442:463–76.

Cordain, L., Brand Miller, J., Eaton, S. B., Mann, N., Holt, S. H. A., and Speth, J. D. "Plant to animal subsistence ratios and macronutrient energy estimations in worldwide hunter-gatherer diets." *American Journal of Clinical Nutrition,* 2000; 71:682–92.

Cordain, L., Eaton, S. B., Brand Miller, J., Mann, N., and Hill, K. "The paradoxical nature of hunter-gatherer diets: meat-based, yet non-atherogenic." *European Journal of Clinical Nutrition,* 2002; 56 (suppl 1):S42–S52.

Cordain, L., Watkins, B. A., and Mann, N. J. "Fatty acid composition and energy density of foods available to African hominids: evolutionary implications for human brain development." *World Rev Nutrition Diet,* 2001; 90:144–61.

de Heinzelin, J., Clark, J. D., White, T., Hart, W., Renne, P., WoldeGabriel, G., Beyene, Y., and Vrba, E. "Environment and behavior of 2.5-million-year-old Bouri hominids." *Science,* 1999 Apr 23; 284(5414):625–29.

Driskell, J. A. *Sports Nutrition.* New York: CRC Press, 2000.

Eaton, S. B., Strassman, B. I., Nesse, R. M., Neel, J. V., Ewald, P. W., Williams, G. C., Weder, A. B., Eaton, S. B. III, Lindeberg, S., Konner, M. J., Mysterud, I., and Cordain, L. "Evolutionary health promotion." *Preventive Medicine,* 2002; 34:109–18.

Emken, R. A., Adlof, R. O., Rohwedder, W. K., and Gulley, R. M. "Comparison of linolenic and linoleic acid metabolism in man: influence of dietary linoleic acid." In *Essential Fatty Acids and Eicosanoids: Invited Papers from the Third International Conference.* A. Sinclair and R. Gibson, eds., pp. 23–25. Champaign, IL: AOCS Press, 1992.

French, L., and Kendall, S. "Does a high-fiber diet prevent colon cancer in at-risk patients?" *Journal of Family Practice,* 2003 Nov; 52(11):892–93.

Gray, J. P. "A corrected ethnographic atlas." *World Cultures Journal,* 1999; 10:24–85.

Hawkes, K., Hill, K., and O'Connell, J. F. "Why hunters gather: optimal foraging and the Ache of eastern Paraguay." *American Ethnologist,* 1982; 9:379–98.

Hu, F. B., Stampfer, M. J., Rimm, E. B., Manson, J. E., Ascherio, A., Colditz, G. A., Rosner, B. A., Spiegelman, D., Speizer, F. E., Sacks, F. M., Hennekens, C. H., and Willett, W. C. "A prospective study of egg consumption and risk of cardiovascular disease in men and women." *Journal of the American Medical Association,* 1999; 281(15):1387–94.

Katan, M. B. "Trans fatty acids and plasma lipoproteins." *Nutrition Review,* 2000; 58(6):188–91.

Knopf, K., Sturman, J. A., Armstrong, M., and Hayes, K. C. "Taurine: an essential nutrient for the cat." *Journal of Nutrition,* 1978; 108773–78.

Kuhn, S. L., and Stiner, M. C. "The antiquity of hunter-gatherers." In *Hunter-Gatherers, An Interdisciplinary Perspective.* Panter-Brick, C., Layton, R. H., and Rowley-Conwy, P., eds., pp. 99–129. Cambridge: Cambridge University Press, 2001.

Laidlaw, S. A., Shultz, T. D., Cecchino, J. T., and Kopple, J. D. "Plasma and urine taurine levels in vegans." *American Journal of Clinical Nutrition,* 1988; 47:660–63.

Lee, R. B. "What hunters do for a living, or how to make out on scarce resources." In *Man the Hunter.* Lee, R. B., and DeVore, I., eds., pp. 30–48. Chicago: Aldine, (1968).

Lee-Thorp, J., Thackeray, J. F., and van der Merwe, N. "The hunters and the hunted revisited." *Journal of Human Evolution,* 2000 Dec; 39(6):565–76.

Leonard, W. R., and Robertson, M. L. "Evolutionary perspectives on human nutrition: the influence of brain and body size on diet and metabolism." *American Journal of Human Biology,* 1994; 6:77–88.

Lieb, C. W. "The effects on human beings of a twelve months' exclusive meat diet." *Journal of the American Medical Association,* 1929; 93:20–22.

MacDonald, M. L., Rogers, Q. R., and Morris, J. G. "Nutrition of the domestic cat, a mammalian carnivore." *Annual Review of Nutrition,* 1984; 4:521–62.

McArdle, W. D., Katch, F. I., and Katch, V. L. *Sports and Exercise Nutrition.* New York: Lippincott Williams & Wilkins, 1999.

Movius, H. L. "A wooden spear of third interglacial age from lower Saxony." *Southwest Journal of Anthropology,* 1950; 6:139–42.

Murdock, G. P. "Ethnographic atlas: a summary." *Ethnology,* 1967; 6:109–236.

Nishikimi, M., and Yagi, K. "Molecular basis for the deficiency in humans of gulonolactone oxidase, a key enzyme for ascorbic acid biosynthesis." *American Journal of Clinical Nutrition,* 1991; 54(6 Suppl):1203S-08S.

Noli, D., and Avery, G. "Protein poisoning and coastal subsistence." *Journal of Archaeological Science,* 1988; 15:395–401.

Pawlosky, R., Barnes, A., and Salem, N. "Essential fatty acid metabolism in the feline: relationship between liver and brain production of long-chain polyunsaturated fatty acids." *Journal of Lipid Research,* 1994; 35:2032–40.

Pitts, G. C., and Bullard, T. R. "Some interspecific aspects of body composition in mammals." In *Body Composition in Animals and Man.* Pp. 45–70. National Academy of Sciences Publication 1598, National Academy of Sciences, Washington, DC, 1968.

Richards, M. P., and Hedges, R. M. "Focus: Gough's Cave and Sun Hole Cave human stable isotope values indicate a high animal protein diet in the British Upper Palaeolithic." *Journal of Archaeology Science,* 2000; 27:1–3.

Richards, M. P., Pettitt, P. B., Trinkaus, E., Smith, F. H., Paunovic, M., and Karavanic, I. "Neanderthal diet at Vindija and Neanderthal predation: the evidence from stable isotopes." *Proceedings of the National Academy of Sciences,* 2000; 97:7663–66.

Rosser, Z. H., Zerjal, T., Hurles, M. E., Adojaan, M., et al. "Y-chromosomal diversity in Europe is clinal and influenced primarily by geography, rather than by language." *American Journal of Human Genetics,* 2000; 67(6):1526–43.

Rudman, D., DiFulco, T. J., Galambos, J. T., Smith, R. B., Salam, A. A., and Warren, W. D. "Maximal rates of excretion and synthesis of urea in normal and cirrhotic subjects." *Journal of Clinical Investigation,* 1973; 52:2241–49.

Semaw, S., Rogers, M. J., Quade, J., Renne, P. R., Butler, R. F., Dominguez-Rodrigo, M., Stout, D., Hart, W. S., Pickering, T., and Simpson, S. W. "2.6-million-year-old stone tools and associated bones from OGS-6 and OGS-7, Gona, Afar, Ethiopia." *Journal of Human Evolution,* 2003; 45(2):169–77.

Shipman, P., and Rose, J. "Early hominid butchering and carcass-processing behaviors: approaches to the fossil record." *Journal of Anthropological Archaeology,* 1983; 2:57–98.

Shipman, P. "Scavenging or hunting in early hominids: theoretical framework and tests." *American Anthropologist,* 1986; 88:27–43.

Simon, H. B. "My husband subscribes to *Harvard Men's Health Watch,* but I read it even more than he does. I hope you can help us resolve a disagreement. He wants to have pizza two to three times a week for his prostate, but I don't think it's a healthy food. Who is right?" *Harvard Men's Health Watch,* 2003 Jun; 7(11):8.

Speth, J. D. "Early hominid hunting and scavenging: the role of meat as an energy source." *Journal of Human Evolution,* 1989; 18:329–43.

Speth, J. D., and Spielmann, K. A. "Energy source, protein metabolism, and hunter-gatherer subsistence strategies." *Journal of Anthropological Archaeology,* 1983; 2:1–31.

Stanford, C. B. "The hunting ecology of wild chimpanzees; implications for the behavioral ecology of Pliocene hominids." *American Anthropologist,* 1996; 98:96–113.

Stanford, C. B., Wallis, J., Matama, H., and Goodall, J. "Patterns of predation by chimpanzees on red colobus monkeys in Gombe National Park, 1982–1991." *American Journal of Physiological Anthropology,* 1994 Jun; 94(2):213–28.

Sturman, J. A., Hepner, G. W., Hofmann, A. F., and Thomas, P. J. "Metabolism of [35S] taurine in man." *Journal of Nutrition,* 1975; 105:1206–14.

Thieme, H. "Lower Palaeolithic hunting spears from Germany." *Nature,* 1997 Feb 27; 385(6619):807–10.

Wildman, D. E., Uddin, M., Liu, G., Grossman, L. I., and Goodman, M. "Implications of natural selection in shaping 99.4% nonsynonymous DNA identity between humans and chimpanzees: enlarging genus *Homo.*" *Proceedings of the National Academy of Sciences USA,* 2003; 100(12):7181–88.

Willett, W. C., and Stampfer, M. J. "Rebuilding the food pyramid." *Scientific American,* 2003 Jan; 288(1):64–71.

Winterhalder, B. P. "Optimal foraging strategies and hunter-gatherer research in anthropology: theories and models." In *Hunter-Gatherer Foraging Strategies.* Winterhalder, B. P., and Smith, E. A., eds, pp. 13–35. Chicago: University of Chicago, 1981.

Wood, B. "Hominid revelations from Chad." *Nature,* 2002; 418(6894):133–35.

CHAPTER 9

Cordain, L. "The nutritional characteristics of a contemporary diet based upon Paleolithic food groups." *Journal of American Neutraceutical Association,* 2002; 5:15–24.

Cordain, L. *The Paleo Diet.* New York: John Wiley & Sons, 2002.

Cordain, L., Brand Miller, J., Eaton, S. B., Mann, N., Holt, S. H. A., and Speth, J. D. "Plant to animal subsistence ratios and macronutrient energy estimations in world wide hunter-gatherer diets." *American Journal of Clinical Nutrition,* 2000; 71:682–92.

Cordain, L., Eaton, S. B., Brand Miller, J., Mann, N., and Hill, K. "The paradoxical nature of hunter-gatherer diets: meat-based, yet non-atherogenic." *European Journal of Clinical Nutrition,* 2002; 56 (suppl 1):S42–S52.

Cordain, L., Gotshall, R. W., and Eaton, S. B. "Physical activity, energy expenditure and fitness: an evolutionary perspective." *International Journal of Sports Medicine,* 1998; 19:328–35.

Cordain, L., Watkins, B. A., Florant, G. L., Kehler, M., Rogers, L., and Li, Y. "Fatty acid analysis of wild ruminant tissues: Evolutionary implications for reducing diet-related chronic disease." *European Journal of Clinical Nutrition,* 2002; 56:181–91.

de Heinzelin, J., Clark, J. D., White, T., Hart, W., Renne, P., Wolde Gabriel, G., Beyene, Y., and Vrba, E. "Environment and behavior of 2.5-million-year-old Bouri hominids." *Science,* 1999; 284:625–29.

Dominguez-Rodrigo, M. "Meat-eating by early hominids at the FLK 22 Zinjanthropus site, Olduvai Gorge (Tanzania): an experimental approach using cut-mark data." *Journal of Human Evolution,* 1997; 33:669–90.

Feskanich, D., Willett, W. C., Stampfer, M. J., and Colditz, G. A. "Milk, dietary calcium, and bone fractures in women: a 12-year prospective study." *American Journal of Public Health,* 1997; 87:992–97.

Foster-Powell, K., Holt, S. H., and Brand-Miller, J. C. "International table of glycemic index and glycemic load values: 2002." *American Journal of Clinical Nutrition,* 2002; 76(1):5–56.

Gannon, M. C., Nuttall, F. Q., Saeed, A., Jordan, K., and Hoover, H. "An increase in dietary protein improves the blood glucose response in persons with type 2 diabetes." *American Journal of Clinical Nutrition,* 2003; 78:734–41.

Gerrior, S., and Bente, I. "Nutrient Content of the US Food Supply, 1909–99: A Summary Report." USDA Center for Nutrition Policy and Promotion. *Home Economics Research Report No. 55*, 2002.

Hu, F. B., Manson, J. E., and Willett, W. C. "Types of dietary fat and risk of coronary heart disease: a critical review." *Journal of American College of Nutrition*, 2001; 20:5–19.

Krauss, R. M., Eckel, R. H., Howard, B., Appel, L. J., Daniels, S. R., Deckelbaum, R. J., et al. "AHA Dietary Guidelines: revision 2000: A statement for healthcare professionals from the Nutrition Committee of the American Heart Association." *Circulation*, 2000; 102:2284–99.

Kris-Etherton, P. M., and Yu, S. "Individual fatty acid effects on plasma lipids and lipoproteins: human studies." *American Journal of Clinical Nutrition*, 1997; 65(5 Suppl):1628S–44S.

Layman, D. K., Boileau, R. A., Erickson, D. J., Painter, J. E., Shiue, H., Sather, C., and Christou, D. D. "A reduced ratio of dietary carbohydrate to protein improves body composition and blood lipid profiles during weight loss in adult women." *Journal of Nutrition*, 2003; 133:411–17.

Layman, D. K., Shiue, H., Sather, C., Erickson, D. J., and Baum, J. "Increased dietary protein modifies glucose and insulin homeostasis in adult women during weight loss." *Journal of Nutrition*, 2003; 133(2):405–10.

Lee, K. W., and Lip, G. Y. "The role of omega-3 fatty acids in the secondary prevention of cardiovascular disease." *QJM: Monthly Journal of the Association of Physicians*, 2003; 96:465–80.

Nelson, G. J., Schmidt, P. C., and Kelley, D. S. "Low-fat diets do not lower plasma cholesterol levels in healthy men compared to high-fat diets with similar fatty acid composition at constant caloric intake." *Lipids*, 1995; 30:969–76.

O'Dea, K., Traianedes, K., Chisholm, K., Leyden, H., and Sinclair, A. J. "Cholesterol-lowering effect of a low-fat diet containing lean beef is reversed by the addition of beef fat." *American Journal of Clinical Nutrition*, 1990; 52:491–94.

Ostman, E. M., Liljeberg Elmstahl, H. G., and Bjorck, I. M. "Inconsistency between glycemic and insulinemic responses to regular and fermented milk products." *American Journal of Clinical Nutrition*, 2001; 74:96–100.

Perez-Jimenez, F., Lopez-Miranda, J., and Mata, P. "Protective effect of dietary monounsaturated fat on arteriosclerosis: beyond cholesterol." *Atherosclerosis*, 2002; 163(2):385–98.

Richards, M. P., and Hedges, R. M. "Focus: Gough's Cave and Sun Hole Cave human stable isotope values indicate a high animal protein diet in the British Upper Palaeolithic. *Journal of Archaeological Science*, 2000; 27:1–3.

Richards, M. P., Pettitt, P. B., Trinkaus, E., Smith, F. H., Paunovic, M., and Karavanic, I. "Neanderthal diet at Vindija and Neanderthal predation: the evidence from stable isotopes." *Proceedings of the National Acadamy of Sciences*, 2000; 97:7663–66.

Rudman, D., DiFulco, T. J., Galambos, J. T., Smith, R. B. III, Salam, A. A., and Warren, W. D. "Maximal rates of excretion and synthesis of urea in normal and cirrhotic subjects." *Journal of Clinical Investigation*, 1973; 52:2241–49.

Wolfe, B. M., and Giovannetti, P. M. "Short-term effects of substituting protein for carbohydrate in the diets of moderately hypercholesterolemic human subjects." *Metabolism*, 1991; 40:338–43.

Wolfe, B. M., and Piche, L. A. "Replacement of carbohydrate by protein in a conventional-fat diet reduces cholesterol and triglyceride concentrations in healthy normolipidemic subjects." *Clinical Investigations of Medicine*, 1999; 22:140–48.

CHAPTER 10

Bowerman, W. J., and Harris, W. E. *Jogging.* New York: Grosset and Dunlap, 1967.

Cordain, L., Gotshall, R.W., and Eaton, S.B. "Evolutionary aspects of exercise." *World Review of Nutrition and Diet,* 1997; 81:49–60.

Cordain, L., Gotshall, R. W., and Eaton, S. B. "Physical activity, energy expenditure and fitness: an evolutionary perspective." *International Journal of Sports Medicine,* 1998; 19:328–35.

Counsilman, J. E. *The Science of Swimming.* New York: Prentice Hall, 1968.

Hill K., and Hurtado, A. M. *Ache Life History.* New York: Aldine De Gruyter, 1995.

Kraemer, W. J., Ratamess, N. A., and French, D. N. "Resistance training for health and performance." *Current Sports Medicine Report,* 2002 Jun; 1(3):165–71.

Loy, S. F., Hoffmann, J. J., and Holland, G. J. "Benefits and practical use of cross-training in sports." *Sports Medicine,* 1995 Jan; 19(1):1–8.

Millet, G. P., Candau, R. B., Barbier, B., Busso, T., Rouillon, J. D., and Chatard, J. C. "Modelling the transfers of training effects on performance in elite triathletes." *International Journal of Sports Medicine,* 2002 Jan; 23(1):55–63.

White, L. J., Dressendorfer, R. H., Muller, S. M., and Ferguson, M. A. "Effectiveness of cycle cross-training between competitive seasons in female distance runners." *Journal of Strength Conditioning Research,* 2003 May; 17(2):319–23.

CHAPTER 11

Alderson, L. M., Hayes, K. C., and Nicolosi, R. J. "Peanut oil reduces diet-induced atherosclerosis in cynomolgus monkeys." *Arteriosclerosis,* 1986; 6:465–74.

Baker, B. P., Benbrook, C. M., Groth, E. III, and Lutz Benbrook, K. "Pesticide residues in conventional, integrated pest management (IPM)-grown and organic foods: insights from three US data sets." *Food Additives and Contaminants,* 2002 May; 19(5):427–46.

Bamshad, M., Kivisild, T., Watkins, W. S., Dixon, M. E., Ricker, C. E., Rao, B. B., Naidu, J. M., Prasad, B. V., Reddy, P. G., Rasanayagam, A., Papiha, S. S., Villems, R., Redd, A. J., Hammer, M. F., Nguyen, S. V., Carroll, M. L., Batzer, M. A., and Jorde, L. B. "Genetic evidence on the origins of Indian caste populations." *Genome Research,* 2001 Jun; 11(6):994–1,004.

Begom, R., and Singh, R. B. "Prevalence of coronary artery disease and its risk factors in the urban population of South and North India." *Acta Cardiology,* 1995; 50(3):227–40.

Bhopal, R.,Unwin, N., White, M., Yallop, J., Walker, L., Alberti, K. G., Harland, J., Patel, S., Ahmad, N., Turner, C., Watson, B., Kaur, D., Kulkarni, A., Laker, M., and Tavridou, A. "Heterogeneity of coronary heart disease risk factors in Indian, Pakistani, Bangladeshi, and European origin populations: cross sectional study." *British Medical Journal,* 1999; 319:215–20.

Bourne, D., and Prescott, J. "A comparison of the nutritional value, sensory qualities, and food safety of organically and conventionally produced foods." *Critical Review of Food Science Nutrition,* 2002; 42:1–34.

Boyle, E. M., Lille, S. T., Allaire, E., Clowes, A. W., and Verrier, E. D. "Endothelial cell injury in cardiovascular surgery: Atherosclerosis." *Annual of Thoracic Surgery,* 1997; 64:S47–56.

Childs, M. T., Dorsett, C. S., King, I. B., Ostrander, J. G., and Yamanaka, W. K. "Effects of shellfish consumption on lipoproteins in normolipidemic men." *American Journal of Clinical Nutrition,* 1990 Jun; 51(6):1020–27.

Cordain, L., Watkins, B. A., Florant, G. L., Kehler, M., Rogers, L., and Li, Y. "Fatty acid analysis of wild ruminant tissues: Evolutionary implications for reducing diet-related chronic disease." *European Journal of Clinical Nutrition,* 2002; 56:181–91.

De Oliveira e Silva, E. R., Seidman, C. E., Tian, J. J., Hudgins, L. C., Sacks, F. M., and Breslow, J. L. "Effects of shrimp consumption on plasma lipoproteins." *American Journal of Clinical Nutrition,* 1996 Nov; 64(5):712–17.

Freed, D. L. "Lectins in food: their importance in health and disease." *Journal of Nutritional Medicine,* 1991; 2:45–64.

Gresham, G. A., and Howard, A. N. "The independent production of atherosclerosis and thrombosis in the rat." *British Journal of Experimental Pathology,* 1960; 41:395–402.

Howell, W. H., McNamara, D. J., Tosca, M. A., Smith, B. T., and Gaines, J. A. "Plasma lipid and lipoprotein responses to dietary fat and cholesterol: a meta-analysis." *American Journal of Clinical Nutrition,* 1997 Jun; 65(6):1747–64.

Hu, F. B., Stampfer, M. J., Manson, J. E., Rimm, E. B., Colditz, G. A., Rosner, B. A., Speizer, F. E., Hennekens, C. H., and Willett, W. C. "Frequent nut consumption and risk of coronary heart disease in women: prospective cohort study." *British Medical Journal,* 1998 Nov 14; 317(7169):1341–45.

Kritchevsky, D., Davidson, L. M., Shapiro, I. L., Kim, H. K., Kitagawa, M., Malhotra, S., Nair, P. P., Clarkson, T. B., Bersohn, I., and Winter, P. A. "Lipid metabolism and experimental atherosclerosis in baboons—influence of cholesterol free, semi-synthetic diets." *American Journal of Clinical Nutrition,* 1974; 27:29–50.

Kritchevsky, D., Davidson, L. M., Weight, M., Kriek, N. P., and du Plessis, J. P. "Influence of native and randomized peanut oil on lipid metabolism and aortic sudanophilia in the vervet monkey." *Atherosclerosis,* 1982; 42:53–58.

Kritchevsky, D., Tepper, S. A., and Klurfeld, D. M. "Lectin may contribute to the atherogenicity of peanut oil." *Lipids,* 1998 Aug; 33(8):821–23.

Magkos, F., Arvaniti, F., and Zampelas, A. "Organic food: nutritious food or food for thought? A review of the evidence." *International Journal of Food Science Nutrition,* 2003; 54:357–71.

Mensinga, T. T., Speijers, G. J., and Meulenbelt, J. "Health implications of exposure to environmental nitrogenous compounds." *Toxicology Review,* 2003; 22(1):41–51.

Misra, A., Cherukupalli, R., Reddy, K. S., Mohan, A., and Bajaj, J. S. "Hyperinsulinemia and dyslipidemia in non-obese, normotensive offspring of hypertensive parents in northern India." *Blood Pressure,* 1998 Nov; 7(5–6):286–90.

Ramachandran, A., Snehalatha, C., Kapur, A., Vijay, V., Mohan, V., Das, A. K., Rao, P. V., Yajnik, C. S., Prasanna Kumar, K. M., and Nair, J. D. "High prevalence of diabetes and impaired glucose tolerance in India: National Urban Diabetes Survey." *Diabetologia,* 2001 Sep; 44(9):1094–101.

Rule, D. C., Broughton, K. S., Shellito, S. M., and Maiorano, G. "Comparison of muscle fatty acid profiles and cholesterol concentrations of bison, beef cattle, elk, and chicken." *Journal of Animal Science,* 2002 May; 80(5):1202–11.

Sanford, G. L., and Harris-Hooker, S. "Stimulation of vascular proliferation by beta-galactoside specific lectins." *The FASEB Journal,* 1990; 4:2912–18.

Scott, R. F., Morrison, E. S., Thomas, W. A., Jones, R., and Nam, S. C. "Short-term feeding of unsaturated vs. saturated fat in the production of atherosclerosis and thrombosis in the rat." *Experimental Molecular Pathology,* 1964; 3:421–43.

Wang, Q., Yu, L. G., Campbell, B. J., Milton, J. D., and Rhodes, J. M. "Identification of intact peanut lectin in peripheral venous blood." *Lancet,* 1998 Dec 5; 352(9143):1831–32.

Ward, M. H., Mark, S. D., Cantor, K. P., Weisenburger, D. D., Correa-Villasenor, A., and Zahm, S. H. "Drinking water nitrate and the risk of non-Hodgkin's lymphoma." *Epidemiology,* 1996 Sep; 7(5):465–71.

Williams, C. M. "Nutritional quality of organic food: shades of grey or shades of green?" *Proceedings of the Nutrition Society,* 2002; 61:19–24.

Wissler, R. W., et al. "Aortic lesions and blood lipids in monkeys fed three food fats." *Federation Proceedings,* 1967; 26:371.

Woese, K., Lange, D., Boess, C., and Bogl, K. W. "A comparison of organically and conventionally grown foods—Results of a review of the relevant literature." *Journal of Science Food Agriculture,* 1997; 74:281–93.

Worthington, V. "Effect of agricultural methods on nutritional quality: a comparison of organic with conventional crops." *Alternative Therapies,* 1998; 4:58–68.

Worthington, V. "Nutritional quality of organic versus conventional fruits, vegetables, and grains." *Journal of Alternative Complementary Medicine,* 2001; 2:161–73.

Zahm, S. H., and Ward, M. H. "Pesticides and childhood cancer." *Environmental Health Perspective,* 1998 Jun; 106 Suppl 3:893–908.

CHAPTER 12

Burke, L. M., and Read, R. S. "Dietary supplements in sport." *Sports Medicine,* 1993; 15(1): 43–65.

Costill, D. L. "Sweating: its composition and effects on body fluids." *Annals of New York Academy of Science,* 1977; 301:160–74.

Mao, I. F., Chen, M. L., and Ko, Y. C. "Electrolyte loss in sweat and iodine deficiency in a hot environment." *Archives of Environmental Health,* 2001; 56(3):271–77.

Noakes, T. "Hyponatremia in distance runners: Fluid and sodium balance during exercise." *Current Sports Medicine Report,* 2002; 1(4):197–207.

O'Toole, M. L., Douglas, P. S., Laird, R. H., and Hiller, D. B. "Fluid and electrolyte status in athletes receiving medical care at an ultradistance triathlon." *Clinical Journal of Sport Medicine,* 1995; 5(2):116–22.

Shirreffs, S. M., and Maughan, R. J. "Whole body sweat collection in humans: an improved method with preliminary data on electrolyte content." *Journal of Applied Physiology,* 1997; 82(1): 336–41.

Speedy, D. B., Faris, J. G., Hamlin, M., Gallagher, P. G., and Campbell, R. G. "Hyponatremia and weight changes in an ultradistance triathlon." *Clinical Journal of Sport Medicine,* 1997; 7(3): 180–84.

Index

Boldface page references indicate illustrations and graphs.
Underscored references indicate boxed text and tables.

INDEX

About the Authors

Loren Cordain, PhD, is a professor in the health and exercise science department at Colorado State University in Fort Collins. His research emphasis is in evolutionary medicine, and he is nationally and internationally recognized for his expertise in the study of Paleolithic diets and how they relate to the health and well-being of modern humans. He has contributed more than 120 publications to the medical, nutritional, and scientific literature in the past 25 years, and he is the author of the popular diet book *The Paleo Diet.* He is a member of the American Institute of Nutrition, the American Society for Clinical Nutrition, and the International Society for the Study of Fatty Acids and Lipids. Dr. Cordain's research is pushing the envelope regarding the role of diet and disease. His recent paper linking diet to acne in the prestigious *Archives of Dermatology* in December 2002 made headlines worldwide and is characteristic of the international notoriety that his scientific research generates. He recently received the Scholarly Excellence award at Colorado State University for his contributions to understanding optimal human nutrition. He has lectured extensively on the Paleolithic nutrition concept worldwide. For more information, visit Dr. Cordain's Web site: www.thepaleo diet.com.

Joe Friel has coached endurance athletes since 1980, including runners, triathletes, duathletes, road cyclists, mountain bikers, swimmers, rowers, Nordic skiers, and endurance horse racers. These men and women ranged from novice to Olympian and included national champions, world-championship competitors, elite age-group athletes, and those who simply wanted to be in better shape, and have included teens, students, senior citizens, business owners, lawyers, doctors, line workers, and professional athletes. He has a master's degree in exercise science and is a recognized authority on training for endurance sports, having written five other books on the subject and serving as a columnist for two national sports publications for a decade. He is a widely sought-after speaker on the subject of training and consults with national sports governing bodies on the preparation of athletes for world competitions and the Olympics. Friel is also the founder and president of two successful businesses: Ultrafit Associates, a sports training company with coaches in three countries; and Training Peaks.com, a World Wide Web–based business that provides training tools for athletes and coaches. For more information, go to www.ultrafit.com.